CASEBOOK SERIES

Tennyson: *In Memoriam*

Tennyson

In Memoriam

A CASEBOOK

EDITED BY

JOHN DIXON HUNT

MACMILLAN

Selection and editorial matter © John Dixon Hunt 1970

First published 1970 by
MACMILLAN AND CO LTD
Little Essex Street London WC2
and also at Bombay Calcutta and Madras
Macmillan South Africa (Publishers) Pty Ltd Johannesburg
The Macmillan Company of Australia Pty Ltd Melbourne
The Macmillan Company of Canada Ltd Toronto
Gill and Macmillan Ltd Dublin

SBN (boards) 333 02532 6
      (paper) 333 06251 5

Printed in Great Britain by
WESTERN PRINTING SERVICES LTD
Bristol

FOR DOUGLAS

CONTENTS

ACKNOWLEDGEMENTS

T. S. Eliot, '*In Memoriam*', from *Selected Essays*, new ed. (Faber & Faber Ltd and Harcourt, Brace & World Inc.; © Harcourt, Brace & World Inc., 1932, 1936, 1950; © T. S. Eliot, 1960, 1964); Graham Hough, 'The Natural Theology of *In Memoriam*', from the *Review of English Studies*, XXIII (1947) 244–56 (Clarendon Press); 'Tennyson as a Modern Poet', from *University of Toronto Quarterly*, XIX (Professor Arthur J. Carr and the University of Toronto Press); Humphry House, '*In Memoriam*', from *All in Due Time* (1955) (Rupert Hart-Davis Ltd); 'Behind the Veil: A Distinction between Poetic and Scientific Language in Tennyson, Lyell, and Darwin', from *Victorian Studies*, II (1958) 60–8 (Professor Walker Gibson and *Victorian Studies*); '*In Memoriam*: The Way of the Poet', from *Victorian Studies*, II (1958) 139–48 (Professor E. D. H. Johnson and *Victorian Studies*); 'The Two Kingdoms of *In Memoriam*', from the *Journal of English and Germanic Philology*, LVIII, no. 2 (April 1959) 228–40 (Professor John D. Rosenberg and the University of Illinois Press); Jerome H. Buckley, *Tennyson: The Growth of a Poet* (1960) (Harvard University Press); 'The Unity of *In Memoriam*', from *The Victorian Newsletter*, no. 21 (Spring 1962) pp. 9–14 (Professor Jonathan Bishop and *The Victorian Newsletter*); 'Faith, Doubt and Mystical Experience in *In Memoriam*', from *Victorian Studies*, VII (1963) 155–69 (Professor Carlisle Moore and *Victorian Studies*); '*In Memoriam*: An Aspect of Form', from *University of Toronto Quarterly*, XXXV (1965) 22–46 (Professor J. C. C. Mays and the University of Toronto Press).

GENERAL EDITOR'S PREFACE

EACH of this series of Casebooks concerns either one well-known and influential work of literature or two or three closely linked works. The main section consists of critical readings, mostly modern, brought together from journals and books. A selection of reviews and comments by the author's contemporaries is also included, and sometimes comments from the author himself. The Editor's Introduction charts the reputation of the work from its first appearance until the present time.

What is the purpose of such a collection? Chiefly, to assist reading. Our first response to literature may be, or seem to be, 'personal'. Certain qualities of vigour, profundity, beauty or 'truth to experience' strike us, and the work gains a foothold in our mind. Later, an isolated phrase or passage may return to haunt or illuminate. Where did we hear that? we wonder – it could scarcely be better put.

In these and similar ways appreciation begins, but major literature prompts to very much more. There are certain facts we need to know if we are to understand properly. Who were the author's original readers, and what assumptions did he share with them? What was his theory of literature? Was he committed to a particular historical situation, or to a set of beliefs? We need historians as well as critics to help us with this. But there are also more purely literary factors to take account of: the work's structure and rhetoric; its symbols and archetypes; its tone, genre and texture; its use of language; the words on the page. In all these matters critics can inform and enrich our individual responses by offering imaginative recreations of their own.

For the life of a book is not, after all, merely 'personal'; it is more like a tripartite dialogue, between a writer living 'then', a reader living 'now', and whatever forces of survival and honour link the two. Criticism is the public manifestation of this dialogue, a witness to the continuing power of literature to arouse and excite. It illuminates the possibilities and rewards of the dialogue, pushing 'interpretation' as far forward as it can go.

And here, indeed, is the rub: how far can it go? Where does 'interpretation' end and nonsense begin? Why is one interpretation superior to another, and why does each age need to interpret for itself? The critic knows that his insights have value only in so far as they serve the text, and that he must take account of views differing sharply from his own. He knows that his own writing will be judged as well as the work he writes about, so that he cannot simply assert inner illumination or a differing taste.

The critical forum is a place of vigorous conflict and disagreement, but there is nothing in this to cause dismay. What is attested is the complexity of human experience and the richness of literature, not any chaos or relativity of taste. A critic is better seen, no doubt, as an explorer than as an 'authority', but explorers ought to be, and usually are, well equipped. The effect of good criticism is to convince us of what C. S. Lewis called 'the enormous extension of our being which we owe to authors'. A Casebook will be justified only if it helps to promote the same end.

A single volume can represent no more than a small selection of critical opinions. Some critics have been excluded for reasons of space, and it is hoped that readers will follow up the further suggestions in the Select Bibliography. Other contributions have been severed from their original context, to which some readers may wish to return. Indeed, if they take a hint from the critics represented here, they certainly will.

A. E. DYSON

INTRODUCTION

ARTHUR HALLAM died in Vienna on 15 September 1833, while travelling on the Continent with his father. The news reached the Tennysons at Somersby on 1 October. During the 1830s Alfred Tennyson had been under constant emotional pressure as a result of hostile reviews, the spectacle of his favourite brother becoming an opium addict and another brother suffering a nervous breakdown; but Hallam's death was certainly the greatest shock and challenge of all. It fell to Alfred to sustain the whole family, who had grown deeply attached to Hallam on his various visits to Somersby since the Christmas vacation of 1829. Emily, who had been engaged to him, was in need of special attention. Outwardly Alfred seems to have been less disturbed than either Emily or Frederick, but he had much to occupy him as head of the family and, equally, he very obviously kept his grief to himself. It is not easy to establish the historical quality and progress of his sorrow very exactly; yet it does appear fairly certain that real depression – 'my heart seemed too crushed and all my energies too paralysed' – came later, in 1834.

We know that he was unable to provide Hallam's father with some memorial account of his friend, for on 14 February 1834 Tennyson wrote to Mr Hallam:

I attempted to draw up a memoir of his life and character, but I failed to do him justice. I failed even to please myself. I could scarcely have pleased you. I hope to be able at a future period to concentrate whatever powers I may possess on the construction of some tribute to those high speculative endowments and comprehensive sympathies which I ever loved to contemplate. . . .

Yet some of his feelings had been immediately released into

writing, for by early in 1834 several poems prompted by Hallam's death were already in draft. There were 'The Two Voices' or, as it was then called, 'Thoughts of a Suicide'; 'Ulysses', which Tennyson said gave his 'feelings about the need of going forward and bearing the struggle of life perhaps more simply than anything in *In Memoriam*' – an emotion at the opposite extreme from thoughts of suicide and more obviously in keeping with his role as *pater familias*; the companion piece to 'Ulysses', 'Tithonus'; and 'Morte D'Arthur', written in a manuscript book among versions of five sections of *In Memoriam*, IX ('Fair ship, that from the Italian shore') which in one manuscript is dated 6 October 1833 (five days after the news reached him), XXX ('With trembling fingers did we weave'), XXXI ('When Lazarus left his charnel-cave'), LXXXV ('This truth came borne with bier and pall') and XXVIII ('The time draws near the birth of Christ').

The poems that were to become part of *In Memoriam* continued to accumulate in various notebooks and were, according to Tennyson, 'written at many different places, and as the phases of our intercourse came to my memory and suggested them'. At what stage this accumulation of 'Elegies', as they were known in the family and among Tennyson's closest friends, were thought of as parts of a longer poem is uncertain. Tennyson said that he did not write them with 'any view of weaving them into a whole, or for publication, until I found that I had written so many'. In any case he issued three other volumes of poetry between Hallam's death and the appearance of *In Memoriam* in 1850: he broke ten years of silence in 1842 with a two-volume collection of *Poems* and followed this with *The Princess* in 1847. One story credits his publisher, Moxon, with urging the publication of the 'Elegies' when he was shown them in 1849, although Tennyson still explained that they were written for his 'own relief and private satisfaction'. In February 1850 Tennyson nearly lost the 'long, butcher ledger-like book' in which the poems were copied, but Coventry Patmore recovered it from a food cupboard in the poet's former lodgings – undoubtedly Patmore's major contribution to Victorian poetry. In March Tennyson had the poem privately printed in a trial issue for circulation among friends;

this is often cited as *Fragments of an Elegy*, a title which Tennyson certainly considered, but which did *not* appear on the title-page of this trial issue. And on 1 June, with several changes and additions, *In Memoriam* was published anonymously. Within eighteen months it had reached a fifth edition.

II

The early reviews were not as wholly sympathetic as either those quick editions or the poem's later popularity suggest. Most reviewers at once recognised its author, although one curiously surmised that the poems 'evidently come from the full heart of the widow of a military man'! The reservations were many: one reviewer resented the 'shallow art spent on the tenderness shown to an Amaryllis of the Chancery Bar', and *The Times* (infra, p. 105) found the amorousness disquieting. Both *The Times* and *Sharpe's London Journal* criticised the 'far-fetched and . . . painfully elaborated' expression of emotions and the poem's obscurity. Understandably, the High Church *English Review* (infra, pp. 90 ff) anticipated T. S. Eliot's scepticism (infra, p. 135) about the quality of Tennyson's faith.

But the reservations and strictures were balanced and soon outweighed by the enthusiasm and applause. *In Memoriam* was compared favourably with Milton's *Lycidas*, with Dante and with the sonnets of Petrarch and Shakespeare. The *Examiner* told its readers of a

pathetic tale of real human sorrow, suggested rather than told. It exhibits the influence of a sudden and appalling shock, and lasting bereavement, in the formation of character and opinion. . . . It is perhaps the author's greatest achievement. A passion, deep-felt throughout it, has informed his ever subtle thoughts and delicate imagery with a massive grandeur and a substantial interest.[1]

A more informal sense of the triumphant impact that *In*

[1] For this and other contemporary reviews of the poem I am indebted to the relevant chapter of E. F. Shannon Jr, *Tennyson and the Reviewers* (Hamden, Conn., 1967).

Memoriam made (or, retrospectively, seemed to have made) upon
its first readers is amusingly conveyed in a scene from Arthur
Gray Butler's *The Three Friends: a story of Rugby in the forties*:

'It is one of the Immortals.' And he handed him, as he sat down,
a little brown volume, from which Arnold read eagerly, '*In
Memoriam, A.H.H.* No author! Who is A.H.H.?'

'They say it is Arthur Hallam,' replied [Clough], 'and the
author shines out in every line. It must be Tennyson. Read
number 56!' . . .

Meanwhile Arnold was heard murmuring to himself, 'Beautiful! Luminous! A new metre! A masterpiece! It must be Alfred.'
Then at last turning to Clough, and handing him the book, he
said, with faltering voice, all the light playfulness, with which he
cloaked real earnestness, departed, 'Read! My voice is wasted in
much teaching.' And pointing with his finger, 'There.' And
Clough read, in a soft low voice, like far-off music . . .

'Another,' said Arnold, lying back, and playing with the great
staghound's ears, 'another!' And again Clough read, not as pick-
ing out favourites, but letting eyes and fingers choose for him,
one after another of those immortal poems, which took the heart
of England by storm, and have been the delight and strength of
the English-speaking race ever since.[1]

Various reasons for the poem's appeal are announced in that
passage – the emotional *timbre* of the verses, their delightful and
accomplished technical virtuosity, the comforting strength of the
poem's faith.

What is perhaps particularly surprising and significant to us
now is the *breadth* of the appeal made by the poem's 'faith'. It
drew from the *Wesleyan-Methodist Magazine* the encomium that
the poem represented:

The refining, elevating, spiritualizing, and chastening influence
which Christianity has exercised upon modern poetry, – furnish-
ing it with nobler ethics; inspiring, but not to disappoint, 'immortal longings'; and infusing the spirit of heaven-ward faith and
charity.

[1] Quoted in G. and K. Tillotson, *Mid-Victorian Studies* (1965)
p. 183. The novel was published in 1900.

Similarly Bishop Westcott admired its

splendid faith (in the face of the frankest acknowledgement of every difficulty) in the growing purpose of the sum of life, and in the noble destiny of the individual man as he offers himself for the fulfilment of his little part.

Yet *In Memoriam* could also draw applause from those who welcomed its honest and rigorous scepticism. The poet's son records in the *Memoir* of his father how 'scientific leaders like Herschel, Owen, Sidgwick and Tyndall regarded him as a champion of Science, and cheered him with words of genuine admiration for his love of Nature, for the eagerness with which he welcomed all the latest scientific discoveries, and for his trust in truth'. Sidgwick's letter to the poet's son (infra, pp. 122 ff) records how *In Memoriam* encouraged them by its defence of 'honest doubt', especially the Prologue's determination to reconcile knowledge and faith. Even more explicit is Froude, who explained how the poem became the authoritative expression of sincere doubt:

The best and bravest of my contemporaries determined to have done with insincerity, to find ground under their feet, to let the uncertain remain uncertain, but to learn how much and what we could honestly regard as true, and to believe that and live by it. Tennyson became the voice of this feeling in poetry. . . . Tennyson's . . . group of poems which closed with *In Memoriam* became to many of us what *The Christian Year* was to orthodox Churchmen. We read them, and they became part of our minds, the expression, in exquisite language of the feelings which were working in ourselves.

That the poem could endorse such a spread of theological opinion reflects both Tennyson's determination to anticipate various responses to the poem and the very real intellectual and spiritual tensions that it tries to accommodate.

But perhaps it is not unfair to claim that the most widespread reaction to the poem and to the poem's faith is that typified by Queen Victoria. During the early months of her widowhood she allowed the Duke of Argyll to inform Tennyson that 'She is finding much that she loves to dwell on in your *In Memoriam*.

She especially desired me to tell you this last night, and she gave
me her copy to show "how well it was read" and how many the
passages she had marked. It will touch you, I think, to know that
she had substituted "widow" for "widower" and "her" for "his"
in the lines "Tears of a widower".'

As for their Queen ('Next to the Bible *In Memoriam* is my
comfort'), so for many of her subjects, the poem became virtually
a book of devotions. This was especially true, as Sidgwick recognised, when the 'great issues between Agnostic Science and
Faith' grew more prominent in the second half of the century. Its
lyrics were used as hymns in church;[1] its verses became the
texts of sermons, and Frederick Robertson affirmed that 'the
most satisfactory things that have been said on the future state are
contained in this poem'. As such a remark implies, an imaginative
reading of the work has been displaced by the urge to find in it
a treatise of faith and comfortable wisdom. Commentaries and
handbooks on the poem were a flourishing industry by the end
of the century. Although they acknowledged what Sidgwick
called its 'poetic charm', their endeavour was often to isolate and
explain the messages that it contained and to communicate its
wisdom in prose paraphrase. The most famous is probably
A. C. Bradley's commentary of 1901; he himself is aware of the
dangerous tendency in separating the 'so-called substance' of the
poem from how it is presented, yet his section by section commentary and a chapter on 'The Ideas Used in the Poem' do not
entirely avoid that same danger.

III

The reaction was inevitable. Long before A. C. Bradley himself
lectured to the British Academy in 1916 on *The Reaction against
Tennyson* the dissent had been heard – from Swinburne, Hopkins,
Bagehot, among others. In his *Autobiographies* W. B. Yeats
complained that Tennyson filled his work 'with what I called
"impurities", curiosities about politics, about science, about

[1] See Peter Hall's note, 'Tennyson in Church', in the first issue of
the *Tennyson Research Bulletin* (Lincoln, 1967).

history, about religion'. And later he records Verlaine's stricture on *In Memoriam*: 'Tennyson is too noble, too *anglais*; when he should have been broken-hearted, he had many reminiscences' (2nd ed., 1955, pp. 167, 342). Another famous reaction to Tennyson's Victorian reputation came in Max Beerbohm's mischievous cartoon in *The Poet's Corner* (1904) of 'Mr Tennyson reading *In Memoriam* to his sovereign'. Across a vast expanse of carpet a sprawling Poet Laureate, with large gesticulation, reads aloud from his manuscript to the diminutive, black-robed figure of his sovereign. The huge, bare drawing-room, presided over by the portrait of the late Prince Consort, reduces the private and compelling literary moment and the apparent frenzy of its bard to an empty, public formality. It is a satire which rehearses the late Victorian mistrust of Tennyson's oracular pose, into which he was himself tempted as well as pushed; at the same time it wittily identifies the Victorian mistreatment of the poem. For *In Memoriam* was not a product of the Laureateship (bestowed upon its author in 1850 *after* the success of the elegies), but a document of a much younger and more insecure man. Yet the poem became an ineluctable part of Tennyson's sage-like orthodoxy, partly for reasons which his contemporaries have already been quoted to explain, partly because its author himself chose to adopt the oracular voice – in explaining, for example, that the 'I' of his poem 'is not always the author speaking of himself, but the voice of the human race speaking through him'.

The hostility to *In Memoriam* as a supreme document of Victorian confidence (some say, complacency) has continued into this century. Hugh I'Anson Fausset, the author of *Tennyson: a modern portrait* (1923), dismisses Tennyson's wedding of art to a 'false morality' which is 'either sentimental or utilitarian' in a poem 'too diffuse and too mechanical' to compel any response. In the same year Harold Nicolson issued his *Tennyson: aspects of his life, character and poetry*, which established the classic manœuvre by which most subsequent criticism has approached its subject. Nicolson postulated a progress from the 'unhappy mystic of the Lincolnshire wolds' to the 'prosperous Isle of Wight Victorian'; he then rescued mainly the poetry of the earlier stages. By this strategy Tennyson can be accepted as England's 'best poet of melancholy', while the Eminent Victorian can be conveniently neglected. This procedure was followed by T. S. Eliot who applauded Tennyson's doubt but not his faith and by W. H. Auden who praised his treatment of melancholia but thought him otherwise the 'stupidest' of English poets.

There were those, like Humbert Wolfe, who rejected the fallacy of Tennyson's decline into tired aphorism and civic gesture. But any movement back towards a juster estimate of Tennyson was frustrated by the current literary-critical fashion which took its cue from I. A. Richards and sought in poetry the tensions and complexities of which irony was the most obvious mode. Tennyson was judged too simple and straightforward for this sophisticated critical method: F. R. Leavis explained his exclusion from *Revaluation* (1936) by saying he offered little opportunity for local analysis. Yet, inevitably, some attempt to reclaim Tennyson by the very critical method which generally rejected him soon took place. In *The Well-Wrought Urn* (1949) Cleanth Brooks suggested by a most subtle and intricate analysis of 'Tears, Idle Tears' that Tennyson's poetry was of the order that worked via ambiguity and paradox and so was hospitable to close scrutiny. Although Brooks was right to call in question the tradition of a simple and straightforward poetry, he distorted it in another direction by making Tennyson an honorary member of the Metaphysical School – and incidentally by reading 'Tears, Idle Tears' out of its extremely intricate Victorian context in *The Princess*.

IV

It is only recently that scholarship has provided more coherent and informed pictures of the Victorian age, which have in their turn promoted more substantial and measured criticism of the poems themselves. The studies chosen for this volume suggest something of these developments in their attention to the evolutionary ideas *used* in the poem, to its structure, and – above all – to the detailed movement and texture of the poetry.

In 1936 T. S. Eliot still cherishes the Nicolson image of the
split poetic personality. His claims for Tennyson's 'greatness'
seem a little dutiful, and he appears to find the Victorian age
something of an oddity. Although elsewhere in his criticism he
attends closely to a text, with Tennyson he offers little detailed
reading and the suggestive ideas he floats by the end of the essay
remain unrelated to the poems: how, for example, *is* the 'technical
accomplishment . . . intimate with his depths' (infra, p. 136)?
Curiously, in his objection to the poem's confused theology,
Eliot even seems to harbour the Victorian notion that it is the
poem's ideas that really matter. However, in his rather gnomic
claim that Tennyson was 'the most instinctive rebel against the
society in which he was the most perfect conformist' he anticipates what would now be valued as a more accurate picture of
Tennyson's involvement with his age.

In 1952 E. D. H. Johnson, who is represented here by his essay
on Tennyson's attitudes towards his own poetic role, published
The Alien Vision of Victorian Poetry. In it he argued that Tennyson, Arnold and Browning were in crucial matters at odds with
their times, locating their own enthusiasms and authority in resources of individual being rather than in an existing social order;
that they sought to accommodate private insights to contemporary currents of thought without materially falsifying them;
that their concern to communicate with the age and not retire
into private fantasy and introspection led them to perfect remarkable techniques for such accommodation. Something of this
more intricate sense of Tennyson's career is available behind the
essays here. Rosenberg, for example, reminds us not only that
Tennyson's was an exceptional intelligence, but that he exercised
it in annexing the Victorian confidence in evolutionary progress[1]

[1] Many different notions of progress seemed interchangeable during
the nineteenth century. John Stuart Mill, for example, said that with
his wife 'self-improvement, progress in the highest and in all senses,
was a law of her nature'. While David G. Ritchie in *Darwin and Hegel*
(1893) wrote: 'In the present age the most conspicuously advancing
science is biology; and the categories of organism and evolution are
freely transferred to philosophy with the great advantage of lifting it
out of the more abstract conceptions of mathematics or mechanics.'

to articulate the less tangible Christian hope of man's redemption. Buckley, too, in the chapter from which his contribution here is selected, considers how the 'deeply personal analysis' becomes a public document. Mays takes this a crucial stage further by suggesting the tensions between communication or the *form* his meditations take and the essentially inarticulate nature of these private apprehensions.

Between 1947, when Hough is concerned with the lack of clarity in the 'one far-off divine event', and the most recent of these essays by Mays in 1965 there has developed a valuable sense of Tennyson's unexpected closeness to T. S. Eliot's own poetry and to that symbolist vision which celebrates (in Eliot's words) 'raid[s] on the inarticulate' and the 'communication[s] of the dead . . . tongued with fire beyond the language of the living'. Much of the reaction to *In Memoriam* around the turn of the century came from a new symbolist aesthetic (Yeats was one of its spokesmen) that could see only trivial anecdote and scientific opinion in the poem. Now we recognise at least as firmly Tennyson's mystical temperament and symbolist affinities and we should be prepared further, I believe, to stress how *In Memoriam* moves from an anxious hankering after definition, 'knowledge' and willed certainties towards a wisdom or noumenous insight, achieved at best through dream and trance. But, in this context, it is worth remarking how nineteenth-century criticism of the poem anticipates most possibilities canvassed today. In this case it was the *North British Review* that identified in 'every phrase' of the poem 'the translation to immortality of some hitherto evanescent and unobserved affection; the outward world exists only as a magazine of symbols for revealing the inner world of man . . .' Further support came from Bradley's emphasis on the poem's transcendental nature and from the *Athenaeum*, which noticed Tennyson's reliance on a child's apprehension to penetrate beyond mere intellect (infra, p. 64).

So some of these essays disclose Tennyson's continuity with modern literature, notably Eliot. Buckley's valuable invocation of Kierkegaard also contributes to this connection, as does Rosenberg's consideration of the often obnoxiously personal tones which make *In Memoriam* 'unique and distressingly modern' among English elegies. But in the opposite direction we are made aware of Victorian poetry as a continuation of Romanticism. Hough writes of the influence of Coleridge upon Tennyson's generation, especially upon F. D. Maurice's regard for 'the preciousness of truths as distinct from facts'. From other studies[1] we have been made aware of *In Memoriam*'s sustained dialogue with the themes and central images of romantic poetry. Benziger (see Select Bibliography, 4 (viii)) suggests some Romantic continuities from Shelley and Wordsworth in Tennyson's poetry and the ways in which he separates himself from them. Tennyson could not, of course, have known *The Prelude: or the Growth of a Poet's Mind* – it was published posthumously one month after *In Memoriam*; but, as Johnson's essay here implies, Tennyson maintains a typical Romantic inquiry into the poetic process, though with less confidence and more anxiety about the efficacy of the imagination. Finally, it seems to me that when Mays suggests that Tennyson's poem represents a direction, not a destination, the fruits of honesty, not tidiness, he is isolating a quality of *In Memoriam* that emphasises its important place in the English romantic tradition from Wordsworth and Blake to Eliot and Yeats.

Hough decided that Tennyson did the best he could in the personal and historical circumstances. As more has been learnt of both, the estimate, certainly of the intricacies, often of the success, of *In Memoriam* has risen. Hough himself provides the first of several essays here on Tennyson's relationship with early nineteenth-century evolutionary thought. As he insists, we must not imagine that the poem has anything to do with monkeys. Nor should we, as too many commentaries seem to imply, think of the poem as *about* even pre-Darwinian evolution. Hough's essay, despite its important reminder that the poem's development is strictly emotional, may itself leave the impression that what we have is a poem of general thought, a literary work that somehow is all 'background'. Tennyson himself is not entirely blameless in

[1] See items by Foakes, Benziger and Mattes in the Select Bibliography, 4 and 1.

contributing to that impression, and it is the poem's attention to
religious and scientific matters that has of course sanctioned the
discussions of them by Hough and others. But it is important to
ask *why* the poem concerns itself with them; and any answer will
necessarily involve some consideration of the figure without
whom the poem would not exist – Arthur Hallam.

Tennyson's relationship with Hallam was a complex one and
to understand this is to appreciate why the poem in his memory
had to be full of what Yeats misjudged 'impurities'. He told his
friend's father that his eventual memorial to Arthur would celebrate 'high speculative endowments and comprehensive sympathies'. The phrase suggests Hallam's specifically private virtues
and his larger and more general significance for Tennyson. By
its very subject, an elegy for Hallam would sanction the movement into wider issues. It is certainly in the elegiac tradition –
think of *Lycidas* or *Adonais* – for the immediate object of the
poem to be displaced by larger considerations; but Tennyson was
not motivated by tradition, although he was doubtless well aware
of working within one. Unlike Edward King's loss to Milton or
Keats's to Shelley, Hallam's death was profoundly felt by Tennyson on both emotional and intellectual grounds, as a private *and*
a 'public' loss. Even in the ostensibly personal feelings for Hallam
there can always be discerned some hint of these larger, supra-
personal matters. 'The Gardener's Daughter', composed during
the happy summer of 1833, evidently reflects Tennyson's relationship with Hallam:

> I and he,
> Brothers in Art; a friendship so complete
> Portion'd in halves between us, that we grew
> The fable of the city where we dwelt.

The total involvement of personalities is apparent, too, in
Frederick Tennyson's account of how the whole family had
'looked forward to his society and support through life in sorrow
and in joy, with the fondest hopes, for never was there a human
being better calculated to sympathize with and make allowance
for those peculiarities and those failings to which we are liable . . .'

The loss extends through the affections to a sense of Hallam's spiritual and intellectual leadership.

Friendship with Hallam gave Tennyson really the first opportunity to direct his morbidly introspective nature beyond itself; it had been encouraged to do that because Hallam furnished an intellectual example that the intensely subjectivist poet had never managed. It has been well demonstrated that Tennyson needed external psychological support 'to take him out of himself, to drain off the poisonous emotion which clogged his spirit, to confirm and vitalize his faith'.[1] He himself recognised the need for such a relationship, as a sonnet on Hallam reveals; it is worth quoting in full.

> If I were loved, as I desire to be,
> What is there in the great sphere of the earth,
> And range of evil between death and birth,
> That I should fear, – if I were loved by thee?
> All the inner, all the outer world of pain
> Clear Love would pierce and cleave, if thou wert mine,
> As I have heard that, somewhere in the main,
> Fresh-water springs come up through bitter brine.
> 'Twere joy, not fear, claspt hand-in-hand with thee,
> To wait for death – mute – careless of all ills,
> Apart upon a mountain, though the surge
> Of some new deluge from a thousand hills
> Flung leagues of roaring foam into the gorge
> Below us, as far on as the eye could see.

Not only does Tennyson desire to be loved, he needs the security of another's confident appraisal of the world. And Hallam, in whom Gladstone praised 'the rapid, full, and rich development of his ever-searching mind', could offer his friend much of a moral and spiritual scheme already formulated.

It is often argued that Tennyson inherited from his evangelical mother her convictions that the ultimate reality was spiritual

[1] R. W. Rader, *Tennyson's 'Maud': The Biographical Genesis* (Berkeley and Los Angeles, 1963) pp. 96–7. Rader also suggests that after Hallam's death Tennyson sought the same psychological support in other relationships with two young ladies in neighbouring society in Lincolnshire.

not material and that love was the central force in the universe.
I think that this undoubted inheritance was emotional and instinctive, while what Tennyson needed and discovered in Hallam
was an *intellectual* statement of such positions. This volume in-
cludes an example of Hallam's formulation of ideas, to which, I
suggest, Tennyson responded so enthusiastically; indeed, it was
upon his recommendation that Hallam's father included *Theodicaea Novissima* in the literary and philosophical *Remains* of his
son that were issued in 1834.

The *Theodicaea*'s most significant argument for Tennyson's
mystical nature was that man's reason alone will not establish
God's existence. This must have seemed to the poet the most
reassuring formal sanction of his own visionary perceptions and
it probably ensured that some of *In Memoriam*'s resonant climaxes involve the power of trance and dream. In 'The Two
Voices', written just after Hallam's death, this appeal above and
beyond reason was also briefly canvassed:

> 'Moreover, something is or seems,
> That touches me with mystic gleams,
> Like glimpses of forgotten dreams –
>
> 'Of something felt, like something here;
> Of something done, I know not where;
> Such as no language may declare.'

The *Theodicaea* argues further that God is Love, which,
though an obvious and traditional notion, must have impressed
Tennyson coming from a man of Hallam's intellectual temper and
sanctioned his own internal convictions and – this, above all –
his own love or sympathy ('the simple affection of the soul', in
Hallam's words) for his friend. But Hallam takes the idea further:
he claims that in 'order to love God perfectly we must love what
He loves; but Christ is the grand object of His love; therefore we
must love Christ before we can attain that love of the Father,
which alone is life everlasting' (infra, p. 48); and yet a further
stage in Hallam's argument represents Christ as the 'lowest
point' in nature that God's Being has realised. Tennyson himself

saw Hallam as an example of man's highest attainment, and so
their joint reflections are responsible for the movement of *In
Memoriam*, the 'stepping-stones . . . to higher things': from love
of Hallam, via the mysterious metamorphosis of the dead friend
into a Christ-like figure,[1] to a new love of the Infinite Being.

In 1851 *The Times* noted, but, perhaps through embarrassment, failed to appreciate, that love is a dominant theme of the
poem. Bradley explored the idea more thoroughly and discovered
that the poem's movement originates in the 'change in the love
felt by the living for the dead, and upon a corresponding change
in the idea of the dead'. With the modern attention to Hallam's
writings and their influence upon *In Memoriam* has come a more
just estimate of the poem's vision of love. A recent critic[2] has
most reasonably suggested that the theme of love goes a long way
to explain why Tennyson chose to compare his poem with
Dante: his remark that *In Memoriam* was designed as 'a kind of
Divina Commedia, ending with happiness' has offended many
critics by its arrogance and critical misjudgement. Yet 'for Dante
the way from loss to the experience of the highest things was by
way of love' (Pitt, p. 114) and Tennyson is undoubtedly identifying a similar progress in his own poem. The comparison with
Dante would have been peculiarly apt, too, for Tennyson: from
Hallam, who studied Italian poetry and translated Dante's early
work, *La Vita Nuova*, he would have learnt how the redemptive
powers of God's love became manifest to Dante through the
blessedness of human love.

So it was that Tennyson's endeavour to establish a memorial
for his friend took him into those areas which Hallam's more inquiring and philosophical mind had already explored. Having
relied upon his friend's formulations of belief, he was left in 1833
without any specific, coherent ideas of his own. This, added to
the intensely personal loss, was the real catastrophe. It was not
that Tennyson's faith in creeds was demolished; it was that he was
forced for the first time to establish his own, or, in T. S. Eliot's

[1] On this fascinating theme in the poem, see the essay by Ryals
noted in the Select Bibliography, 4 (iv).
[2] See the book by Pitt in Select Bibliography, 1.

words, 'to construct something/Upon which to rejoice'; *In Memoriam* is, in this respect at least, like Eliot's later poetry, especially *Four Quartets*. Springing from and recording the poet's catastrophic loss, it moves towards establishing in the best fashion of which Tennyson was capable the necessary scheme of belief to replace Hallam's. And inevitably, Tennyson draws upon his friend's own theodicy, sometimes directly, sometimes blending Hallam's inspiration with similar ideas and discussions that were alive in the 1830s and 1840s.

The evolutionary material, for example, was absorbed into the poem during its long composition because in two startling respects Hallam had seemed to have anticipated ideas that Tennyson discovered later. As early as 1832 in the sonnet to Hallam, already quoted, Tennyson invokes the geological theory of catastrophism, against which Hallam's love would strengthen and sustain him. He kept up his geological and biological studies and incorporated certain ideas of this reading into sections of *In Memoriam*. Then in 1844 he saw a review of Robert Chambers's *Vestiges of the Natural History of Creation* and sent for a copy; ideas in it confirmed his previous studies in Lyell's *Principles of Geology*. But more resonantly they must have recalled ideas from his dead friend's writings as well as the example of Hallam's life itself. Chambers, like Lyell before him, considered that the individual 'is to the Author of Nature a consideration of inferior moment'; Hallam's *Theodicaea* had also recorded its author's sense of humanity as mere 'atoms in the immense scheme', yet had reaffirmed beyond reason the ineffable power of Divine Love for that humanity. Chambers also speculated whether

our race [is] but the initial of the grand crowning type? Are there yet to be species superior to us in organization, purer in feeling, more powerful in device and act. . . . There may then be occasion for a nobler type of humanity, which shall complete the zoological circle on this planet, and realize some of the dreams of the purest spirits of the present race.

This, as I have already suggested, was part of Tennyson's sense of Hallam when alive. His mythopœic faculty had by 1844, when he came to read Chambers, made of Hallam in death an exemplar or type of the new and nobler race that Chambers so mistily predicted. Hallam appeared, as the 'Epilogue' asserts, 'ere the times were ripe' to lead Tennyson towards his own vision of the world.

V

It is sometimes argued that *In Memoriam* is the result of constant pressure, mainly by Tennyson's reviewers, to compose a long philosophical poem, some worthy Victorian successor to Wordsworth's unfinished *Excursion*. In 1842 'The Two Voices' had been praised for its advance in that direction, and as late as 1849 Tennyson had been urged by the *Christian Remembrancer* to 'aspire to the rank of a prophet'. Now it is at times in *In Memoriam* quite apparent that Tennyson succumbed to such pressures. Furthermore, with Hallam's example as abstract thinker before him, Tennyson must inevitably have been tempted by the discursive and expository manner. Yet basically, I believe, *In Memoriam* is not this kind of sage's poem. It is the work of a young man anxiously establishing how and in what he may believe: right up to *after* the trial issue of March 1850 Tennyson was adjusting the poem's emphasis by adding sections LV ('I falter where I firmly trod') and XCVI ('There lives more faith in honest doubt') to give greater emphasis to the sceptical character of the poem. Above all, *In Memoriam* is the work of one who had Hallam constantly and reverentially in mind. Now, not only did Hallam sanction the appeal to God's existence beyond reason and knowledge, but he had himself in an early review of Tennyson's poetry argued effectively for 'poets of sensation rather than reflection' (infra, p. 52). He had also warned against endeavouring to articulate sensations in terms of the reason:

for a man whose reveries take a reasoning turn, and who is accustomed to measure his ideas by their logical relations rather than the congruity of the sentiments to which they refer, will be apt to mistake the pleasure he has in knowing a thing to be true, for the pleasure he would have in knowing it to be beautiful, and so will pile his thoughts in a rhetorical battery, that they may convince, instead of letting them flow in a natural course of contemplation, that they may enrapture (infra, pp. 51–2).

He identifies the very danger into which several critics (see House's essay, for example, infra, pp. 166 ff) think Tennyson falls. It is a warning that Tennyson would surely not have wilfully neglected in a poem about the man who uttered it. Hallam's words, in fact, suggest a more authentic fashion in which to read the poem's contemplative flow, an attention to poetic texture rather than a concentration upon its more formal structure of ideas; the method is tried by much of the criticism in this volume.

Whether or not Hallam's shrewd identification of these tendencies in the early review of his friend's poems actually confirmed them in Tennyson's later work, they may certainly be invoked now to suggest the kind of literary sensibility that is displayed in *In Memoriam*. Most relevant perhaps of Hallam's remarks, written long before Matthew Arnold made the same diagnosis of modern culture, is when he points to the 'return of the mind upon itself and the habit of seeking relief in idiosyncrasies rather than community of interest' (infra, pp. 56–7); *In Memoriam* is a monument to such solipsist tendencies and to their rewards. But the elegies further share the qualities that Hallam saw as peculiar to a 'remarkable point on the progress of literature' (infra, p. 53): namely, the congruence of sensual impressions and a train of active thought, those 'feelings of music' where sensation and reflection conjoin.

Section xcv would be an example of *In Memoriam*'s successful movement along the lines Hallam identified as his friend's characteristic ability. Hallam is surely correct to stress the 'picturesque delineation of objects' (infra, p. 58) that are nevertheless 'fused . . . in a medium of strong emotion' and thus *imply* (Hallam's word) the elevated habits of thought for which Tennyson was so much esteemed among his contemporaries. The movement of section xcv, its account of the poet's new process of growth, begins with a curious, almost surrealist attention to details – dry grass underfoot, the woolly breasts of the skimming bats – which define the start of new visions; the memory of such details remains as the poet moves through the intricate and less exactly stated impact of re-reading the letters, tracking 'Suggestion to her inmost cell' and into his trance; and then the reversion from vision to the noumenous details of the landscape – the 'heavy-folded rose' and the waving lilies.

A good deal of Tennyson's attention in this section is directed towards registering the strangeness of his experience. The whole poem, of course, is controlled by a subtle and continuously shifting sense of the poet's relationship with his dead friend and an analogous movement in his relationships with society. Here this theme is brilliantly invoked: the family gathering to sing old songs is used to declare Tennyson's inability to perform his proper and ordinary role in the household and to contrast with his more resonant visionary experiences. Yet these very experiences return him to a world of which he is more electrically aware than ever before – the breeze gathering *freshlier* overhead and the startling intimations of 'boundless day'. But the boundlessness of his new experience after the trance has been in part prepared for by the poet's inability to define, to articulate, his visionary grace:

> how hard to frame
> In matter-moulded forms of speech,
> Or ev'n for intellect to reach
> Thro' memory that which I became.

The loss of an adequate vocabulary at key moments of the poem derives from the general background of a poetry that can recover neither the true language of pastoral and its assumptions of harmony between man and nature nor the full philosophical implications of Dante's amatory language to explain his relationship with Hallam. The expressions of love used between man and woman are often awkward when invoked in *In Memoriam*, but they perhaps represent Tennyson's difficulty in finding a sufficiently general currency in which to communicate the unusual and the unique.

A similar awkwardness characterises its utterance as a religious poem. Moore's essay in this volume attends to *In Memoriam* as a religious poem, but not particularly to the religious poem that recommended itself to Victorian readers. Certainly, as F. W. Robertson remarks (infra, p. 117), the *undertones* of the poem are Christian. But its overt account of the progress of faith does not really rely upon Christian vocabulary and insight; Franklin Lushington pointed in his review of the poem (infra, p. 75) to the highly *personal* feelings and expression that contribute to the 'progressive enlargement of faith'. This was also, I believe, the difficulty that Emily Sellwood experienced with the poem and with its author's religion. At first, we know, she felt that they 'moved in worlds of religious thought so different'; it took *In Memoriam*, which she read 'through and through' in 1850, to persuade her that Tennyson was a 'true seer' (itself not a straightforward claim). As the poem's vocabulary and explanations grew upon her, she recognised in it 'ever more and more a spiritual movement grand and beautiful, in whose presence I feel admiration and delight, not unmixed with awe'. It was she who suggested its title, *In Memoriam*, and perhaps this was a consequence of her new understanding of how Tennyson's seventeen-year-long dialogue with Hallam's spirit and example had provided her fiancé with a new language of religious insight. Benziger reminds us in an essay (see Select Bibliography) of similar stratagems of the spirit by which some Victorians replaced traditional religious forms. While Moore's account of the mystical nature of Tennyson's imagination should remind us that this mysticism finds at least some of its vocabulary in certain of the resources – trance, dream, music, the cries of children – that we have come to identify as symbolist.[1]

One particularly interesting aspect of Tennyson's symbolist imagination deserves brief discussion. The *Spectator*, in its review of *In Memoriam* in June 1850, first pointed to the fashion in which the structure of the poem was 'favourable to those pictures of common landscape and of daily life, redeemed from triviality by genial feeling and a perception of the lurking beautiful'. As

[1] A discussion of the poem's affinities with symbolism is contained in this editor's 'The Symbolist Vision of *In Memoriam*', *Victorian Poetry* (1970).

section xcv shows, Tennyson can focus his inarticulate visions in detailed *pictures*; the apparently trivial becomes the noumenous vocabulary of trance and new insight. He was, a modern critic has observed,[1] 'pre-eminently equipped to spiritualize the commonplace', while the *North British Review* equally stressed Tennyson's 'exquisitely polished expression of ordinary thought and sentiment'. But I am inclined to see, especially in Tennyson's attention to the details and ordinary events of existence (which Victorian critics constantly praised), the poet's anxiety to identify himself with a 'community of interest' that Hallam has said was unavailable for the modern poet. But this identification was not merely seized to prevent his own isolation; it served the far more strenuous and legitimately literary purpose of providing a language in which to announce apprehensions beyond ordinary speech.

At its worst this method fabricates a limp sentimentality, infusing into what is otherwise a literal rendering of the Victorian world some spirit or suggestion which the phenomena do not or would not contain.[2] But at its best, as in section xcv, it provides both a public symbolism for his mystical experience and a means of relating himself to general society, which is a central anxiety throughout the poem. His success with this device may be gauged simply by comparing sections xcv, xiii, vii, for example, or the Epilogue, with some paintings from later in the century that borrowed from the Poet Laureate this technique of registering in ordinary events what they hoped was significant and resonant spiritual experience. Frederick Walker's 'Old Letters' provides a neat parallel with xcv, where the girl in the window-seat on a nostalgic summer-day re-reads the letters of an old lover; or Frank Dicksee's 'A Reverie', where a man listening to a melody from the pianoforte recalls those 'Lips that are dead / Sang me that song' (verses quoted in its catalogue entry); or the painting directly derived from *In Memoriam*, Bowler's 'The

[1] Joyce Green, 'Tennyson's Development During the Ten Year Silence', *PMLA* lxvi (1951).

[2] A point made originally by Humphry House, *All In Due Time* (1955) p. 147.

Doubt: "Can These Dry Bones Live?" ', in which the woman
leaning over the tombstone and gazing at the freshly unearthed
skull and bones is caught in a delicate play of light and shade that
suggest, together with other emblematic details, a gentle mixture
of hope and doubt.[1] Moving as these paintings can be, their
appeal is slighter than Tennyson's, their sentimentality more conspicuous. And what they have been unable to imitate is Tennyson's brilliant control, most of the time, of emphasis: familiar
details are identified in the poetry, visible signs of an accustomed
world, yet already coloured by the poet's emotion and ideas and
so incapable of remaining, as in some paintings, merely literal with
only an afterthought of sentiment.

VI

It remains to comment briefly upon the unity of *In Memoriam*,
which first worried *Hogg's Intructor* in 1850 and still eludes consensus. What is easiest to establish is Tennyson's formalist intention, which prevented the elegies from having any merely
biographical structure: as he said, it was 'a poem, *not* an actual
biography'. This is why I find T. S. Eliot's famous comparison
of *In Memoriam* to a diary somewhat misleading in its suggestion
of a literal, daily record of the poet's life. We know that Tennyson continually revised and reconstructed the lyrics and their
possible sequence to contrive an ideal structure of thought and
emotion phased over three years. Thus, as Valerie Pitt has shown
(see Select Bibliography), section cxxxv, probably composed by
the end of 1833 immediately following Hallam's death, is placed
in the poem's fictive chronology in the spring of '1835'; the
following lyric is one composed six years later in 1839 but added
to the 'second year' of the sequence. Perhaps we should not be
too surprised, merely because Victorian readers could interpret it
as a literal record of human experience, that Tennyson could

[1] The three paintings are respectively in the Walker Art Gallery,
Liverpool, the Walker Art Gallery, and the Tate Gallery. The last is
illustrated in Raymond Lister, *Victorian Narrative Painting* (1966),
and the first two in Graham Reynolds, *Victorian Painting* (1966).

dramatise his private world: after all, the other poems written in
1833–4 are all dramatisations either through the dialogue of
'The Two Voices' or the *personae* of poems like 'Ulysses'. And it
is worth recording another of Patmore's services to the poem, for
he was among the first to demonstrate (to a sceptical Aubrey de
Vere) the consistently *arti*ficial qualities of *In Memoriam*.

The difficulties arise over any attempt to define a very rigid
structure for what *The Athenaeum* called Tennyson's 'detailed
mental experiences'. Tennyson's own account of the poem's
structure given to James Knowles was that there were nine
natural divisions: I–VIII, IX–XX, XXI–XXVII, XXVIII–XLIX,
L–LVIII, LIX–LXXI, LXXII–XCVIII, XCIX–CIII, and CIV–CXXXI. A
later and more influential view was that of A. C. Bradley, who
saw the long spiritual journey of the poet as marked by the recurring Christmases and anniversaries (the former insistence, of
course, contriving more support for the straightforward Christian character of the poem). At least one critic in this volume,
E. D. H. Johnson, finds Bradley's sense of the structure wholly
convincing. Yet it is a little difficult to accept any scheme that
makes one precise pattern of the poem rather than allowing more
scope to the less systematic emotional and intellectual currents
that run beneath its formal attempts at chronology. Hallam was
saying something prophetically relevant to the structure of *In
Memoriam* when in an essay on Cicero he described that 'mood of
feeling which conjoins all mental states that pass in review before
it'. T. S. Eliot is probably directing us to the same end by his
suggestion that what unity the poem achieves comes via its
'lyrical resourcefulness' (infra, p. 130). Two other essays in this
volume specifically provide accounts of the poem's structure that
are attentive to its *montage* and less rational habits of progress:
Mays emphasises how the form of *In Memoriam* springs from a
dialectic process of self-realisation; Bishop, by attending to the
theme of change, finds maybe the most satisfactory principle by
which to explain the poem's movement.

There is one other attempt at unity that the poem makes,
which is related to other points in this introduction. Namely, that
the whole movement of Tennyson's imagination is controlled

quite consistently by his effort to put private grief into perspective; the poet himself told James Knowles that it was 'a
very impersonal poem as well as personal'. He tried consistently
to render highly individual experiences in terms of a more public
typology. Hence the invocation, as the *Spectator* originally
noticed, of a common landscape and daily detail by which he
could fix his private insights. In the Epilogue, for example, the
wedding is offered in very general terms, in almost the clichés of
such events, rather than with any specific and local detail; this is
simply because it was needed as a *type* that recurs in life and art, a
symbol of the new growth and larger future that Hallam revealed
to Tennyson and towards which the poet himself moved. The
marriage, like other Victorian types in the poem, helps Tennyson
to generalise and to move nearer what his dead friend had defined
as the nature of the true poet, who addresses the 'common nature
of us all' (infra, p. 55). That is, I believe, the effort, if not always
the consistent achievement, of this poem.

JOHN DIXON HUNT

PART ONE

Two Essays
by Arthur Hallam

In her study of various influences that shaped In Memoriam *(see Select Bibliography) Miss E. B. Mattes draws attention to the probable impact upon Tennyson of various pieces of Hallam's writing. There were, as she herself argues, other influences on* In Memoriam*; but we might presume, as the Introduction to this Casebook suggests, that little could have been more eloquent for Tennyson than the work of the man whose life and death he commemorates. Accordingly, it seemed that a service which this volume could perform for readers of* In Memoriam *was to make extracts of two of Hallam's essays more accessible than they are to support Miss Mattes's and subsequent accounts of the poem.*

The first is Theodicaea Novissima. *Almost certainly an essay that Hallam read to the Cambridge 'Apostles' in October 1831, it was included by Hallam senior in the volume of his son's* Remains *(1834) on Tennyson's insistence. The second is Hallam's review of his friend's* Poems, Chiefly Lyrical *of 1830, that had appeared in* Moxon's Englishman's Magazine, *August 1831. Some of the most interesting and relevant points from these extracts are discussed in the Introduction.*

THEODICAEA NOVISSIMA *or Hints for an Effectual Construction of the Higher Philosophy on the Basis of Revelation*

I AM about to meet the discussion of the most serious of all subjects, and I am entitled to ask that it may be seriously considered. In these times, when knowledge is increased, and many go to and fro on the earth to spread it, those who are not against

the cause of Christianity must be anxious to give a reason for the
faith that is in them, not only that the assaults of infidel opinion
may be repelled, but for the sake also of knowledge itself, that a
right value may be set on all portions of truth, and those which
really are most elevated, most pregnant with consequences, may
not be defrauded of their full and legitimate estimation. This
seems to be well understood by many recent writers on the
subject. Christianity is no longer generally treated as a topic apart
from intellectual inquiry, but is viewed in its connection with
other elements of knowledge, and especially with the main facts
of our moral and rational constitution. In throwing together then
some thoughts, which have occurred to my own mind, while
employed in such meditations, I wish to contribute what little I
can to the completion of a true intellectual system. . . .

Can man by searching find out God? I believe not. I believe
that the unassisted efforts of man's reason have not established
the existence and attributes of Deity on so sure a basis as the
Deist imagines. However sublime may be the notion of a supreme
original mind, and however naturally human feelings adhered to
it, the reasons by which it was justified were not, in my opinion,
sufficient to clear it from considerable doubt and confusion. Between the opposing weight of reasonings, equally inalienable
from the structure of our intellect, the scale hung with doubtful
inclination, until the Bible turned it. I hesitate not to say that I
derive from Revelation a conviction of Theism, which without
that assistance would have been but a dark and ambiguous hope.
I see that the Bible fits into every fold of the human heart. I am a
man, and I believe it to be God's book because it is man's book.
It is true that the Bible affords me no additional means of demon-
strating the falsity of Atheism; if mind had nothing to do with the
formation of the Universe, doubtless *whatever had* was competent
also to make the Bible; but I have gained this advantage, that my
feelings and thoughts can no longer refuse their assent to *what
is evidently framed to engage that assent*; and what is it to me that
I cannot disprove the bare logical possibility of my whole nature
being fallacious? To seek for a certainty above certainty, an
evidence beyond necessary belief, is the very lunacy of scepticism:

we must trust our own faculties, or we can put no trust in anything, save that moment we call the present, which escapes us while we articulate its name. I am determined therefore to receive the Bible as divinely authorized, and the scheme of human and divine things which it contains, as essentially true. I consider it as an axioma, or law, to which I have ascended by legitimate induction of particulars, and from which I am entitled to descend with increased knowledge on the heap of remaining phenomena.

Now what is the scheme of Christian philosophy? What account does it give of the reasons for which God created us? I find in the Bible that 'man is created in the image of God'. I find also these words, 'God is love.' 'In Christ alone God loved the world.' 'By Christ and for Christ all things consist.' 'Through Christ God constituted the ages.' 'He is the well beloved Son in whom the Father is well pleased.' 'He is the express image of His person.' 'He was made perfect through sufferings.' 'He came into the world to destroy the works of the devil.' From these and several other passages I collect the following scheme, which I am prepared to show is consistent with facts and reason as well as with Scripture, and is liable to no objection that does not bear with equal force against Deism.

GOD IS LOVE. What do these words mean? Some will say they signify the general benevolence of God's nature, his wish to see all his creatures happy. Undoubtedly they include this; but is this all? I think not. Since man is in the image of God, and since nothing can be more essential to man, as an intelligent being, than to act upon a motive, some motive must have actuated the Supreme Being in his original fiat of creation. Now have we any knowledge, or can we form any reasonable conjecture, what that motive was? The Deist would probably answer; it was a wish to enjoy the happiness of multitudes, to see everywhere around him his own capacity of existence and delight communicated to forms of his creation. Unfortunately however, 'Je vois le mal sur la terre' [Rousseau]: how comes that? The Deist answers that he does not know, but that if we suppose it impossible for finite beings to attain certain measures of felicity without previous pain, the existence of evil will be no impeachment of the Sovereign

Goodness. Upon which I shall only make this remark, that we have here three hypotheses made in the dark, which for anything we know may be in direct contradiction to the nature of things. First the hypothesis with respect to God's chief end is in creation. Secondly, the hypothesis that certain degrees of happiness cannot be attained without previous torment. Thirdly, the hypothesis that, even if the second were true, the creation of suffering would be no impeachment to Divine Mercy. Now then what says the Bible? It seems to me to declare emphatically, that the motive which drew God from eternity into time was *the love of Christ*.

We know that in the human mind, passions, of which the objects are remote, general, or vague, do not interest, or excite to action nearly so often as objects of immediate and concentrated allurements. Why else do all passions, the evil and the good, the self regarding as well as, alas! more than, the disinterested and conscientious, uniformly prevail over the calmer emotions excited by views of balanced interest and reasonable advantage? Why else, which is more to the present purpose, do the affections of domestic and friendly intercourse overcome our diffusive sentiments of philanthropy? Why is love exclusive and absorbing in its tendencies, so that, whenever it exists in greatest perfection in our bosoms, we feel it sin and sacrilege to withdraw any considerable portion of our heart from the adored object?

Philosophers, who have fallen in love, and lovers who have acquired philosophy by reflecting on their peculiar states of consciousness, tell us that the passion is grounded on a conviction, true or false, of similarity, and consequent irresistible desire of union or rather identification, as though we had suddenly found a bit of ourselves that had been dropt by mischance as we descended upon earth. The same philosophic persons have been strenuous maintainers of the doctrine, that this erotic feeling is of origin peculiarly divine, and raises the soul to heights of existence, which no other passion is permitted to attain. It should follow then from their opinion, that while we consider human thought, design, volition, &c., as images of qualities somehow resembling these, though at infinite distance, in the Divine Mind, a passion so manifestly the noblest attribute of our nature should also be considered as representing some principle equally eminent in the Supreme Character.

If it be answered, God is without passions; He has no need of any other being; His felicity is supreme, independent, unalterable; I ask, whether or not God has created the Universe? If he has, he must have had some motive, some desire of some object to be attained by action. If his motive was the desire of creating happy beings, as is commonly said, this was a feeling just as much as the motive I have supposed, and implied a want no less. If the analogy of man does not deceive us, the feeling would indeed be weaker than on my supposition; but does a sentiment become unworthy of God by becoming intense, and is it not evident the objection arises from the ambiguous sense of the word 'passion', which is generally used to denote unreasonable or dangerous feelings? In our frail nature strong feeling is prone to error; but are we afraid for God? It is mere abuse of terms to talk of God as wrapt in independent felicity; we should not be here to say it, if he were.

Having thus disposed of this objection, I revert to my former conclusion, that love, by which I mean direct, immediate, absorbing affection for one object, on the ground of similarity perceived, and with a view to more complete union, as it is the noblest quality of the human soul, must represent the noblest affection of the Divine Nature. And here the words of St John meet us, 'God is love.' Are we at a loss to interpret them right? Let us place beside them the words of the blessed Jesus, when in solemn prayer to His Father he said, 'Thou lovedst me before the foundation of the world.'

Surely these views throw light on the assertion that Christ is God. He is God, not in that highest sense in which the Absolute, the ʽO ʼΩN is God: but as the object of that Infinite Being's love, the necessary completion of his being, the reproduction of Him, without which His nature could not have been fulfilled, because He is love. The generation of this reflex being is manifestly eternal, since God's nature is eternal, and the only possible thought of God on his own being must have comprised the thought of the necessity of Christ's existence. I believe this; but I believe also, that the Godhead of the Son has not been a fixed, invariable thing from the beginning: he is more God now than he was once; and will be perfectly united to God hereafter, when he has put all enemies under his feet. Is this heterodox? Yet the Scriptures say it plainly; 'He is made perfect through sufferings.' That which is already perfect hath no need to be made so. I will explain myself further.

Similarity, it has been said, is an essential condition of love, and it is equally true that reciprocity is implied in its idea. I do not mean that it is impossible truly to love a person, who does not return the affection, but that it is impossible to love without desiring such return, and without feeling the nature and purpose of love to be unfulfilled so long as it is confined to one party. Is it not reasonable therefore to conclude that the love of the Eternal Being will require similarity in the object that excites it, and a proportionable return of it, when once excited? But here arises a difficulty. Whatever personality is generated by God out of His substance must be essentially subordinate to God. I say not how subordinate, or to what extent; I contend for the plain truth that he must be so in one sense, and that an important one. Elevate and magnify the Son, as you will: he is the Son still, and not in all points or in all senses equal to the Father. A personality derived must be wonderfully different from one self-existent and original. How then will the requisite similarity be possible, since the nature of God is Infinite, Absolute, Perfect? And how will the Reciprocity be possible, since the attributes of God are all infinite, and that great attribute so infinite to Him, that the Apostle asserts it to be His essence, must be altogether illimitable?

I believe the Universe, as it exists, full of sin and sorrow, is the solution of this difficulty. The supposition that no being, not properly self-existent, can attain conformity of character with the Supreme God, except by a contest with evil, seems admirably adapted to explain existing phenomena, and is not without antecedent probability. The strength of love in sublunary concerns is manifested by collision with opposing principles. When amidst doubt and ignorance and suffering, and temptation, a heart perseveres in love, we may be sure of the indomitable character of that heart's affection.

It may be said, that although the force of love is thus manifested to our human apprehension, God, who sees all things, could see the whole extent and capacity of a heart without this process of trial. I answer that, until we know more clearly the nature of sentient being, and the ground of that mysterious principle we term personality, we have no power to determine, whether the very existence of exalted love in any Being, short of Absolute Deity, may not depend on collision with evil. Doubtless the mere consideration, that 'the course of true love never doth run smooth' in this mortal condition, is of itself no proof that such is the intrinsic nature of that sentiment: but at the same time it is no proof, or shadow of proof, to the contrary; and it leaves the field of dispute freely open to those accumulated probabilities, which are supplied by the language of the Scripture, the apparently natural suggestions of our own most affectionate moods, and the conditions of the great problem which we have to solve, and which no other method can solve without more postulates than are here required.

If these thoughts have any foundation, evil may have been called into existence and power, because it was the necessary and only condition of Christ's being enabled to exert the highest acts of love, that any generated Being could perform, and thereby attaining that high degree of conformity comprised in the Divine Idea of his existence, and that high degree of reciprocate affection required by the eternal love of his Father. Whether then we consider evil merely as a negation, or choose to acquiesce in the opinion of a personal ill principle, the purpose of its existence is equally clear; and since that purpose is the fulfilment of the Eternal Nature by completing those conditions, without which Christ could not have been the object of Supreme Love, and the first self affirmation of God would have become contradictory and impossible, who will dare to maintain that the existence of evil impugns, rather than establishes, the Divine attributes?

It may still perhaps be asked 'How could the pure mind of the most holy God conceive the idea of evil? Is it not blasphemy to make God the author of sin?' Undoubtedly it would be blasphemous to assert that sin exists in virtue of the particular approbation, and according to the desire of God: but to say that it exists in virtue of His power, as the perpetual shadow of His light, for the purpose of fulfilling a nature perfectly opposite to itself, and which could not be fulfilled without this contrast, what is there in this contrary to religious veneration?

It is obvious that in the idea of perfect obedience must have been included the possibility of disobedience; and the power, inscrutable and incomprehensible as it must ever be to man, by which God could set beyond the limits of His own personality another individual spirit, capable of separate love, may well be presumed to extend even to the formation of a froward soul, capable of swerving from the sovereign will. It should seem too that pain, at once cause and effect of sin, is inalienable from the source of all enjoyment: we talk of the supreme happiness of God, and doubtless He hath within Himself a capacity of infinite pleasure; but I say, leaning on the Bible, the full satisfaction of this capacity is future, not actual, not always identical. Is not God love? and is not privation essential to that feeling, until it hath passed out of the sphere of desire into that of gratification? Moreover pain is a component part of all desire; and were we to substitute any other motive of creation for the scriptural and rational one, it would remain equally true, that the sense of need or privation is part of the creative spirit.

But the plain answer to all objections, drawn from logical definitions of God is – Look at the facts: here is a world overrun with sin and suffering; how did they get here except by Divine permission? Every system of theism must make God the author of sin in this sense: the question is, whether it is better to run away from a truth which remains steadfast, whether we look at it or no, or to shew that that truth redounds, like all others, yea more than all others, to His glory, who is 'the Creator and Saviour, with whom is none'.

I will then suppose it granted that the purpose of Christ's existence could not have been attained, and the essential nature of God could not have been fulfilled, without an actual contest be-

tween Christ and the powers of evil. It may be asked why this
warfare could not have been carried on and brought to conclusion
directly and face to face, without involving other created spirits
in its terrible proceedings. I think I see three reasons for the
course that has actually been taken.

In the first place, ignorant as we are concerning the nature of
personal being, it seems highly probable from the little knowledge
we have, that the highest possible power must be that which can
control the springs of personal agency; and therefore, if the object was to exalt that Evil Principle to a very high degree of
dominion, in order that more exalted love might be called forth
for his overthrow, it is obvious that this particular species of
power, namely, over the hearts, the grounds of character, in a
plurality of sentient beings, would be the very kind we should
expect would be entrusted to that Evil Principle. A further step
has then been taken in the argument, and I am enabled to ask why
the Divine Goodness may not be considered as established rather
than impeached, by the fact of a ruined world, a number of souls
enthralled by a principle of sin inherent in their original formation. I may further observe, that however much we should rejoice to discover that the eternal scheme of God, the necessary
completion, let us remember, of His Almighty Nature, did not
require the absolute perdition of any spirit called by Him into
existence, we are certainly not entitled to consider the perpetual
misery of many individuals as incompatible with sovereign love.
If Christ could attain the requisite degree of exaltation without the
concession of so much power to evil, there is no doubt everlasting torment would not be, because God is love, and can have
no delight in inflicting pain for its own sake; but if the loss of
certain souls was necessary to Christ's triumph over the evil that
opposed him, most certainly on the principles I have laid down,
God must have included it in His plan, and a contrary mode of
proceeding would have been contradictory to that infinite love
which constitutes his moral nature.

My second reason is this; love that is infinite must embrace all
objects calculated to excite any degree of that holy feeling. However slight the similarity perceived, however faint the reciprocity

obtained, yet if a minimum only of these qualities exist, proportionable love will be aroused by them. God therefore, since His idea of Christ did not include the ideas of other possible spirits, had love in His infinite self for them all; for there must be some similarity in all beings formed after His own image, all that are capable of love. Incomparably less must these emotions have been than the great feeling for Christ, which arose from the idea of complete similarity and union actually to be realised in him, yet small as they were in comparison, and incapable of influencing his preference, they were yet parts of His Eternal Nature; and as such must be imitated by Christ before his conformity to the Father could be complete. By choosing this mode therefore of warfare with evil, Christ effected another part of the necessary conformity, since he displayed a perfect love for the lost souls of men, and, by living for them, procured salvation for as many as the Father gave him. His character became conformed to that of God by two things, a full return of God's love for him, and a manifestation of exalted love towards inferior spirits.

There is yet a third reason which renders the existence of such spirits necessary to the conflict and triumph of Christ. However complete the return of affection in his heart for the original love of the Father, one point of similarity never could, by possibility, be attained by him. He never could be the unselfish lover of himself. Yet it is surely to be conceived that the holy love of God would receive gratification and fulfilment from the existence of a parallel love to itself, a love that is for Christ. Hence the third manifestation of Godhead, the manifestation of the Holy Spirit, became necessary to complete the Eternal Nature, so that Christ might be loved, so to speak, from below as well as from above, and to him as the one object might tend the energies of everything that was not himself.

Let us cease then to complain of the hard condition of this world, and to draw from it arguments against the existence of Overruling Goodness: for, if the positions I have endeavoured to establish are, as I believe, the most probable that our reason presents to us after a full survey of all the facts we can command, ought we not to acquiesce with cheerfulness in the sight of calamities which alone render the existence of happiness possible, of iniquity, without which the very being of a holy God would be a contradiction?

I shall now pass to a different and less important part of the subject, and offer a few observations on the manner in which I conceive the self abasement and sacrifice of Christ procured redemption for fallen man. The momentous point to be settled is that this redemption has been procured: the manner, I repeat, is less important, yet the enquiry into it will be attended with benefit, since it has been hindered and perplexed from the beginning with many human errors, some of which and those not the least dangerous, may be avoided by keeping steadily in sight the principles I have laid down.

In the Supreme Nature those two capacities of Perfect Love and Perfect Joy are indivisible. Holiness and Happiness, says an old Divine, are two several notions of one thing. Equally inseparable are the notions of Opposition to Love and Opposition to Bliss. Unless therefore the heart of a created being is at one with the heart of God, it cannot but be miserable. Moreover, there is no possibility of continuing for ever partly with God and partly against Him: we must either be capable by our nature of entire accordance with His will, or we must be incapable of anything but misery, further than He may for awhile 'not impute our trespasses to us', that is, He may interpose some temporary barrier between sin and its attendant pain. For in the Eternal Idea of God a created spirit is perhaps not seen, as a series of successive states, of which some that are evil might be compensated by others that are good, but as one indivisible object of these almost infinitely divisible modes, and that either in accordance with His own nature, or in opposition to it. But I have no wish to enter into these abstruse considerations: there is no novelty in the doctrine that incapability of perfect love for God is incapability of happy existence; and for this belief the experience of the human soul in all ages, echoed by the Bible, affords ample reason.

But God, we have seen, is love; love for all spirits in His image, but above all, far above all, for His Son. In order to love God perfectly we must love what He loves; but Christ is the grand object of His love; therefore we must love Christ before we can attain that love of the Father, which alone is life everlasting. Before the Gospel was preached to man, how could a human soul have this love, and this consequent life? I see no way; but now that Christ has excited our love for him by shewing unutterable love for us; now that we know him as an Elder Brother, a being of like thoughts, feelings, sensations, sufferings, with ourselves, it has become possible to love as God loves, that is, to love Christ and thus to become united in heart to God. Besides Christ is the express image of God's person: in loving him we are sure we are in a state of readiness to love the Father, whom we see, he tells us, when we see him. Nor is this all: the tendency of love is towards a union so intimate, as virtually to amount to identification; when then by affection towards Christ we have become blended with his being, the beams of Eternal Love falling, as ever, on the one beloved object will include us in him, and their returning flashes of love out of his personality will carry along with them some from our own, since ours has become confused with his, and so shall we be one with Christ and through Christ with God.

Thus then we see the great effect of the Incarnation, as far as our nature is concerned, was to render human love for the Most High a possible thing. The Law had said 'thou shalt love the Lord thy God, with all thy soul, and with all thy mind, and with all thy strength'; and could men have lived by law, 'which is the strength of sin', verily righteousness and life would have been by that law. But it was not possible, and all were concluded under sin, that in Christ might be the deliverance of all. I believe that Redemption is universal, in so far as it left no obstacle between man and God, but man's own will: that indeed is in the power of God's election, with whom alone rest the abysmal secrets of personality, but as far as Christ is concerned, his death was for all, since his intentions and affections were equally directed to all, and 'none who come to him will be in any wise cast out'.

From what I have said, the efficacy of Christ's death will be apparent, and those Apostolic expressions, which ascribe much more to it than to his previous life, will appear fully warranted and perfectly intelligible. That death was the crowning act of his faith in God. The whole force of evil was then brought to bear upon his holy soul, and he resisted to the last. Severest agony and most fearful temptation were thrown across his being; but he bore up against them, trusting in God, even when God seemed to have forsaken him. Thus in his death the seal was set to the conformity he had struggled to attain; and while on one side the possibility of life accrued to helpless humanity, on the other God beheld his perfect Son, his true Μονογενης, and the First Great Problem of the Eternal Nature was solved.

And now a few words in conclusion to opponents of a different kind – those who are ready to accuse me of having sacrificed too little instead of too much to reason. After all, these may say, it can be but a fanciful dream, a piece of romantic extravagance, to suppose the Being of beings, whose nature is so infinitely removed from our apprehension, can be possessed by love for one individual product of His Almightiness, and can have been induced by passion for that single object to create this admirable multiplicity of contrivances we call the Universe!

I answer that the infinite superiority of God to man is the very truth, which renders it far more probable to my judgment that God should act from a regard to a Being nearest to His Supreme Nature, and immeasurably exalted above our frail condition, than that the astonishing facts of a creation involving evil, an incarnation, and a redemption, should have ultimate reference to such atoms in the immense scheme as ourselves. Christ indeed is one, and inferior spirits, of whom we perhaps are the lowest, may be innumerable; yet in excellence and plenitude of existence, in nearness to God and adequacy to the absorption of His glorious love, what are the myriads of created beings, when weighed against that Only begotten Son, the express image of the Father's person? It is not easy perhaps, on the common scheme, to prevent a feeling of pride in beholding the counsel of God revolve about this little earth like the sun in the system of Ptolemy: but when we come to regard our extreme lowness of nature as a fact involved in the great truth of Christ's having abased himself to the lowest point of disadvantage, in order that the triumph of his faith in God might be more complete, 'where is boasting then? It is excluded.'

The philosophical Deist however, who very willingly concedes the incongruity of the established system, may challenge me to meet him on his own ground, and may assert that a God animated by emotions resembling our own, and for whatever reason, mixing himself up with our passions, and caring for our love, is a figment of presumptuous imagination, and can stand no comparison with that pure intellect, which he delights to contemplate as the pervading principle of his stupendous whole. I have already remarked that no system of Theism can subsist without the notion of some emotive principle in the Deity.

Experience, I think, fairly warrants the conclusion that no such principle is nobler than love. The great error of the Deistical mode of arguing is the assumption that intellect is something more pure and akin to Divinity, than emotion. The truth, however, remains steadfast, 'τὸ τέλος οὐ γνῶσις, ἀλλα πρᾶξις': that capacity of the human soul by which it is capable of action, and according to the exercise of which praise or blame is bestowed, must be the image of the highest capacity in God. Certainly, when we call it the image, we speak only of similarity in effect: the constitution of feeling in a self-existent Being, must be infinitely dissimilar and superior to that in man: but so it is also with intellect; and we have not the slightest reason for supposing that the operations of our thoughts approach nearer to the modes of Divine Knowledge, than the affections of our hearts to that Love, which God is.

These are the thoughts I have encouraged myself to lay before you: doubtless others are included in them, which further reflection may bring to light. Again, before I conclude, I deprecate any hasty rejection of them, as novelties. Christianity is indeed, as St Augustine says, 'pulchritudo tam antiqua'; but he adds, 'tam nova', and it is capable of presenting to every mind a new face of truth. The great doctrine, which in my judgment these observations tend to strengthen and illumine, the doctrine of personal love for a personal God is assuredly no novelty, but has in all times been the vital principle of the church. Many are the forms of antichristian heresy, which for a season have depressed and obscured that principle of life: but its nature is conflictive and resurgent; and neither the Papal Hierarchy with its pomp of systematised errors, nor the worse apostacy of latitudinarian Protestantism, have ever so far prevailed, but that many from age to age have proclaimed and vindicated the eternal Gospel of love, believing, as I too firmly believe, that any opinion which tends to keep out of sight the living and loving God, whether it substitute for Him an idol, an occult agency, or a formal creed, can be nothing better than a vain and portentous shadow projected from the selfish darkness of unregenerate man.

(1831)

ON SOME OF THE CHARACTERISTICS OF MODERN POETRY, *and on the Lyrical Poems of Alfred Tennyson*

IT is not true, as [Wordsworth's] exclusive admirers would have it, that the highest species of poetry is the reflective; it is a gross fallacy, that because certain opinions are acute or profound, the expression of them by the imagination must be eminently beautiful. Whenever the mind of the artist suffers itself to be occupied, during its periods of creation, by any other predominant motive than the desire of beauty, the result is false in art.

Now there is undoubtedly no reason why he may not find beauty in those moods of emotion, which arise from the combinations of reflective thought; and it is possible that he may delineate these with fidelity, and not be led astray by any suggestions of an unpoetical mood. But though possible, it is hardly probable; for a man whose reveries take a reasoning turn, and who is accustomed to measure his ideas by their logical relations rather than the congruity of the sentiments to which they refer, will be apt to mistake the pleasure he has in knowing a thing to be true, for the pleasure he would have in knowing it to be beautiful, and so will pile his thoughts in a rhetorical battery, that they may convince, instead of letting them flow in a natural course of contemplation, that they may enrapture.

It would not be difficult to shew, by reference to the most admired poems of Wordsworth, that he is frequently chargeable with this error; and that much has been said by him which is good as philosophy, powerful as rhetoric, but false as poetry. Perhaps this very distortion of the truth did more in the peculiar juncture of our literary affairs to enlarge and liberalize the genius of our age, than could have been effected by a less sectarian temper.

However this may be, a new school of reformers soon began to attract attention, who, professing the same independence of immediate favour, took their stand on a different region of Parnassus from that occupied by the Lakers, and one, in our opinion, much less liable to perturbing currents of air from ungenial climates. We shall not hesitate to express our conviction, that the cockney school (as it was termed in derision from a cursory view of its accidental circumstances) contained more genuine inspiration, and adhered more steadily to that portion of truth which it embraced, than any *form* of art that has existed in this country since the days of Milton. Their *caposetta* was Mr Leigh Hunt, who did little more than point the way, and was diverted from his aim by a thousand personal predilections and political habits of thought.

But he was followed by two men of very superior make; men who were born poets, lived poets, and went poets to their untimely graves. Shelley and Keats were indeed of opposite genius; that of the one was vast, impetuous, and sublime, the other seemed to be 'fed with honeydew', and to have 'drunk the milk of Paradise'. Even the softness of Shelley comes out in bold, rapid, comprehensive strokes; he has no patience for minute beauties, unless they can be massed into a general effect of grandeur. On the other hand, the tenderness of Keats cannot sustain a lofty flight; he does not generalize or allegorize Nature; his imagination works with few symbols, and reposes willingly on what is given freely.

Yet in this formal opposition of character there is, it seems to us, a groundwork of similarity sufficient for the purposes of classification, and constituting a remarkable point in the progress of literature. They are both poets of sensation rather than reflection. Susceptible of the slightest impulse from external nature their fine organs trembled into emotion at colours, and sounds, and movements, unperceived or unregarded by duller temperaments. Rich and clear were their perceptions of visible forms; full and deep their feelings of music. So vivid was the delight attending the simple exertions of eye and ear, that it became mingled more and more with their trains of active thought, and tended to absorb their whole being into the energy of sense. Other poets *seek* for images to illustrate their conceptions; these men had no need to seek; they lived in a world of images; for the most important and extensive portion of their life consisted in those emotions which are immediately conversant with the sensation. Like the hero of Goethe's novel, they would hardly have been affected by what is called the pathetic parts of a book; but the *merely beautiful* passages, 'those from which the spirit of the author looks clearly and mildly forth', would have melted them to tears. Hence they are not descriptive, they are picturesque. They are not smooth and *negatively* harmonious; they are full of deep and varied melodies.

This powerful tendency of imagination to a life of immediate sympathy with the external universe, is not nearly so liable to false views of art as the opposite disposition of purely intellectual contemplation. For where beauty is constantly passing before 'that inward eye, which is the bliss of solitude'; where the soul seeks it as a perpetual and necessary refreshment to the sources of activity and intuition; where all the other sacred ideas of our nature, the idea of good, the idea of perfection, the idea of truth, are habitually contemplated through the medium of this predominant mood, so that they assume its colour, and are subject to its peculiar laws, there is little danger that the ruling passion of the whole mind will cease to direct its creative operations, or the energetic principle of love for the beautiful sink, even for a brief period, to the level of a mere notion in the understanding.

We do not deny that it is, on other accounts, dangerous for frail humanity to linger with fond attachment in the vicinity of sense. Minds of this description are especially liable to moral temptations; and upon them, more than any, it is incumbent to remember, that their mission as men, which they share with their fellow-beings, is of infinitely higher interest than their mission as artists, which they possess by rare and exclusive privilege. But it is obvious that, critically speaking, such temptations are of slight moment. Not the gross and evident passions of our nature, but the elevated and less separable desires, are the dangerous enemies which misguide the poetic spirit in its attempts at self-cultivation. That delicate sense of fitness which grows with the growth of artist feelings, and strengthens with their strength, until it acquires a celerity and weight of decision hardly inferior to the correspondent judgments of conscience, is weakened by every indulgence of heterogeneous aspirations, however pure they may be, however lofty, however suitable to human nature.

We are therefore decidedly of opinion that the heights and depths of art are most within the reach of those who have received from nature the 'fearful and wonderful' constitution we have described, whose poetry is a sort of magic, producing a number of impressions, too multiplied, too minute, and too diversified to allow of our tracing them to their causes, because just such was the effect, even so boundless and so bewildering, produced on their imaginations by the real appearance of Nature.

These things being so, our friends of the new school had evidently much reason to recur to the maxim laid down by Mr Wordsworth, and to appeal from the immediate judgment of lettered or unlettered contemporaries to the decision of a more equitable posterity. How should they be popular, whose senses told them a richer and ampler tale than most men could understand, and who constantly expressed, because they constantly felt, sentiments of exquisite pleasure or pain, which most men were not permitted to experience? The public very naturally derided them as visionaries, and gibbeted *in terrorem* those inaccuracies of diction occasioned sometimes by the speed of their conceptions, sometimes by the inadequacy of language to their peculiar conditions of thought.

But it may be asked, does not this line of argument prove too much? Does it not prove that there is a barrier between these poets and all other persons so strong and immovable, that, as has been said of the Supreme Essence, we must be themselves before we can understand them in the least? Not only are they not liable to sudden and vulgar estimation, but the lapse of ages, it seems, will not consolidate their fame, nor the suffrages of the wise few produce any impression, however remote or slow matured, on the judgment of the incapacitated many.

We answer, this is not the import of our argument. Undoubtedly the true poet addresses himself, in all his conceptions, to the common nature of us all. Art is a lofty tree, and may shoot up far beyond our grasp, but its roots are in daily life and experience. Every bosom contains the elements of those complex emotions which the artist feels, and every head can, to a certain extent, go over in itself the process of their combination, so as to understand his expressions and sympathize with his state. But this requires exertion; more or less, indeed, according to the difference of occasion, but always some degree of exertion. For since the emotions of the poet, during composition, follow a regular law of association, it follows that to accompany their progress up to the harmonious prospect of the whole, and to perceive the proper dependence of every step on that which preceded, it is absolutely necessary *to start from the same point*, i.e. clearly to apprehend that leading sentiment of the poet's mind, by their conformity to which the host of suggestions are arranged.

Now this requisite exertion is not willingly made by the large majority of readers. It is so easy to judge capriciously, and according to indolent impulse! For very many, therefore, it has become *morally* impossible to attain the author's point of vision, on account of their habits, or their prejudices, or their circumstances; but it is never *physically* impossible, because nature has placed in every man the simple elements, of which art is the sublimation. Since then this demand on the reader for activity, when he wants to peruse his author in a luxurious passiveness, is the very thing that moves his bile, it is obvious that those writers will be always most popular who require the least degree of exertion. Hence, whatever is mixed up with art, and appears under its semblance, is always more favorably regarded than art free and unalloyed. Hence, half the fashionable poems in the world are mere rhetoric, and half the remainder are, perhaps, not liked by the generality for their substantial merits. Hence, likewise, of the really pure compositions, those are most universally agreeable which take for their primary subject the *usual* passions of the heart, and deal with them in a simple state, without applying the transforming powers of high imagination. Love, friendship, ambition, religion, &c., are matters of daily experience even amongst unimaginative tempers. The forces of association, therefore, are ready to work in these directions, and little effort of will is necessary to follow the artist. . . .

The age in which we live comes late in our national progress. That first raciness and juvenile vigor of literature, when nature 'wantoned as in her prime, and played at will her virgin fancies' is gone, never to return. Since that day we have undergone a period of degradation. 'Every handicraftsman has worn the mask of Poesy.' It would be tedious to repeat the tale so often related of the French contagion and the heresies of the Popian school.

With the close of the last century came an era of reaction, an era of painful struggle to bring our over-civilised condition of thought into union with the fresh productive spirit that brightened the morning of our literature. But repentance is unlike innocence; the laborious endeavour to restore has more complicated methods of action than the freedom of untainted nature. Those different powers of poetic disposition, the energies of Sensitive, of Reflective, of Passionate Emotion, which in former times were intermingled, and derived from mutual support an extensive empire over the feelings of men, were now restrained within separate spheres of agency. The whole system no longer worked harmoniously, and by intrinsic harmony acquired external freedom; but there arose a violent and unusual action in the several component functions, each for itself, all striving to reproduce the regular power which the whole had once enjoyed.

Hence the melancholy which so evidently characterises the spirit of modern poetry; hence that return of the mind upon itself and the habit of seeking relief in idiosyncrasies rather than community of interest. In the old times the poetic impulse went along with the general impulse of the nation; in these it is a reaction against it, a check acting for conservation against a propulsion towards change.

We have indeed seen it urged in some of our fashionable publications, that the diffusion of poetry must be in the direct ratio of the diffusion of machinery, because a highly civilized people must have new objects of interest, and thus a new field will be open to description. But this notable argument forgets that against this *objective* amelioration may be set the decrease of *subjective* power, arising from a prevalence of social activity, and a continual absorption of the higher feelings into the palpable interests of ordinary life. The French Revolution may be a finer theme than the war of Troy; but it does not so evidently follow that Homer is to find his superior.

Our inference, therefore, from this change in the relative position of artists to the rest of the community is, that modern poetry in proportion to its depth and truth is likely to have little immediate authority over public opinion. Admirers it will have; sects consequently it will form; and these strong under-currents will in time sensibly affect the principal stream. Those writers whose genius, though great, is not strictly and essentially poetic, become mediators between the votaries of art and the careless cravers for excitement. Art herself, less manifestly glorious than in her periods of undisputed supremacy, retains her essential prerogatives, and forgets not to raise up chosen spirits who may minister to her state and vindicate her title.

One of the faithful Islâm, a poet in the truest and highest sense, we are anxious to present to our readers. He has yet written little and published less; but in these 'preludes of a loftier strain' we recognize the inspiring god. Mr Tennyson belongs decidedly to the class we have already described as Poets of Sensation. He sees all the forms of nature with the 'eruditus oculus', and his ear has a fairy fineness. There is a strange earnestness in his worship of beauty which throws a charm over his impassioned song, more easily felt than described, and not to be escaped by those who

have once felt it. We think he has more definiteness and round-
ness of general conception than the late Mr Keats, and is much
more free from blemishes of diction and hasty capriccios of
fancy. He has also this advantage over that poet and his friend
Shelley, that he comes before the public unconnected with any
political party or peculiar system of opinions. Nevertheless, true
to the theory we have stated, we believe his participation in their
characteristic excellences is sufficient to secure him a share of
their unpopularity. . . .

We have remarked five distinctive excellencies of his own
manner. First, his luxuriance of imagination, and at the same time
his control over it. Secondly his power of embodying himself in
ideal characters, or rather moods of character, with such extreme
accuracy of adjustment, that the circumstances of the narration
seem to have a natural correspondence with the predominant
feeling, and, as it were, to be evolved from it by assimilative
force. Thirdly, his vivid picturesque delineation of objects, and
the peculiar skill with which he holds all of them *fused*, to bor-
row a metaphor from science, in a medium of strong emotion.
Fourthly, the variety of his lyrical measures, and exquisite modu-
lation of harmonious words and cadences to the swell and fall of
the feelings expressed. Fifthly, the elevated habits of thought, implied in these compositions, and imparting a mellow soberness
of tone, more impressive, to our minds, than if the author had
drawn up a set of opinions in verse, and sought to instruct the
understanding rather than to communicate the love of beauty to
the heart. . . .

The *Confessions of a Second-rate, Sensitive Mind* are full of
deep insight into human nature, and into those particular trials
which are sure to beset men who think and feel for themselves at
this epoch of social development. The title is perhaps ill-chosen.
Not only has it an appearance of quaintness which has no sufficient reason, but it seems to us incorrect. The mood portrayed in
this poem, unless the admirable skill of delineation has deceived
us, is rather the clouded season of a strong mind than the habitual
condition of one feeble and 'second-rate'. Ordinary tempers
build up fortresses of opinion on one side or another; they will

see only what they choose to see. The distant glimpse of such an agony as is here brought out to view is sufficient to keep them for ever in illusions, voluntarily raised at first, but soon trusted in with full reliance as inseparable parts of self.

Mr Tennyson's mode of 'rating' is different from ours. He may esteem none worthy of the first order who has not attained a complete universality of thought, and such trustful reliance on a principle of repose which lies beyond the war of conflicting opinions, that the grand ideas, *'qui planent sans cesse au dessus de l'humanité'*, cease to affect him with bewildering impulses of hope and fear. We have not space to enter further into this topic; but we should not despair of convincing Mr Tennyson that such a position of intellect would not be the most elevated, not even the most conducive to perfection of art.

The 'How' and the 'Why' appears to present the reverse of the same picture. It is the same mind still: the sensitive sceptic, whom we have looked upon in his hour of distress, now scoffing at his own state with an earnest mirth that borders on sorrow. It is exquisitely beautiful to see in this, as in the former portrait, how the feeling of art is kept ascendant in our minds over distressful realities, by constant reference to images of tranquil beauty, whether touched pathetically, as the Ox and the Lamb in the first piece, or with fine humour, as the 'great bird' and 'little bird' in the second.

(1831)

PART TWO

Victorian Reviews
and Reactions

The first six items here are from reviews of the poem in the year or so after its appearance. Almost all were published anonymously, and authors' names have been added where they are known or conjectured. Many reviews quoted large sections of the poem as an indication to their readers of the characteristics of In Memoriam; *these have generally been omitted and the modern section numbers noted in square brackets.*

The two remaining pieces are a spirited response to the review in The Times, *and a letter from Professor Henry Sidgwick, addressed to Tennyson's son and quoted by him in the* Memoir *of his father (1897), which rehearses some important contemporary feelings about Tennyson's place in and contribution to the religious ideas of the time.*

J. Westland Marston

THE various poems which are included under the general title of *In Memoriam* are formally distinguished from each other only by being divided into sections, and are all written in the same stanza. Taking the bereavement recorded at the commencement for their key-note, they embody all the phases of feeling and speculation which such a loss induces. So elemental are most of these out-pourings, that the mere intellect scarcely furnishes any clue to their beauty and their reality. We recognize their power less by any mental estimate than by their vibration on the deepest and most mysterious chords of the heart, – and their effect is analo-gous to that produced by the unexpected sound of some long absent voice reviving in the breast of manhood the dormant and forgotten sensibilities of the child. They come upon us with all the truthfulness of a diary: – but it is the diary of a love so profound, that though using the largest symbols of imagination, they appear to us as direct and true as the homeliest language. The beauty and melody of illustration are so absorbed in the pervading feeling, that we become fully conscious of the former attributes only by a recurrence to the poems. So deep is the basis of earnestness in the strains which we are about to quote, that we feel no sense of hyperbole when the Poet demands that the very elements shall be solemnized in sympathy while the freight of death passes over the waters ... [ix and x].

(from an unsigned review in *The Athenaeum*,
Saturday, 15 June 1850)

G. H. Lewes

SACRED to the memory of one long loved and early dead, this tablet bears neither the name of the deceased nor of the affectionate hand that raised it. Our readers have already been informed that it is erected by our greatest living poet – Alfred Tennyson – to the memory of Arthur Hallam. On first announcing the volume we stated our belief that it was unique in the annals of literature. The only poems that occurred to us as resembling it were the *Lament of Bion*, by Moschus; *Lycidas*, by Milton; and *Adonais*, by Shelley; but these are all distinguished from it both by structural peculiarities, and by the spirit which animates them. They may fitly be compared with each other, because they are all rather the products of sorrowing Fancy than of genuine sorrow. Herein note a fundamental difference from *In Memoriam*, which is the iterated chant of a bereaved soul always uttering one plaint, through all the varying moods of sorrow. There is iteration in Moschus, and it is effective; but this ever-recurring burden,

ἄρχετε Σικελικαὶ τῶ πένθεος, ἄρχετε Μοῖσαι,

is not the 'trick of grief' but the trick of art. The unity and recurrence in Tennyson lie deeper – they are internal, not external.
Tennyson does not, like Moschus, Milton, and Shelley, call upon
the woods and streams, the nymphs and men, to weep for his
lost Arthur; he weeps himself. He does not call upon his fancy
for images of woe; he lets his own desolate heart break forth in
sobs of music. The three great poets are superior to him in what
the world vulgarly calls poetry, in the graceful arabesque of
fancy, when the mind at ease plays with a grief that is just strong
enough to stimulate it, not strong enough to sombre it; but they are
all three immeasurably below him in strength, depth, and passion,
consequently in the effect produced upon the minds of others. To
read Moschus is a critical delight; beautiful conceits are so beauti-
fully expressed, that our admiration at the poet's *skill* is intense;
but who believes in the poet's grief? who is saddened by his
mournfulness, or solaced by his hope? The first twelve lines are
exquisite, and even the conceit,

> Now, Hyacinth, give all thy letters voice,
> And more than ever call 'Alas! alas!'

νῦν ὑάκινθε λαλει τὰ σὰ γράμματα, καὶ πλέον ἄι ἄι λάμβανε σοῖς
πετάλοισι,

is felt to be in proper keeping with the spirit of the whole; and so
is the beautiful line wherein he says that Echo, hidden among the
reeds, fed on Bion's songs: –

> Ἀχὼ δ' ἐν δονάκεσσι τεὰς ἐπιβοσκετ' ἀοιδάς.

But from first to last you feel that he is playing with his subject,
and *si vis me flere*, &c. Milton, again, has nobly imitated his
favourite classics, and drawn from the wealthier stores of his own
capacious mind, images which will live for ever; but the only
passage recurring to memories of friendship is that famous one, –

> Together both, ere the high lawns appeared
> Under the opening eyelids of the morn,
> We drove afield ...

Every one knows the 'beauties' of this poem: the passage about
Amaryllis in the shade, and that about Alpheus, set to noble music;

but there is one passage we have not seen quoted, and as, in our estimation, it is the most beautiful in the poem, we will give it here: –

> There entertain him all the saints above
> In solemn troops and sweet societies,
> That sing, *and, singing, in their glory move,*
> *And wipe the tears for ever from his eyes.*

What potency of language, image, rhythm!

The reader sees it is not lightly, or irreverently to Milton's genius, that we have placed *Lycidas* below *In Memoriam*. The comparison is not here of genius, but of feeling. Tennyson sings a deeper sorrow, utters a more truthful passion, and, singing truly, gains the predominance of passion over mere sentiment.

In mere amplitude *In Memoriam* differs from all its predecessors. It is not *one* expression of bereavement; it is the slow gathering of seventeen years, and bears within it the varying traces of those varying moods which a long-enduring sorrow would necessarily assume. Our criticism need not be long. The elegiac mournfulness bears the impress of genuine feeling; it is the musical utterance of a noble loving heart. Instead of criticising, let us suppose the reader has an observing pencil, and that we are looking over his shoulder exchanging remarks. We first bid him notice – perhaps we are fanciful, but the remark comes spontaneously – how exquisitely adapted the music of the poem is to its burden; the stanza chosen, with its mingling rhymes, and its slow yet not imposing march, seems to us the very perfection of stanzas for the purpose. We then bid him notice how free from 'conceits' (and what magazine poets call 'poetry') the whole volume is, and yet how abundant the felicities of diction and image, painting by one energetic word a picture which fills the mind, – as in this sea-burial

> His *heavy-shotted* hammock-shroud
> *Drops in his vast and wandering grave.*

Never was the wild, mysterious, indefinite idea of sea-burial more grandly pictured than in the incomparable felicity of those words, 'vast and wandering grave', wherein the rhythm partakes of the feeling of the image, and seems to bear away the corpse into infinity.

Then, again,

> Calm on the seas and silver sleep,
> And waves that sway themselves in rest,
> And dead calm in that noble breast
> Which heaves but with the heaving deep.

Or such touches as

> The rooks are *blown* about the skies.

Or as this of

> Some dead lake
> That holds the shadow of a lark
> Hung in the shadow of a heaven.

Or this: –

> And hush'd my deepest grief of all,
> When fill'd with tears that cannot fall,
> *I brim with sorrow drowning song.*

Or this: –

> Her eyes are homes of silent prayer.

Or this larger landscape: –

> Till now the doubtful dusk reveal'd
> The knolls once more, where, couch'd at ease,
> The white kine glimmer'd, and the trees
> Laid their dark arms about the field;
>
> And, suck'd from out the distant gloom,
> A breeze began to tremble o'er
> The large leaves of the sycamore,
> And fluctuate all the still perfume;
>
> And gathering freshlier overhead,
> Rock'd the full-foliaged elms, and swung
> The heavy-folded rose, and flung
> The lilies to and fro, and said,

'The dawn, the dawn!' and died away;
    And East and West, without a breath,
    Mixt their dim lights, like life and death,
To broaden into boundless day.

While you, reader, are pencilling in this way with so much
love, do not forget to place a mark of disapproval against the
insufferable rhymes which three times mar the beauty of the page:
again, to rhyme with *then*, must be vulgarized into *agen*; and
Christ, to rhyme with *mist*, and elsewhere with Evange*list*, can
only be accepted upon a total change in our pronunciation. Certain prosaisms and obscurities may be better defended; false
rhymes admit of no defence.

But how beautiful, how simple, and how touching are the
poems when you read them uncritically, giving full sway to the
feelings which that music rouses in you! Who does not feel with
him. [Here follow sections v, viii, x, xiii, lxxii, civ and lxvi,
from *In Memoriam*.]

From the specimens already given you may estimate the beauty
of the volume. We shall be surprised if it does not become the
solace and delight of every house where poetry is loved. A true
and hopeful spirit breathes from its pages. Sorrow has purified
him. Its lessons are no ungenerous or repining thoughts; and truly
does he say,

            I hold it true, whate'er befal;
                I feel it, when I sorrow most
                'Tis better to have loved and lost,
            Than never to have loved at all.

And elsewhere: –

            O last regret, Regret can die!
                No – mixt with all this mystic frame,
                Her deep relations are the same;
            But with long use her tears are dry.

Sorrow is the deepest teacher; it opens the portals of worlds
which otherwise were unexplored; it mingles with our life, en-
larges our capacity of feeling, deepens our sympathy, corrects the
egotism of our nature, and raises our moral development. All who

have sorrowed will listen with delight to the chastened strains here poured forth *In Memoriam*.

(from an unsigned review of 'Tennyson's New Poem', in *The Leader*, 22 June 1850)

North British Review

THE second volume of Mr Tennyson's *Poems* abounds with metrical excellence of every variety; the blank verse of *The Princess*, and the marvellously beautiful songs (most of which are introduced only in the third edition of that poem) are worthy of all praise in this respect. But probably the most striking instance of thorough knowledge and pure feeling for metre which has been displayed by a modern poet, is shewn in the choice of the metre of *In Memoriam*. We introduce our account of this metre by an example of its use, in one of the most musical poems in the volume.

> Sweet after showers, ambrosial air,
>   That rollest from the gorgeous gloom
>   Of evening, over brake, and bloom,
> And meadow, slowly breathing bare
>
> The round of space, and rapt below
>   Through all the dewy-tassell'd wood,
>   And shadowing down the horned flood
> In ripples, fan my brows and blow
>
> The fever from my cheek, and sigh
>   The full new life that feeds thy breath
>   Throughout my frame, till doubt and death,
> Ill brethren, let the fancy fly
>
> From belt to belt of crimson seas
>   On leagues of odour streaming far,
>   To where in yonder orient star
> A hundred spirits whisper 'Peace'.

This seems to us to be one of the most perfect rhymed measures for continuous verse ever invented. The divisions are scarcely to be regarded as stanzas, for the beauty of the measure mainly depends upon its adaptation to lengthy phrases. A stanza ought to contain a completed phrase: stanzas of any but the shortest lengths should terminate in a full stop; and no good metrist would separate even the brief ballad-stanzas, unless for some rare and striking effect, with less than the semicolon. The punctuation in the above metre, however, takes no congizance of the termination of the rhymed compartments; the continuity between them being even more entire than that between couplets or quatrains printed in succession. In these the last rhyme always carries the principal weight; but in the metre of *In Memoriam*, the rhyme which concludes the division is so far from its fellow, that the additional importance thus acquired by it, although marked by a typographical space, is more than balanced by the intervening couplet. Terminal effect is thus wholly abolished, and this metre has the continuity of Dante's *terza rime*, without its great fault of not allowing a conclusion without a deficiency in the last set of rhymes, and of taking away one's breath, as it were, by the obligation of pursuing the never-terminating rhyme, without reference to, and in despite of, the terminations of sense. The adaptation of this, not only most unepigrammatical, but antiepigrammatical metre, to the mournful tenor of the poem, is admirable; and not less praiseworthy is the strictness with which the author has adhered all through the work to the simple laws of his measure. It is easy enough for a middling poet to be strictly metrical in form, because he will purchase accuracy of metre by license of language. In this case, however metrical the form of the verse, the effect will be wholly unmetrical. Perfection of metre must go hand in hand with perfection of language, or it will be good for nothing but to gauge the defects of the latter. When the language of the versifier is incomplete, he will do well, therefore, to adopt a licentious style of metre; but when the words are perfect, every additional stringency of form is less an addition to, than a multiplication of their beauty.

In closing this portion of our remarks, we should add that the metre of *In Memoriam*, as far as regards length of verse and arrangement of rhyme, is probably not the invention of the author of this poem. George Puttenham, if we remember rightly, in his ancient and famous work on the *Art of English Poetry*, gives formulæ for all possible stanzas, within certain limits of complexity; and we fancy, moreover, that this particular form had been used, on one or two occasions, prior to Mr Tennyson's first employment of it in his *Collection of Minor Poems*. The mere invention and accidental use of so simple a form amounts to nothing: it is the perception of its peculiar capabilities when employed upon a large scale, and treated, not as a stanza, but as a continuous metre, that stamps the author of *In Memoriam* as a skilful metrist.

(abridged from a review published in August 1850)

Franklin Lushington

WITHOUT assuming for the present age either an unprecedented sharpness of curiosity or an unparalleled acuteness of criticism, we may safely assert that the most unostentatious publication, the most exemplary secrecy, and the blankest title-page, could not long have kept the public in doubt as to the authorship of these poems. No one moderately conversant with the style, diction, and deep thought of the other works of the gifted writer could have read many pages without becoming aware of their parentage. No one endowed with a perception of what poetry is, could have closed the volume without a full conviction that it was the creation of the first poet of the day.

Such a trial of its merits was, however, not reserved for *In Memoriam*. The thin veil was lifted by too curious hands. Before the lapse of twenty-four hours, the circulating libraries had advertised the new birth in large type. The attractive announcement of 'Fifty copies of Tennyson's new poem this day in circulation!' undoubtedly paid its own expenses. The close of the first week brought with it the notices of the various Sunday papers;

not, indeed, destitute of misconceptions and misconstructions, but all (except in one instance, where the literal tendencies of the critic discovered a female hand, and hailed the rising of a new poetical star in a widow's cap) assuming the notoriety of the authorship, and of all, or more than all, the facts connected with the production of these poems. On the whole, we do not complain of the premature solution of the mystery, as, in fact, it may be considered rather convenient than otherwise. That considerable portion of the public which is content to defer entirely to the influence of authority in matters of poetical opinion is, by the announcement of a well-known name, spared the thankless labour of exercising an unbiassed judgment, the expression of which might possibly hereafter have been found inconsistent with its received formulas of criticism. Those who are ready and willing to use the Protestant right of private opinion, and therefore are less liable to be prejudicially affected by this disclosure, have had their attention earlier drawn to the pleasure and profit which this volume had in store for them, than if the secret had oozed out more gradually.

Nevertheless, we are glad to record our full sympathy with the feelings which prompted the author to omit his own name on the title-page; and we feel it to be, if not our bounden duty, at any rate our better course, to treat this work as it appears, *per se*; to consider it without any unnecessary reference to his earlier poems; and, as far as is possible, without the *prestige* attaching to his established reputation. And we have no hesitation in saying, not only that *In Memoriam* contains finer passages of poetical thought than have been published for many years, but that it is perfect and unique as a whole, to a degree and in a style very rarely reached. It is one of the most touching and exquisite monuments ever raised to a departed friend – the pure and unaffected expression of the truest and most perfect love; and as such, it ought to be, and (unless some great and sudden psychological convulsion overlays and buries, throughout the whole human world, the present fabric of poetical sympathies and conceptions), will be, a memorial more lasting than bronze.

Taking into our account nothing beyond the facts which come

out on the internal evidence of the poems themselves, and relying on these implicitly, the history of *In Memoriam* may be given briefly as follows:— A. H. H. was the dearest friend of the poet, and betrothed to one of his sisters. He was endowed with singularly clear and comprehensive intellectual powers: loved and revered among his college contemporaries for the truth and earnestness of his views, and by old and young alike for the irresistible grace and gentleness which clothed their expression. He had quitted college, and commenced the study of the law; his friends were anticipating a brilliant political future for the exercise of his noble talents; when, in the autumn of 1833, he died suddenly at Vienna. His remains were conveyed to England, and interred on the banks of the Severn.

So runs the round of life from hour to hour.

It is the fate of many men of promise to die early – of many more to be prevented by bad fortune from attaining the eminence of which their powers were worthy, and for which the aspirations of their contemporaries had already destined them; but to few of them is allowed the compensating glory of being associated in life and after death with the deepest and dearest thoughts of so great a writer. Indeed, the interest of such a memorial arises, not merely from the exercise of the highest genius, but from the irresistible truth and strength of feeling, arguing so forcibly the enduring impression made by the character and the continual influence exerted by the memory of A. H. H. on his friend. The Sicilian muses may begin and end the bucolic strain – the sisters of the sacred well may sweep the string loudly or lowly for their loved Lycidas; we must always linger gladly in the charm of their divine melody; but neither the Daphnis of Theocritus, nor 'Mr King, son of Sir John King, Secretary for Ireland', have for us any durable personal interest beyond the mere beauty of the elegies which are sacred to their *manes*. To this very day, the personality of 'Mr W. H., the only begetter of Shakspeare's sonnets', is an unresolved problem. Even the wonderful lyrical passion and prophetic melancholy of the *Adonais* of Shelley cannot enlarge our love and regret for Keats. The interest of Laura is

entirely derived from her permanent influence on the character of
Petrarch; and our vivid persuasion of the charms of Beatrice
(for we will not believe her to be Theology 'whate'er the faithless
people say'), from the sense that Dante's passion for her was the
origin and life of the *Vita Nuova*, while it gave form and colour
to the *Divine Comedy*. It is not only the momentary absorption of
self in the contemplation of that which has been loved and lost,
but the entire and enduring devotion to the self-imposed task of
recording its excellences, which still has, after the lapse of five
hundred years,

> Virtù di far piangere altrui.

We have said that, in reviewing *In Memoriam*, we would not
make any unnecessary reference to the earlier works of the same
author; but we must begin by recalling to the attention of our
readers one of the sonnets in his first collection, published in
1830. We mean that entitled 'Love and Death'. Love is turned
out of the 'thymy plots of Paradise' by Death, who, with the
insolence of a mortal 'man in possession', is talking to himself
beneath a yew. Love submits to the temporary ejectment with a
sorrowful but confident protest: –

> 'This hour is thine:
> Thou art the shadow of life, and as the tree
>   Stands in the sun and shadows all beneath,
> So in the light of great eternity
>   Life eminent creates the shade of death:
> The shadow passeth when the tree shall fall,
> But I shall reign for ever over all.'

Sun and shadow, love and death, yew-trees and thymy plots,
are the contrasts of which the world is make. The sonnet of 1830,
filled with the imaginative hopefulness of a young artist, passes
lightly over the sting of Death, and the victory of the Grave, to
dwell on the glorious end of the contest. The aim of *In Memoriam* is identical with the moral deduced in the youthful Paradise-
picture; but the interval has turned the imagination of grief into
the stern consciousness of experience. Years of toil and danger
are required to change the recruit into the veteran; and the simple

assertion of our 'sure and certain hope' is very different from the actual struggle which must be gone through before overcoming the shock of pain and despair consequent on a sudden bereavement. It is one thing to deny a fear of ghosts, and another to face and lay the spectres of the mind.

In a late article, we had occasion to refer to Goethe as being in the habit of writing calm reviews of his past feelings, and even, in certain cases, writing himself deliberately out of a waning phase, in contrast to Wordsworth, whose practice it was to set down a pure and simple transcript of his then present mood. In the composition of *In Memoriam* we have to remark an intermediate principle, the result of which is the reconciliation and harmonious fusion of the two methods. Each separate poem of the series is a true expression of the particular shade of feeling under which it was written; but each poem is also a necessary link in the great chain of thought by which the progressive enlargement of faith is worked out. The various moods of hope and sorrow often contradict each other; but they all lead towards the same end. The despair of the moment is fixed and deep; but in its very depth there is a vague but irresistible longing to look forward. As the final state of perfect resignation cannot be immediately reached by a simple submission to reason, it must be gradually won by the actual workings of the feelings themselves; and it is only from the full and simple frankness with which these workings are confessed, and their inevitable contradictions grappled with, that we can unreservedly sympathise in the reconciliation of love and destiny. The process is slow, but sure; and to the very last the rights of the original feelings are asserted, so as to maintain satisfactorily what we may term the personal identity of the soul.

With such a text we might write many a sermon; but we prefer to illustrate our meaning by quoting the first poem of the series, in which the ground-plan of the whole is indicated. The author referred to in the first stanza is, as our readers will see, Goethe himself. . . .

The general law enunciated by the German poet – that we may rise on stepping-stones 'of our dead selves' – had been theoretically accepted; but the application of it to the practice of life must be modified by the opposition of our deepest and most divine feelings, or its proud logic will fail. The 'large discourse' of sight with which we are made must not, in 'looking before and after', stoically overlook the present; or we may run the risk of falling where we thought to rise. The higher the tower of intellect rises the broader moral base does it require. There can be no true security for the future where all the past 'is overworn'. But there are times when the blind despair of sorrow almost overpowers faith, alternating with the strong reaction of reason, which prompts the suffered to 'crush her like a vice of blood'. The purely physical revulsions of feeling, from the weary passiveness of midnight to the stronger pulse of waking manhood in the morning, are drawn by the rigid hand of iron experience in the poem numbered IV. Under such pressure, it is an unmingled good for the overburdened heart to betake itself to the relief of song. It is the most natural substitute for the Gaelic moaning or the Greek wail over the dead. The best answer (if any is needed) to the objections of all who hold that if a man is merry he should sing only psalms, and that his singing anything whatever is a proof of the unreality of his sadness, is to be found in the following lines . . . [v].

Where so mutual an interchange of love had bound together the writer and the object of *In Memoriam*, it is not wonderful that every familiar place, every returning anniversary, every strain of thought or feeling, should 'breathe some gracious memory' of his friend. Each poem is a record of some single affectionate fancy, some tender detail of past years, some well-known picture in which the two friends had been prominent figures, some high or deep thought or yearning evoked by the terrible contrast of present circumstances. The subject runs through the whole diapason of human sympathy; the founts of sorrow and love are always flowing, for every one that thirsteth to come to the waters.

Here and there the poems naturally arrange themselves into smaller self-contained systems. The succession of feelings and fancies, while waiting for the arrival of the ship which conveyed the remains to England, forms the matter of a most beautiful and touching series. The mind, strained by indefinite expectation, falls into the most contradictory moods, of which, nevertheless, the music is as true and deep as that produced by the fusion of the clashing discords of Beethoven. The 'wild unrest that lives in woe' alternates with calm despair; the longing which annihilates space spends itself in forming the most distinct pictures of the vessel sailing under southern skies, and dwells with magnetic attraction upon the sacred relics nearing their native land; till the reaction of fancy almost brings back the bitter-sweet hope that the present sorrow is a dream, and refuses to realise the mourner's loss, until the desperate certainty of vision has dispelled his affectionate scepticism. The sad aim and end of the voyage, the final resting-place of the remains, is indicated with a grand simplicity which will find its way to the bosoms of all whose losses have taught them to endow some particular spot with the attributes of a sacred city, the most frequent and revered goal of the heart's silent pilgrimage [xix].

It is through the assertion of these broad relations with nature – colouring with our individual passions the largest features of the universe – that we exercise our most direct (if our most unconscious) action upon the sympathies of our fellow-beings, who are creatures of time and space like ourselves. The simplest and most familiar images are those which flatter most our home-bred fancies, and, consequently, those through which the artist can work on us most easily. The illustration of the deepest feelings through the commonest uses of daily life, through the most necessary and primeval (and therefore the widest) laws of society, will awake the most distant echoes between 'the slumber of the poles'. The shepherd in the plains of Chaldæa, the ferryman over the waters of the Euphrates, the most untaught agricultural intellect that ever stepped behind an English plough, would all be able to see dimly and in part the beauties of the terrestrial imagery contained in the following verses [cxxi].

We should take especial delight in pointing out to the Chaldæan shepherd, whose astronomical tendencies are matter of the world's earliest history, how the simplicity of the local images prevents them from unduly interfering with the fixed contemplation

of the star. The whole earth is reduced to a single point, on
which the spirit may stand while gazing through the heavens. To
our present readers we need hardly remark the beauty of the love
which enshrines its object in so glorious a likeness, or the imitation of the celebrated epigram of Plato –

Thou, that did'st shine a morning star among the living,
Now shinest dead among the dead, the star of even.

The English poet carries the analogy one step farther; after the
dusk of death, and the night of doubt, the serene hope of reunion brings back to its place in heaven the fallen star of the
morning.

We have quoted these lines earlier than their place in the volume, or, indeed, their relations in time and feeling, may apparently justify us in doing, to illustrate the witchcraft that lies in the
indication of landscape by a few broad touches. For a specimen of
a very opposite manner of painting, where the infinities of perspective are drawn with a careful truth of graduation not surpassed
by Claude, we must return to one of the earlier series, written
during the homeward voyage of the sacred ship. We look beyond
the forcible and characteristic foreground over the mellowing
colours and blending details of the middle distance, back to the
extreme horizon of the sea, where it is lost under the harmonious
airy canopy which embraces all [xi].

The same power of accurate delineation of the charms of an
English landscape is visible everywhere through the volume; but
the peculiar handling of this description of autumn strikes us as
displaying a wonderful mastery over the materials of art. It is
an almost unique instance of transferring into a word-picture the
magic of the pencil. There is, however, a pendant to it, in the
aerial perspective of the following 'Frühlingslied' [cxv].

We now return to an analysis of the story, for such, although
the incidents are few, it may well be called; or rather a most intricate history of the growth of love and faith. The ship has
reached the port; the mortal relics are interred in English ground;
the vague dreams of an unwilling fancy have yielded to the stern
certainty which accompanies the sound of the dropped handful of

emblematic dust; but the mourner lingers still. He has no present aim in life, except to prolong the sad farewell — to sing to him that rests below. He takes no heed of the sneers or wonder of the unsympathising crowd, or answers them with the shortness of sorrow, strong in the rights of necessity: —

> Behold, ye speak an idle thing —
> Ye never knew the sacred dust;
> I do but sing because I must,
> And pipe but as the linnets sing;
>
> And unto one her note is gay,
> For now her little ones have ranged;
> And unto one her note is changed,
> Because her brood is stolen away.

He reviews the years of their sweet companionship, bright with the joy of youth and love; he recalls in vain the happy trust in the goodness of all created things, the emulation of mutual fancy, the unwearied freshness of spirit, the gaiety of endless sunshine, which lightened the necessary burdens of life; but all the avenues of recollection converge to the Valley of the Shadow of Death. It is only by a firm but agonised clinging to the faith that man is made in the Divine image that he can reconcile his grief to the confession: —

> I hold it true, whate'er befall;
> I feel it, when I sorrow most;
> 'Tis better to have loved and lost
> Than never to have loved at all.

The first return of Christmas, with its sacred household festivities, now so sad, or, at any rate, so changed, by the loss of the beloved partaker, as to raise the doubt whether they would be more honoured in the breach or the observance, excites mingled feelings in the mourning circle. The well-known games, songs, and dances are gone through at first with the ghastly hollowness of pretended merriment, till finally the overwrought nerves are roused into the temporary exaltation of lyrical enthusiasm. The holly boughs and the yule-log are at once melancholy reminders of the past, and vague whispers of a more cheerful future; but most of all, the village bells. That simple music, of which the associations stretch over the world – 'the merry, merry bells of Yule' – brings to the troubled spirit 'sorrow touched with joy'. How should it be otherwise? In spite of all the songs, good, bad, and indifferent, that have been written and sung on the subject of village bells, there is an invincible freshness in their merry peal. In spite of the 'Lied der Glocke', one of the few among Schiller's poems for which we can prophecy immortality, there is yet infinite and most excellent fancy to be drawn out of the inexhaustible theme. Ignorant as we are of the scientific mysteries of ringing, we yet feel a pathos associated with the very name of a triple bob-major. The unimaginative sailor in the calms of the tropics, and the *blasé* wanderer in the Syrian desert, hear the distant notes of the church-bells of England booming through the thin air, and are changed by the magnetic influence of the illusion into unalloyed masses of poetical feeling. Even those of our readers whose unhappy tympana have ever vibrated to the *scherzi, fantasie involontarie*, and general *charivari* of a Maltese festa, will pardon us for being slightly sentimental on the topic of village bells.

Between this Christmas and the next point in time which is distinctly marked, the first anniversary of the death, a calmer and more speculative element enters into the spirit of 'these brief lays, of sorrow born'. They touch on all the mysteries of life and death; they unfold 'grave doubts and answers', proposed, not with the dogmatic confidence or irrefragable arguments of professed science, but by the blind inspiration and instinctive reasoning of the heart, which will not submit to the *reductio ad absurdum* of its holiest feelings. Their continuity of thought is often assisted by what is the greatest proof of their unfailing truth, the unsparing revision, in one poem, of the assertions or results contained in the one immediately preceding; as, for instance, in nos XLIX [L] and L [LI]. The natural yearning for the presence and aid of the loved spirit is the *motive* of the first; the severest self-questioning as to the sincerity and reality of this wish is expressed as follows in the second: —

> Do we *indeed* desire the dead
>> Should still be near us at our side?
>> Is there no baseness we would hide?
> No inner vileness that we dread?

when the heart justifies itself by the noble answer:

> I wrong the grave with fears untrue;
>> Shall love be blamed for want of faith?
>> *There must be wisdom with great Death:*
> The dead shall look me through and through.

The same intense honesty and persevering spirit of inquiry is pre-eminent in the 'Natural Theology' of the three poems LIV, LV and LVI.

The touching and graceful modesty of all the comparisons drawn between the writer's self and the 'nobler tone' of the soul which has passed away, reminds us again of the sonnets of Shakspeare. Whether he sighs in solitude, like the

> Poor girl, whose heart is set
> On one whose rank exceeds her own,

or, like the old playmate of 'some divinely-gifted man', who had risen from the 'simple village green' to be 'the pillar of a people's hope, the centre of a world's desire', stands musing in the furrow of the field of his childhood, within which the fate of his own manhood is as firmly bound,

> Does my old friend remember me?

or whether he looks upward in happy trust, like the simple wife of some great philosopher, who, while her husband's weight of learning and abstraction of thought rarely condescend to the expression of playful tenderness, still preserves a fixed faith in the depth of his attachment, and 'darkly feels him great and wise'; we cannot but feel that, however dwarfed the living may appear to the dead, however small a point our own planet occupies in the

realms of space, the earnestness of such love is a warrant for its
being reciprocated on equal terms.

> I loved thee Spirit, and love, nor can
> The soul of Shakspeare love thee more.

It is the soothing certainty of this return of affection which
creates the calm cheerfulness amid general society, so exquisitely
compared to the gaiety of the blind man, whose 'inner day can
never die'. The stillness of night hushes the noise of every-day
life, and lets us hear the whispered communion with the unseen
world [LXVII].

The *dies carbone notandus*, a chilly, stormy, colourless day of
autumn, is quickly followed by the second Christmas. The regret
for the fair guerdon of fame, which, but for the premature death,
must sooner or later have 'burst out into sudden blaze', is con-
soled by the trust that it 'lives and spreads aloft' by the pure eyes
and perfect witness of a higher judge. The old games no longer
jar upon the sense: the tears of sorrow are dry, although 'her deep
relations are the same'. The mind can afford to look forward to
the springing beauty of the new year; to enjoy in anticipation the
colour and scent of the woods, the fresh 'ambrosial air', and the
overflowing passion of the nightingale. But the re-awakening to
a fuller sympathy with the outer world only strengthens and
expands the inner life of love. The hunger for a nearer intercourse,
for some picture more strong than that of memory, some inner
sight more true than that conveyed by the fallible nerves of
vision, grows with the growth of the summer, to an intensity
which, at last, we are told,

> By its own energy fulfilled itself,
> Merged in completion.

Towards the end of the second autumn, the family of the poet
quit the home of their childhood. The memories of infancy are
mingled with the traces of this departed friend into 'one pure
image of regret'. It does not require any abnormal development
of the organ of inhabitativeness to enter thoroughly into the
feeling of the following picture [CI].

On the last night before leaving his first home the poet dreams a dream, into which the presence of his friend is interwoven, here described with the force and grandeur of Dante. The next Christmas is passed in 'the stranger's land', and kept sacred by solemn thoughts alone, instead of song, or dance, or feast, for 'change of place, like growth of time, has broke the bond of dying use'. But in spite of the snapping of local ties, always most strongly felt at such a season, the merry bells of New Year's Eve ring out with a new vigour, and cause a more world-wide echo to thrill over the harp of faith. The prophetic enthusiasm which chants a noble accompaniment to the wild peal culminates in the last stanza: –

> Ring in the valiant man and free,
> The larger heart, the kindlier hand;
> Ring out the darkness of the land,
> Ring in the Christ that is to be.

And so the story draws to a conclusion. The spirit has risen 'to something greater than before'; but what he was is not overworn. The meeting with Death has not paralysed Love, but made him rise on stronger wings. Before the saying of the words which must at last be said, AVE, AVE, DILECTISSIME, he can express, as follows, the sum of his own infinity: –

> Strange friend, past, present, and to be,
> Loved deeplier, darklier understood;
> Behold, I dream a dream of good,
> And mingle all the world with thee.

Only once more, after the lapse of some years, are the same chords touched; the appropriate occasion being the marriage of another of the writer's sisters. The poem which is placed as the preface to the whole series, written after another long interval, is, from its tone and subject, beyond criticism.

We are loth to mingle one or two slight hints of imperfection with the praise of such a book. For those who are content to read poetry only once, a great deal of its beauty must remain unintelligible: even those who are willing to study it as fully as it deserves must, after many readings, find some parts exceedingly hard. The thoughts themselves are not always adequately expressed in clear language, nor is their connexion always so fully within the logical view of the reader as to make him feel sure that all, as in some piece of art, 'is toil co-operant to an end'. There are one or two of the poems from which we should like to cut off the final stanza. The 'grand old name of gentleman', referred to in CIX [CXI], has not only been 'defamed by every charlatan', and 'soiled with all ignoble use' of theatrical and other parodies of the original 'good old song', but has even crossed the seas, and naturalised itself in Paris as *un vrai gentleman*, till, we fear, nothing can be done to retrieve its character. The agonies, and energies, and undulations of CXI [CXIII] remind us too forcibly of the wounded snake that drags its slow length along. We should be glad to ask the Chaldæan shepherd, who should know (potentially) all about mythology as well as astronomy (for the Chaldæans taught the Assyrians, who taught the Egyptians, who taught the Greeks, who taught the world), for the elucidation of a conceit, which, we fear, will otherwise take up its residence in that undiscovered country of Cloudland to which many of the pictures of Turner, with their unearthly limpets and black dogs, emphatically belong. What, O Chaldæan – in *te spes ultima*, is the mystery of 'the crimson-circled star' that falls 'into her father's grave'?

These, however, are but small and almost invisible specks on the beauty of *In Memoriam*; and we can only conclude by repeating what we have said before, and what we trust the feeling of our readers, and of all who already know or may hereafter become acquainted with the work itself will justify, that it is the finest poem the world has seen for very many years. Its title has already become a household word among us. Its deep feeling, its wide sympathies, its exquisite pictures, its true religion, will soon be not less so. The sooner the better.

(unsigned review in *Tait's Edinburgh Magazine*, August 1850)

The English Review

AMIDST the existing trials and troubles of Christ's Church, the progress of poetry, however important in itself to the welfare of a people, may appear at least of minor consequence; among the stirring war-notes of the trump of controversy, the voice of the nightingale may well-nigh be hushed. However, two of the works before us, at least, possess such eminent merit in their respective spheres, that they have won our attention, even at this present crisis. Indeed, we cannot allow such passing troubles, however grievous, to engross our critical attention, or our individual minds: we are convinced that our Anglican branch of the Church Catholic is firmly built upon the One Rock, and that no tempest can uprear her from her strong foundations; and this conviction we are anxious to show forth, by devoting at least our usual amount of space to the literary and other questions of the day. We are not only convinced that 'all things work together for good to God's elect', but also, that our English Church, despite her sins and short-comings, is in possession of the especial presence of her God, and is destined to be the great champion of Christianity in the approaching warfare with the spirit of Antichrist throughout the civilized world: and, in this persuasion, whatever foes assail or friends desert us, we may grieve indeed for the perversity of man, but our cheeks shall not blanch, neither shall our hearts be troubled. We mourn over existing divisions, but are intimately convinced that they subserve some high purpose in God's providence; we work indeed towards the goal of unity; but, *until* this goal is attained, we are content to abide in patience and in hope: 'Heaviness may endure for a night, but joy cometh in the morning!'

And now, enough of this. Turn we from such solemn themes to the more pleasant task before us, – the critical acknowledgment of merits of the highest order. And here let us pause to say that though the name of Taylor stands with those of Tennyson and Browning at the head of this article [the notice deals with Browning's *Christmas-Eve and Easter Day* and a play by Henry

Taylor as well as *In Memoriam*. Ed.], we are very far from rank-
ing the first of these three authors (as our readers may already
know from earlier numbers of our *Review*) with the two latter
bards, whom we have recognized, and do recognize, as 'facile
principes', the undoubted chiefs of their poetic era. We have
already dwelt with love on the exquisite grace and pathos of a
Tennyson, on the passion and power of a Browning; and we have
further acknowledged that they, with Mrs Browning (late Miss
Barrett), may fitly be regarded as the founders of *a new school*,
which, though it combines some of the elements of Wordsworth's and of Shelley's poetry, the former's simplicity and the
latter's brilliancy, have yet produced effects which are altogether
distinct from those of the bards just named; more substantial than
Shelley, more concentrated and powerful than Wordsworth. A
special mannerism, no doubt, does characterize these living ex-
ponents of the beautiful; they are addicted to the use of a certain
half-German phraseology, which is not highly to be commended;
they are more or less mystical in their utterances, and they very
frequently barely suggest where other writers would express; they
have sometimes the air of being laboured and artificial just where
they have most striven to be plain and natural; they all require to
be read more than once before they can be appreciated; their
philosophy and religion are somewhat *dubious*. Their feelings indeed are eminently reverential, and their love for Christianity
appears sincere; but their opinions would seem by no means
formed, and they are more or less wanting in that moral courage,
which boldly proclaims its own perception of the truth, without
the remotest fear of man's censure or the age's ridicule. . . .

No doubt, the very nature of Tennyson's genius in some
measure accounts for this fact [the writer has been considering
the state of the literary and critical culture of the time, especially the
smaller audiences that poetry was commanding, a fact to which he
refers here. Ed.]: he is not calculated, it may be, to be *popular*: and
in so far as that is the case, he is *defective* as a poet: for the greatest
poets, a Homer, a Shakspeare, a Schiller, a Goethe, are, as it were,
the heritage of all! Still we would scarcely call Tennyson's
occasional obscurity a defect; for it is ofttimes a great beauty: but,

at all events, it is not to be commended as his chiefest excellence, or recommended as a fitting model for imitation. We believe and are convinced, that England, – that the human race, in fact, – has the same faculties for the love and appreciation of poetry it ever has possessed, and that a really popular poet might to-morrow find his way to the hearts of the million; might, – and yet *would not*, without *fighting* his way first, in the face of critical coldness, and the assumption on the part of the public, that he must be either nearly unintelligible, – too high for it, – or else, good for nothing!

Tennyson and Browning are great poets, and yet neither of these are really 'household names', as Byron, and Scott, and others have been: one reason is, that they are in some respects superior to Byron or Scott as poets; that they do not descend, as *they* did, to the common level; that their merits are often higher and deeper: (for generally the *highest* genius cannot be recognised at once; we like Strauss's Waltzes on the very first time of hearing, but Beethoven's Symphonies may require more than one audience; Moore's 'Melodies' please a child, but Southey's 'Roderick' will only be *duly* appreciated by one who possesses a good heart and a cultivated understanding): Tennyson and Browning have neither the merits nor the demerits of Scott and Byron, – who, however, should only be classed together, as being both in the highest degree *popular*; for Scott was as superior in artistic unity and sound sense, as he was inferior in power and passion. Our two modern bards have a language and a philosophy of their own, and display, both of them, an hitherto almost unparalleled combination of grace and pathos, – almost unparalleled we say, – for Shakspeare has shown it us before them (he who has done all things), in *Romeo and Juliet*, in the last wonderful scene of *A Winter's Tale*, in Desdemona's last conference with Emilia, in Lear and Cordelia &c. They are, together with Mrs Browning, pre-eminently aristocratic and refined: theirs is indeed the aristocracy of poetic genius, bordering sometimes on affectation, but rarely reaching it. No poets understand better to draw tears, – 'tears', as Southey himself, a master of pathos, expresses it, 'of pleasurable pain'. Their colouring is rich and deep, their language is passionate, and their thoughts and feelings are pre-eminently *real*, even when exaggerated in expression. Indeed, no bards have carried farther, or so far, the combination of the simplest everyday life with the highest order of ideal poetry.

They possess, therefore, the very loftiest merits; but these are scarcely calculated to render them *popular*; and criticism, to speak generally, has done its utmost to retard their progress, whether intentionally or no. In the first place, it was right long before it discovered their respective merits at all, especially those of Tennyson and Browning. The *Quarterly*, which was ready at once to laud a mediocre *Philip von Artevelde* to the skies; the *Edinburgh*, which could scarcely find language to express its, if possible, still more glowing admiration for *Edwin the Fair*, by the same author, and which has recently bestowed some fifty or sixty pages of laborious comment on that unfortunate abortion, Bulwer's *King Arthur*, *had only scorn and ridicule, or total silence, for Tennyson for ten or twelve years*. No doubt his mannerisms did deserve reprehension, but still this lamentable incapacity to discern true poetic merit was the perfectly natural characteristic of both our *presumed* chief literary organs: now, at last, that they *have* learnt to admire, they err just as widely in the opposite direction, praising indiscriminately, and losing themselves in those vague common places, in which mediocrity always takes refuge to conceal its real deficiency of taste and judgment. . . .

Waiving all further introduction, let us at once approach the works before us. The first, *In Memoriam*, is a very singular production, – one continuous monody, we may say, – divided into a hundred and thirty separate strains. It is published without an author's name, but every line, every word bears the Tennysonian impress: the whole constitutes a noble monument to the graces, virtues, and powers, never destined to attain maturity, of 'A. H. H.' (we believe, 'Arthur Henry Hallam', the son of the historian), a great friend of Tennyson's; indeed his 'Pylades', or 'Orestes', which you will (he recognises in his friend the higher spirit!), his college-companion, the betrothed of his sister, the sharer in all his hopes and views and youthful projects. Never has friendship been placed in a loftier and more ideal point of view: we have no doubt, by the by, that hundreds of rhymers will begin to discover from this time forward, that they are all possessed of the dearest bosom-friends in the world! It might be presumed, that such a work, extending to 210 pages, upon the same simple theme, would be monotonous: but this is scarcely the case. At least, if there be any monotony here, the monotony of sorrow, it is so eminently beautiful, that we could not wish it other than it is: but, in truth, the hopes and fears of the poet, as to a Providence and a life beyond the grave, and his general views of human life, are all embodied in this most exquisite collection; an heirloom bequeathed to our nation, and to be treasured by it, as long as the English tongue endures. This, we say, speaking generally, and recording our broad impression; but by no means implying that we imagine this work to be free from faults. Even literary faults, we think, can be discovered in it; philosophical and religious deficiencies are, alas! only too patent.

The poet commences in the dedication (written *last year*, and, therefore, some sixteen springs after the commencement of the series), by addressing himself (to all appearance, at least), to our Blessed Lord, and imploring His forgiveness for his shortcomings. He commences (it will be observed, that he uses small letters where capitals are now *customary*): –

> Strong Son of God, immortal Love,
> Whom we, that have not seen thy face,
> By faith, and faith alone, embrace,
> Believing where we cannot prove:

And he continues: –

> Thou seemest human and divine,
> The highest, holiest manhood, thou:
> Our wills are ours, we know not how;
> Our wills are ours, to make them thine.

Ending: –

> Forgive my grief for one removed,
> Thy creature, whom I found so fair,
> I trust he lives in thee, and there
> I find him worthier to be loved.

> Forgive these wild and wandering cries,
>   Confusions of a wasted youth;
>   Forgive them where they fail in truth,
> And in thy wisdom make me wise.

Is this Mr Tennyson's deliberate faith? or are we rather to regard this prayer as the result of a poetic imagination? We know not: certain it is, that if Mr Tennyson has mustered courage to believe at last (for courage was what was mainly wanting to him!), if he has received revelation as satisfying the highest reason, he has *then* much to answer for in publishing some of the stanzas in this collection, such a poem, for instance, commencing –

> O thou, that after toil and storm,

in which it is most falsely, and, we may add, offensively assumed, that the unbeliever in Christianity can possess a faith of his own, quite as real and as stable as that of the believer!

We do not mean to deny that there are not common-place men of the world by thousands, – we know many such, – who can neither be said to believe nor disbelieve; who stand toward Christianity very much in the attitude of Mr Taylor, whom we shall notice by and by; whose prevailing characteristic is a mild and dull indifferentism. These good folks, if we may so call them, derive a general sense of God's existence and His goodness from that Revelation which they nevertheless ignore, they hold these things because they have been taught them, and because it is pleasant to hold them; and as for the rest, they simply 'let it go'. But there is no logical self-consistency, and no high wisdom in this course; there is merely a mild and self-sufficient selfishness; so characteristic, for instance, of the ordinary statesman of the day. Genius has nothing, or should have nothing, in common with this obtuseness of perception. To set such a 'Gallio', even the *least harmful*, intellectually above an ardent Christian, is not only an absurdity, but also a sin; and to this fact we beseech Mr Tennyson to open his eyes. We can scarcely conceive more dangerous language than *this* of his, – more flattering to the small vanity of a very numerous class already existing among us, and more calculated to lead thousands more astray: –

> O thou, that after toil and storm,
> Mayst *seem* to have reach'd a purer air,

('*Seem*' indeed! – but let us go on!) –

> Whose *faith has centre every where,*

(that is, *no where,*) –

> Nor *cares to fix itself to form,* –

> Leave thou thy sister, when she prays
> Her early heaven, her happy views:

(How condescending!) –

> Nor thou *with shadow'd hint* confuse
> A life that leads melodious days.

Really, we could find it in our hearts to whip this self-conceited rhymester. But we will give the last two mischievous verses without any comment: –

> Her faith thro' form is pure *as thine,*
> Her hands are quicker unto good.
> Oh, sacred be the flesh and blood
> To which *she* links a truth divine!

> See, thou that countest *reason ripe*
> In holding by the *truth within,*
> Thou fail not in a world of sin,
> And even for want of such a type.

Rather ten thousand-fold give us the insolent denunciations and open assaults of a Froude, than such insulting commiseration as this! Honestly, Mr Tennyson, what is it justifies *you* in employing such language? Is it your own firm possession of 'faith – void of form'? *This*, at all events, does not look very much like it!: –

> *So runs my dream: but what am I? –*
> *An infant crying in the night;*
> *An infant crying for the light:*
> *And with no language but a cry!*

This does not *seem* the plenitude of self-contented faith and reason!

We are sorry to appear cruel, but 'we are only cruel to be kind'; and we are bound to consider the interests of many thousands of the poet's readers. *Has Mr Tennyson any perception of truth at all? Does he care for truth? Is he not an exclusive worshipper of the beautiful?* We very much suspect it! He appears to us to have faith or no faith, according to the poetic effect such quality, or the absence of such quality, may have upon his poetry; not consciously perhaps (we do not charge him with baseness), but *really*, and as a matter of fact. Sometimes he questions there being any life beyond the grave; *questions only*, but obviously with a doubt, as in [LVI]. And is it for such helpless ignorance as this, to assume airs of inflated *superiority*? Ignorance, of which our author says: –

> I falter where I firmly trod;
> > *And, falling with my weight of cares*
> > *Upon the great world's altar-stairs*
> *That slope thro' darkness up to God,*
>
> *I stretch lame hands* ...

And which can make such a pitiable confession as *this*: –

> I *trust* I have not wasted breath:
> > I *think* we are not *wholly brain,*
> > *Magnetic mockeries*; not in vain,
> Like Paul with beasts, I fought with death;
>
> Not *only* cunning casts in clay; –
> > *Let science prove we are,* and then,
> > What *matters* science unto men,
> At least to *me*? – I would not stay.
>
> Let him, *the wiser man,* who springs
> > Hereafter, up from childhood shape
> > His action like the greater ape, –
> But I was born to other things.

Is it this faint instinctive hope, trembling on the verge of despair, which is calculated to address faith after the following fashion? The poet speaks, say, to a sister: –

> You say, but with no touch of scorn,
> Sweet-hearted, *you*, whose light-blue eyes
> Are tender over drowning flies,
> You tell me, doubt is devil-born.
>
> I know not: *one* indeed I knew,
> In many a subtle question versed,
> Who touch'd a jarring lyre at first,
> But ever strove to make it true:
>
> Perplext in faith, but pure in deeds;
> At last he beat his music out,
> *There lives more faith in honest doubt,*
> *Believe me, than in half the creeds.*

Now, we repeat, that such language as this is infinitely mischievous. Such things are caught up as the catchwords of unbelievers, and go very far towards justifying them in their own esteem in their vanity and folly. No doubt there *may* be honest doubters, and there *are* hypocritical believers; but the assumption here seems to be, that doubt is almost of necessity a more honest thing than faith! Another very mischievous poem is that commencing, –

> Tho' truths in manhood darkly join,
> Deep-seated in our mystic frame,
> We yield all blessing to the name
> Of him that made them current coin.

That is, of course, of Christ our Lord. This is simply and purely blasphemy! This is the tone of 'Emerson' and his 'confrères'; the tone which Browning, in the admirable poem we shall deal with anon, alludes to, and dismisses so contemptuously. We might quote more to the same effect, but refrain. In other passages the dreams of the author of *Vestiges of Creation* seem to be realized and accepted by the poet, who says, addressing humanity, with reference to its earliest age: –

> Arise and fly
> The reeling fawn, the sensual feast:
> Move upward, *working out the beast*,
> *And let the ape and tiger die.*

But now let us leave this painful theme. We remain undecided as to Mr Tennyson's faith, though we opine, that, strictly speaking, *he has none*, whether negative or affirmative, and advise him, for his soul's good, to try to get one! Let us now deal with the exquisite *poetical* beauties of the volume before us.

Mr Tennyson is not a showy, not a gaudy, poet: he does not carry you by storm; his strain rather creeps gently into the heart, and awakens there a low and long resounding echo. We are rarely dazzled by him at first sight; he has few tulips to exhibit (though, if he likes, he can be gorgeous also), but his violets are wonderfully blue and sweet, and breathe forth such a delicious, though somewhat lingering, fragrance, that they seem to the beholder the very quintessence of all flowers. Here is a *theme*, which, treated by any other poet, would have been mawkish, nay, insupportable: but, treated by Tennyson, we are captivated, we are enchanted, almost against our wills: we think it at last the most natural of occurrences to write a hundred and thirty poems to the memory of one youthful friend.

Perhaps, the very unpassionateness of friendship, in a sense, may make this a subject well adapted for elegiac poetry: the friend seems to have leisure and ability to sound the depths of his loss, to measure the value of the lost one. The blindness and excess of mere passion are not here: the grief felt is real and deep; but it is not so violent and unutterable as *some* griefs, which would scarcely suffer such poetic contemplation. However this may be, we wish to moralize no longer, but to treat, for some little space, of the exquisite beauties before us.

To begin *seriatim*, the opening poems appear to us at present a little mystic and hard of comprehension: we may instance especially, no. III; but V is very natural and striking. We will quote

it, though it is not precisely one of our favourites. We fear this
language may seem very *hard-hearted* to the poet, dealing after
this literary fashion with his heart's emotions; we cannot help it;
we respect, we most sincerely respect, his feelings; but *we* have to
deal with the poet, rather than with the man, and must act
accordingly.

> I sometimes hold it half a sin
>   To put in words the grief I feel;
>   For words, like nature, half reveal
> And half conceal the mind within.
>
> But, for the unquiet heart and brain,
>   A use in measured language lies;
>   *The sad mechanic exercise*
> *Like dull narcotics, numbing pain.*
>
> In words, like weeds, I'll wrap me o'er
>   Like coarsest clothes against the cold;
>   But that large grief which these enfold
> Is given in outline, and no more.

(The italics throughout, we may observe, will be ours, as indi-
cating what *we* consider 'beauties'.) The next, no. VI, is exceedingly beautiful, on the common topics of consolation, and their
vanity. There is no bereaved one who has not felt the truth of the
poet's comment. No. VIII is also admirable. We quote only the
last two verses, for lack of space: –

> So seems it in my deep regret,
>   O my forsaken heart, with thee
>   And this poor flower of *poesy*,
> Which, little cared for, fades not yet.
>
> But, since it pleased a vanish'd eye,
>   I go to plant it on his tomb,
>   That, if it can, it there may bloom;
> Or, dying there, at least may die!

Then follow several very poetical addresses to 'the ship',

bearing young 'Arthur's' remains from a foreign strand, – as we afterwards learn, 'Vienna', – to be buried in his native soil. Most admirable in its keen truthfulness is no. xiv, where the poet declares, that if the report were brought him that the ship had touched the land, if he went down to the harbour, and saw his dead friend stepping from the vessel, striking 'a sudden hand' in his, asking 'a thousand things of home', – he 'should not feel it to be strange'! It is long, indeed, before the heart *realizes* the loss of one who has perished at a distance and unexpectedly. He is brought to England. He is buried near the Severn and the Wye. The cold white monument is raised to his memory. Then, finally, the poet sings [xxi, no italics].

We have given this at full, not so much for its poetic merit (though it has much), as because it is the poet's apology for his series; and it was fitting we should let him speak for himself: but we must be more cautious with our citations in future. Nevertheless the next poem, xxii, tempts us so much, that we must needs extract it. . . .

The sad horror of this has rarely been surpassed. Beautiful are the various 'Christmas' poems: the three of the first year are exquisite, – the first beginning 'The time draws near the birth of Christ', – together with xxix and xxx; especially the latter, anent the Christmas songs and games. Then follow two beautiful sections or tablets (whatever they may be called) on Lazarus and his sister: the second of these is most exquisite and *pious*: but, as if afraid of what he has written, the poet hastens in the obnoxious xxxiii already quoted at full, beginning –

O thou, that after toil and storm,

to undo whatever good he may have thus accomplished. Then follow several melancholy doubting sonnets, the tone of which has been already condemned: the poet at last appears consciencestricken, and at last arraigns himself under the form of a reprimand, addressed by 'Urania' to his 'Melpomene' in xxxvii, where we learn accidentally that these were the views of his departed friend, who would appear to have been rather characterized by a delightfully genial temperament than by any genius of a high

order. Most exquisite is no. XXXIX [XL] though too long for quotation, replete with that sweet quiet pathos, in which Tennyson is
perhaps without an equal. Some compartments of the poem follow in which the bard dwells on the mental superiority of his
friend to himself, a superiority in which we cannot very thoroughly believe.

> I vex my heart with fancies dim:
>   He still outstript me in the race . . .

Very fine is LIII [LIV]: –

> Oh yet we trust that some how good,

ending with a verse we have already cited, proclaiming the poet's
helplessness. Many of the work's sections hereabouts are bitter,
and dark with doubt. LVIII [LIX] is very sweet and touching.
Still more so, perhaps, is LXII [LXIV], which we shall quote
accordingly. . . .

This is exceedingly beautiful, though we cannot but think the
poet rates himself too low, and his friend too high: however, to
true affection this may easily be forgiven. A very singular strain
is that headed LXVII [LXIX], commencing, –

> I dream'd there would be spring no more,

wherein is a species of allegory: the poet describes himself as
wreathing a crown of thorns around his brow, by which he types,
we presume, this series of sad and sorrowful pipings; the world
calls him 'the fool that wears a crown of thorns'; but an angel
touches it into leaf, and breathes a mystic blessing. This is very
admirable of its kind, and will, it is to be hoped, operate as a
warning voice to the vulgar, especially the vulgar *critic*, not to
meddle with what he does not understand! Very beautiful is
LXXIII [LXXV], beginning, –

> I leave thy praises unexpress'd,

an assertion, however, with regard to his lost, and, no doubt, much-loved friend, which our poet is scarcely justified in making. This poem concludes most nobly: –

> Thy leaf has perish'd in the green;
>   And, while we breathe beneath the sun,
>   The world, which credits what is done,
> Is cold to all that might have been!

> So here shall silence guard thy fame;
>   *But somewhere, out of human view,*
>   *Whate'er thy hands are set to do*
> *Is wrought with tumult of acclaim.*

Our poet's friend would seem to have been pre-eminently destined for a *worker*: he is described as likely to become, –

> A life in civic action warm,
>   A soul on highest mission sent,
>   *A potent voice of Parliament,*
> A pillar stedfast in the storm.

Another sweet Christmas memory follows. The text, no. LXXVII [LXXIX], is a very graceful and tender apology to a brother, for an expression dropped before, 'More than my brothers are to me'; concluding, –

> At one dear knee we proffer'd vows,
>   One lesson from one book we learn'd,
>   Ere childhood's flaxen ringlet turn'd
> To black and brown on kindred brows.

> And so my wealth *resembles* thine;
>   But *he* was rich where *I* was poor,
>   And he supplied my want the more
> As his unlikeness fitted mine.

But truly, we must close our citations: we have exquisite reminiscences of past happiness in the family circle when the lost one was present; one charming memory of college, LXXXV [LXXXVII]; another touching series on the departure of the poet and his family from their native home or dwelling; and one most lovely and pathetic poem on a learned and talented husband and

his admiring wife, perhaps, poetically, the most perfect thing in
the book, but it is too long for extraction. One exquisite por-
traiture of the lost 'Arthur' we must however add to our citations.
It forms the no. CVIII [CX]: --

> Thy converse drew us with delight,
>   The men of rathe and riper years;
>   *The feeble soul, a haunt of fears,*
> *Forgot his weakness in thy sight.*
>
> On thee the loyal-hearted hung,
>   *The proud was half disarm'd of pride,*
>   Nor cared the serpent at thy side
> To flicker with his treble tongue.
>
> *The stern were mild when thou wert by,*
>   *The flippant put himself to school*
>   *And heard thee; and the brazen fool*
> *Was soften'd, and he knew not why.*
>
> While I, thy dearest, sat apart,
>   And felt thy triumph was as mine;
>   And loved them more, that they were thine,
> The graceful tact, the Christian art;
>
> Not mine the sweetness or the skill,
>   But mine the love that will not tire;
>   And, born of love, the vague desire
> That spurs an imitative will.

And now let us quote no more, though several of the remaining
poems are also most beautiful. The epilogue, respecting the
marriage of a younger sister of the poet, a child at the period of
his friend's decease, is very exquisite, and will be felt by many,
perhaps, as much if not more than any thing else in the volume:
it is full of a happy, and we might almost say, a holy pathos, which
melts on the heart like dew. And so we bid this work farewell.
Much, much, remains to say concerning it; but we have no space
for further comments. We must add, however, that it is scarcely
possible not to think, that the existence of 'Shakspeare's Sonnets'

in some measure prompted the poet to the composition of his work: he has furnished them with a full worthy counterpart. One magnificent strain we have omitted to notice, on the bells ringing *out* the old, and *in* the new year: we are sorry to find it conclude with an expression, which *may* be interpreted as an endeavour to swell the cry of Carlyle, and Emerson, and 'George Sand', and so many others for the future Antichrist; namely, 'Ring in *the Christ that is to be*'; but one verse should be cited for the sake of its mournful modesty: –

> Ring out the want, the care, the sin,
> The faithless coldness of the times:
> *Ring out, ring out, my mournful rhymes*,
> But ring the fuller minstrel in.

He may long delay his coming: yet such a minstrel there no doubt *may be*; for, as we observed before, despite the really exquisite beauty of much of his writing, Mr Tennyson will always be a *class poet*; he will never be *very generally popular*. Then, too, he *teaches* us nothing; he needs teaching himself; he is rather an exponent of this age's wants, than one who can in any measure undertake to satisfy them. And yet, with all this, we repeat, he is a great poet; and great he for ever will remain.

(abridged from an article published in September 1850)

The Times

'Before I had published, I said to myself, "You and I, Mr Cowper, will not concern ourselves much with what the critics say of our book." ' This was a brave, but a hasty resolve, which Mr Cowper very soon abandoned, and stood before the judge of the chief review in a most uncomfortable state of shiver. He was improved by the suffering. An ingenious person of the last century, the Rhymer of the Leasowes, compared criticism to a turnpike on the road to fame, where authors, after being detained for a few minutes, and relieved of some trifles of baggage, are permitted to proceed on their journey. Of late this critical turn-pike has been very carelessly attended. Authors, finding it left on the jar, or wide open, have daringly carried through it any amount of luggage, contraband or plundered, without question or interruption. The public are not the only losers by this neglect. Few people, intellectually or morally, are benefited by having their own way. A true critic is a physician of the mind, and his treatment strengthens the constitution of an author.

Perhaps of modern poets Mr Tennyson has met with fewest obstacles on the high-road to reputation. The famous horseman of Edmonton did not find his gate thrown back with a more generous abandonment of the tax. It is well that the critical result has not been equally unfortunate with the equestrian. Mr Tennyson, retaining all his packages, grotesque and beautiful, has grown into the most resolute mannerist in England, except Mr Carlyle. His faults of taste and language are stereotyped, and he now writes his affectations in capitals.

Our present remarks upon his errors and his merits will be confined to the latest production of his pen. The book of verses bearing the title of *In Memoriam* is a tribute to the genius and virtues of a most accomplished son of Mr Hallam, the historian. Let the acknowledgment be made at once that the writer dedicated his thoughts to a most difficult task. He has written 200 pages upon one person – in other words he has painted 120 miniatures of the same individual, with much happiness of expression, great bloom and freshness of landscape illustration, and many touching scenes of busy and indoor life. English literature possesses no work which, in compass and unity, can be justly compared with *In Memoriam*.

This interesting field of fancy had not, indeed, been left un-tilled. Two of the most eminent and dear of our poets – Spenser and Milton – have bound up their names with the poetry of sorrow. Spenser's elegies are carefully elaborated, but look more like the exercises than the fruitfulness of his pen. . . .

Milton, in every way, surpassed the Serious Teacher whom he loved. He wept his friends with a more winning sorrow. His Latin elegy on *Deodati* contains two or three exquisite touches of natural description and tenderness. But the full tide of his imaginative regret flowed into the memorial of another friend, Mr King. *Lycidas* is one of the noblest efforts of an author who heard few strains of a higher mood. As a whole, the composition is beyond praise, whether we regard the beauty of the allegory, the solemn lights of the fancy, or the organ-like symphony of the verse, which, however, has in it nothing monotonous. Exquisitely does the writer say –

> He touched the tender stops of various quills.

For at one moment the grandeur and torrent of his inspiration overbear us, and then a sweet, gleeful note calls us to the shade of trees, or the field-side, when the plough moves or the husbandman reposes. The Doric lay variegates the chant, and we step out of a cathedral into a flower garden.

Only one discord in Milton's poetry of grief grates upon the ear and offends it. His anti-church invective reads like an interpolation by Mr W. J. Fox, or a stray note for Mr Binney's sermon. It is worth a remark that the chief spot in the elegy on *Deodati* has likewise a religious connexion. Having placed his friend among the blessed spirits, with a crown about his head and a palm in his hand, he desecrates the scene by a headlong Bacchanal and the tossing of the thyrsus. At a considerable distance from *Lycidas*, in the *Poetry of Sorrow*, we might mention Dryden's tribute to Oldham as being among the most manly and dignified utterances that ever flowed from his full mouth.

It will be seen that Spenser and Milton agree in giving a pastoral tone to their mourning. Their framework is bucolic. With what skill and pathos the similitude is managed in *Lycidas* every reader of it knows. But the interest of the style must always rise out of the handling. We admire the poem not so much because, as in despite of, its plan. The pencil of Claude turns a crook into a sceptre, and makes it kingly. We cannot but think that Johnson's objection was essentially sound, if only he had confined it to the parabolical form of the poem, without shutting his eyes to the grace of the execution. We regard it as a most happy judgment of Mr Tennyson, that he resolved to forget *Lycidas*, and to place the charm of his own longer elegy in its biographical passages and domestic interiors. We hear nothing of Damon, and are thankful for the silence. The age, whether for better or worse, has left the pastoral behind it. Corydon is for ever out of the question with people who have anything to do; the close of the 18th century witnessed his burial. That rather insipid shepherd-swain, whom Pope patronized, will never lead his flock along the banks of the Thames since the South-Western crossed it at Twickenham. Not even Theocritus could have outlived a viaduct.

In turning to consider these verses we will mention on the threshold two leading defects likely, in our opinion, to largely lessen the satisfaction of a reflective and tasteful reader. One is the enormous exaggeration of the grief. We seem to hear of a person unlike ourselves in failings and virtues. The real fades into the legendary. Instead of a memorial we have a myth. Hence the subject suffers loss even from its magnitude. The hero is beyond our sympathy. We think of the difference between Ariosto's charmed knight and Sir John Moore at Corunna. It is not Mr Arthur Hallam, but the Admirable Crichton of the romancer, who appeals to our hearts. A rather apt illustration occurs to us. A friend of ours was once spirited up to try for the medal which Cambridge offered in honour of her deceased Chancellor. Having completed his task he showed it to an accomplished critic, who said, – 'The lines are good, but I should have imagined that instead of a duke dying, the whole world had gone off in convulsions, your lamentation is so tremendous.' The wailings of *In Memoriam* might have drawn forth a similar exclamation. The disproportion of phrase is sometimes ludicrous, and occasionally it borders on blasphemy. Can the writer satisfy his own conscience with respect to these verses?

> But, brooding on the dear one dead,
>   And all he said of things divine,
>   (*And dear as sacramental wine*
> *To dying lips, is all he said.*)

For our part, we should consider no confession of regret too strong for the hardihood that indicted them. Soften it as you will, the feeling of untruthfulness cannot be removed. Nature and identity are wanting. The lost friend stalks along a giant of 11 feet, or moves a spiritual being, with an Eden-halo, through life. The difficulty set before a poet is to reconcile the imaginary with the actual; the epic with the prose of common men. . . .

A second defect, which has painfully come out as often as we take up the volume, is the tone of – may we say so! – amatory tenderness. Surely this is a strange manner of address to a man, even though he be dead: –

> So, dearest, now thy brows are cold,
>   I see thee what thou art, and know
>   Thy likeness to the wise below,
> Thy kindred with the great of old.
>
> But there is more than I can see,
>   And what I see I leave unsaid,
>   Nor speak it, knowing death has made
> His darkness beautiful with thee.

Very sweet and plaintive these verses are; but who would not give them a feminine application? Shakespeare may be considered the founder of this style in English. In classical and Oriental poetry it is unpleasantly familiar. His mysterious sonnets present the startling peculiarity of transferring every epithet of womanly endearment to a masculine friend, – his master-mistress, as he calls him by a compound epithet, harsh as it is disagreeable. We should never expect to hear a young lawyer calling a member of the same inn 'his rose', except in the Middle Temple of Ispahan, with Hafiz for a laureate. Equally objectionable are the following lines in the 42nd sonnet: –

> If I could write the beauty of your eyes,
>   And in fresh numbers number all your graces,
> The age to come would say this poet lies;
>   Such heavenly touches ne'er touched earthly faces.

Is it Petrarch whispering to Laura? We really think that floating remembrances of Shakespeare's sonnets have beguiled Mr Tennyson. Many of these poems seem to be contrived, like

Goldsmith's chest of drawers, 'a double debt to pay', and might
be addressed with perfect propriety, and every assurance of a
favourable reception, to one of those young ladies with melting
blue eyes and a passion for novels whom we found Mr Bennet so
ungallantly denouncing in a recent letter to his children.

We object to a Cantab being styled a 'rose' under any conditions; but do not suppose that we would shut up nature, as a
storehouse of imagery and consolation, from him who laments a
lost companion of his school, or college, or maturer days, with
whom he took sweet counsel and walked as a friend. Let Cowley
weep for Harvey. Most exquisitely does the poet of all joy and
sorrow write –

> So are you to my thoughts as food to life,
> Or as sweet seasoned showers are to the ground.

The harvest of memory will come up abundantly, as the seed
falls up and down life; the shadow of the familiar form glides over
the landscape; the old field-path recalls him; and the warm home-
stead, the meadow stile, the windy sheepwalk, the gray church
tower, the wrangling daw in the quarry, – each is dear and each
has a voice, as having been seen with him and by him. But this
source of interest requires to be opened with a sparing hand. It
easily and quickly is corrupted into sentiment. We can appreciate
the meditative rapture of Burns, who saw his 'Jean' in the flower
under the hedge; but the taste is displeased when every expression
of fondness is sighed out, and the only figure within our view is
Amaryllis of the Chancery Bar.

Another fault is not perculiar to *In Memoriam*; it runs through
all Mr Tennyson's poetry, – we allude to his *obscurity*. We are
prepared to admit that certain kinds of writing are especially ex-
posed to this accusation, and from causes beyond the oversight
of the author. The emotions of the heart and of the fancy have
their own dialect. This is always hard to be understood, – is frequently altogether unintelligible by ruder minds. The muses'
court cherishes particular idioms. ... Again, a magnificent thought
is likely to be obscure to the first glance; a mist hangs round it
and shows its elevation. As in passages of emotional tenderness

and taste there is a reflective light to be thrown from the reader's experience of corresponding sensations, so in images of sublimity a large perspective requires filling up. Perhaps the poetry of the world contains no grander description than Milton's of the advancing God –

> Far off His coming shone.

But the picture loses its splendour unless we people the vast field of time that lies between with legions of heavenly warriors, and light the cloudy edge of distant centuries with the blaze of Cherubim and the chariots of the Eternal. In such cases the obscurity melts before the observer. We will call Mr Tennyson himself in support of our argument [CXXIV]. To that most literal gentleman whom Elia pleasantly ridiculed these verses would be simply so many inscriptions in an unknown tongue; but to the poetical eye their obscurity is the result of the illimitable expanse of mystery over which the poet sweeps. The very dimness helps to impress his mind with immensity.

The following invocation to the departed friend would claim the benefit of the exception: –

> Come; not in watches of the night,
>   But when the sunbeam broodeth warm,
>   Come, *beauteous in thine after form*,
> *And like a finer light on light.*

Perhaps we might even include in this class the contrast in the 24th elegy between the happiness and sorrow of former and present days, where the poet inquires whether it is that the haze of grief magnifies joy –

> Or that the past will always win
>   A glory from its being far;
>   And orb into the perfect star,
> We saw not when we moved therein?

For there is something striking and suggestive in comparing the goneby time to some luminous body riding like a red harvest moon behind us, lighting our path homeward.

Now, for all such cases of obscurity a very liberal allowance is

to be made. The highest beauty does not always lie upon the surface of words. In whatever degree the difficulty of Mr Tennyson's
verse is to be explained by its depth the writer should be acquitted.
But in a large number of passages plea cannot be received. He is
difficult not from excess, but want of meaning. Take a specimen
[xxvi].

We ask seriously if that celebrated collector and critic Mr M.
Scriblerus would not have bought up this stanza at any price?
Unquestionably it is worth its weight in lead for a treatise on
Bathos. Lately we have heard much of keys both from the Flaminian Gate and Piccadilly, but we back this verse against Hobbs.
We dare him to pick it. Mr Moxon may hang it up in his window,
with a £200 prize attached, more safely than a Bramah. That a
Shadow should hold keys at all, is a noticeable circumstance; but
that it should wait with a cloak ready to be thrown over a gentleman in difficulties, is absolutely amazing. There is an allusion,
which soars to the same height above our comprehension: –

> That each, who seems a separate whole,
>   Should move his rounds, and fusing all
>   The skirts of self again, should fall,
> Remerging in the general Soul.

Of the two mysteries, the Shadow with the cloak is probably the
easier. We request the reader, who may be of an analytical turn,
to try the above stanza for himself. Let him resolve it into prose.
We have applied every known test, without detecting the
smallest trace of sense, and are confident that the 'blind clerk' at
the General Post-office would abandon the effort when he came
to *fusing the skirts of self*.

There is a fainter kind of obscurity which ought, so far as
possible, to be cleared away. In this sort, also, Mr Tennyson makes
considerable demands upon our patience. Even a refined and
educated reader is often puzzled to identify his exact allusion.
This uncertainty is always injurious to poetical scenery. When
Mason was writing *Caractacus* he was cautioned by his most
accomplished friend to make every allusion so plain that it might
immediately be understood; because, he said, we are not allowed

to *hint* at things in general or particular history as in the Greek fables, which everybody is supposed to know. This stanza of Mr Tennyson will show our meaning: –

> And seem to lift the form, and glow
>   In azure orbits heavenly wise;
>   And over those ethereal eyes
> *The bar of Michael Angelo.*

We shall not say if we comprehend the closing line. We can keep a secret. But we put it to the last young lady for whom Hayday bound the *Princess* in pink morocco to answer whether the *Bar of Michael Angelo* raises a distinct image to her mind, so distinct that, in her next lesson from Gavazzi, she will be able to put the passage into good Tuscan for the Father?

We may here observe that Mr Tennyson frequently allows his amplitude of coloured and stately phrases to seduce him into line after line of grand sounding dactyls and spondees, out of which it is extremely hard to draw any message of wisdom or utterance of common sense. We string together three passages that might be mistaken for lumps of Statius or Nat Lee in their most turgid or twilight mood. Just listen how they tumble along with a heavy, splashing, and bewildering roll: –

> On thee the loyal-hearted hung,
>   The proud was half disarm'd of pride,
>   *Nor cared the serpent at thy side*
> *To flicker with his treble tongue.* [cx]

> For every grain of sand that runs,
>   And every span of shade that steals,
>   And every hiss of toothed wheels,
> And all the courses of the suns. [cxvii]

> Large elements in order brought,
>   And tracts of calm from tempest made,
>   *And world-wide fluctuation sway'd*
> *In vassal tides that follow'd thought.* [cxii]

What is the meaning of the serpent with the tongue that flickers? and how can a fluctuation be swayed into 'a vassal tide'?

A frequent source of mist and doubtfulness in language is a habit, either wilful or indifferent, of grammatical inaccuracy. Mr Tennyson is quite autocratic in his government of words. Substantives are flung upon the world without the slightest provision for their maintenance; active and passive verbs exchange duties with astonishing ease and boldness, and particles are disbanded by a summary process unknown to Lindley Murray or Dr Latham. Look at these instances out of many: –

I brim with sorrow drowning song. [xix]

Each voice four changes on the wind. [xxviii]

Thine own shall wither in the vast. [lxxvi]

A happy lover, who has come
   To look on her that loves him well;
    Who *lights* and rings the gateway bell,
And learns her gone, and far from home. [viii]

Here it is evident that '*lights*' and '*learns*' are used with extreme incorrectness. The construction requires us to suppose that the lover arrives in a dark evening with a lantern, and gropes about the brick wall until he finds the bell. Just look at the circumstance as Jones might relate it to a young lady in the suburbs – 'I got into the Kennington omnibus yesterday, and in the hope of finding you at home I light and ring the bell, and learn you gone.' Would such an epistle be understandable? If the object of his devotion be a girl of spirit, she will instantly cut off six heads, and send Jones a copy of Mr Edwards' *Progressive English Exercises* by the next post. Will the Germanic and cloud-compelling school permit us to recommend to their patient meditation a short saying of Hobbes, which need not be confined to Mr Tennyson's ear? – 'The order of words, when placed as they ought to be, carries a light before it, whereby a man may foresee the length of his period; as a torch in the night showeth a man the stops and unevenness of the way.'

We turn with very sincere pleasure to notice some of the finer and purer qualities of this book and its author. We wish Mr

Tennyson to number us with his friends. First among his gifts
we should place his mastery of diction. Words many, and of the
finest dyes, from Greece and Italy, are heaped in his treasury.
Whatever be the wants of his muse, her wardrobe is rich in every
article of dress, laid up in myrrh and ivory. A single expression
often shoots a sunbeam into a line and kindles a page. This quality
establishes his claim to the title of a true poet. It stamps every
honoured name of song and distinguishes it from the usurper's.
It is like the hasty touch of Rembrandt, that struck his mind's
life into canvas. The 'shadowy gust' with which Thomson swept
his corn-field was as much beyond the ablest versifier as the
building of Pandemonium. We judge a genius by a word, as we
might try a new mintage by the shape and the ring of its smallest
coin. With these happinesses of expression the present Elegies
are plentifully sprinkled. We gather several, beginning with an
evening cloud-scene: –

> That rises upward always higher,
>   And onward drags a labouring breast,
>   And topples round the *dreary west*,
> A looming bastion fringed with fire. [xv]

> And on the low dark verge of life,
> *The twilight of eternal day.* [l]

> I falter where I firmly trod,
>   And falling with my weight of cares
>   Upon the *great world: Altar stairs*
> *That slope through darkness up to God.* [lv]

> The chestnut *pattering to the ground.* [xi]

> With blasts *that blow the poplar white.* [lxxii]

> The gust that round the garden flew,
> *And tumbled half the mellowing pears.* [lxxxix]

> When summer's hourly-mellowing change
>   May breathe with many roses sweet
>   *Upon the thousand waves of wheat,*
> *That ripple round the lonely grange.* [xci]

> And Autumn laying here and there
> *A fiery finger on the leaves.* [XCIX]

> Unwatched the garden bough shall sway,
>   The tender blossom flutter down,
>   Unloved that *beech will gather brown*,
> This maple burn itself away. [CI]

Sometimes Mr Tennyson is apt to exceed the poetical liberty of reviving ancient manners of speech. Old words are old gold. Dryden, in particular, understood this way of setting his jewels. Its recommendations are strong. A phrase or epithet of early times brings its age with it. A pure Chaucerian is like a fresh nosegay flung suddenly on the table; but the beauty of the word should be decided. It must have something of the past centuries more winning than their wrinkles. In Mr Tennyson's revivals this preciousness is not seldom absent. Take two instances, –

> A thousand wants
> *Gnarr* at the heels of men. [XCVIII]

> Now *burgeons* every maze of quick. [CXV]

We know that both of these words are used by Spenser – the former in the sense of snarling or barking, the latter of springing forth or budding – but they have no merit whatever of their own; Spenser's pen does not consecrate them.

It is not necessary to commend the almost unbroken music of Mr Tennyson's rhythm – nobody denies his ear. You are sure of a sweet sound, though nothing be in it. We will add that he is extremely successful in the endings of the short poems into which the memorial is broken. This is a merit of much importance. When Mason sent his elegy written in a garden to Gray, he objected to the last line as being flat and prosaic, whereas that above every other, he told him, ought to sparkle, or, at least, to shine. Accordingly, Gray exhorted him to twirl the sentiment into an apophthegm, to stick a flower in it, to gild it with a costly expression, and to make it strike the fancy, the ear, or the heart. Mr Tennyson has, however unconsciously, followed the advice. Nor among his word excellencies should we forget the pleasing effect of his word-repetitions – an art which poets of all countries and times have been fond of practising. Ovid's description of Apollo's chariot is a musical example, with its golden axle, its golden beam, and the outward rim of the wheels in gold; where the sound of the *aureus* is like a mellow note continually returning in the strain.

In conclusion, we offer only one observation by way of moral. Small as this book is, it may be abridged with profit. The kindest gift to a poet is a division of '2'. We would not exclude the greatest names from a share in the privilege. What fierce grinning distortions of Dante might be driven out of Purgatory? What succulent episodes of Spenser or Camoens be lopped off? What dry shreds of Milton be tossed into a Baptist magazine? How the noble features of Dryden's genius would shine out if all his trade verses had been treated like Tonson's trade guineas, and *clipped*! Wordsworth's *Excursion* would pleasantly shorten into a summer walk, and Southey's 10 volumes reappear with infinite vivacity in a moderate 8mo. Whatever be the expansion of ancient song, compression is indispensable to a modern versifier. The circulation of his blood is too languid for a large body and scarcely reaches the extremities. His chances of fame in the future may be calculated by the thickness of his volume. Posterity will only preserve the choicer metal. Epic urns, with their glitter and baseness, will be broken up, while the ode and sonnet give forth their little gleams; and he will be the happy rhymer in the coming century, whose grain of gold, disengaged of its impurities, and not swollen out with alloy, has melted quite pure into a locket.

(abridged from an anonymous review, possibly by
Manley Hopkins, under the title, 'The Poetry of Sorrow',
28 November 1851)

[*Editor's general note*. Several of *The Times* critic's strictures on Tennyson's phrasing made the poet modify occasional words in subsequent editions. Full details are given in the notes to *In Memoriam* provided by Christopher Ricks in his edition of the poems: see Select Bibliography.]

F. W. Robertson

THE poem entitled *In Memoriam* is a monument erected by friendship to the memory of a gifted son of the historian Hallam. It is divided into a number of cabinet-like compartments, which, with fine and delicate shades of difference, exhibit the various phases through which the bereaved spirit passes from the first shock of despair, dull, hopeless misery and rebellion, up to the dawn of hope, acquiescent trust, and even calm happiness again. In the meanwhile many a question has been solved, which can only suggest itself when suffering forces the soul to front the realities of our mysterious existence; such as: Is there indeed a life to come? And if there is, will it be a conscious life? Shall I know that I am myself? Will there be mutual recognition? continuance of attachments? Shall friend meet friend, and brother brother, as friends and brothers? Or, again: How comes it that one so gifted was taken away so early, in the maturity of his powers, just at the moment when they seemed about to become available to mankind? What means all this, and is there not something wrong? Is the Law of Creation Love indeed?

By slow degrees, all these doubts, and worse, are answered; not as a philosopher would answer them nor as a theologian, or a metaphysician, but as it is the duty of a poet to reply, by intuitive faculty, in strains in which Imagination predominates over Thought and Memory. And one of the manifold beauties of this exquisite poem, and which is another characteristic of true Poetry, is that, piercing through all the sophistries and over refinements of speculation, and the lifeless scepticism of science, it falls back upon the grand, primary, simple truths of our humanity; those first principles which underlie all creeds, which belong to our earliest childhood, and on which the wisest and best have rested through all ages: that all is right: that darkness shall be clear: that God and Time are the only interpreters: that Love is king: that the Immortal is in us: that – which is the key note of the whole –

– all is well, though Faith and Form
Be sundered in the night of fear.

This is an essential quality of the highest Poetry, whose characteristic is simplicity; not in the sense of being intelligible, like a novel, to every careless reader, without pain or effort: for the best Poetry demands study as severe as mathematics require; and to any one who thinks that it can be treated as a mere relaxation and amusement for an idle hour, this Lecture does not address itself: but simplicity, in the sense of dealing with truths which do not belong to a few fastidious and refined intellects, but are the heritage of the many. The deepest truths are the simplest and the most common. . . .

To a coarser class of minds *In Memoriam* appears too melancholy: one long monotone of grief. It is simply one of the most victorious songs that ever poet chaunted: with the mysterious undertone, no doubt, of sadness which belongs to all human joy, in front of the mysteries of death and sorrow; but that belongs to Paradise Regained as well as to Paradise Lost: to every true note, indeed, of human triumph except a Bacchanalian drinking song. And that it should predominate in a monumental record is not particularly unnatural. But readers who never dream of mastering the plan of a work before they pretend to criticise details can scarcely be expected to perceive that the wail passes into a hymn of solemn and peaceful beauty before it closes.

Another objection, proceeding from the religious periodicals, is, that the subject being a religious one, is not treated religiously; by which they mean theologically. It certainly is neither saturated with Evangelicalism nor Tractarianism; nor does it abound in the routine phrases which, when missed, raise a suspicion of heterodoxy; nor does it seize the happy opportunity afforded for a pious denunciation of the errors of Purgatory and Mariolatry. But the objection to its want of definite theology, – an objection, by the way, brought frequently against Wordsworth by writers of the same school, is, in fact, in favour of the presumption of its poetic merit; for it may be the office of the priest to teach upon authority – of the philosopher according to induction – but the province of the poet is neither to teach by induction nor by authority, but to appeal to those primal intuitions of our being which are eternally and necessarily true.

With one of these criticisms I mean to occupy your time at somewhat further length. Some months ago, *The Times* devoted three or four columns to the work of depreciating Tennyson. I will answer that critique now, as concisely as I can; not because *The Times* can do any permanent harm to Tennyson's reputation, but because it may do a great deal of harm to the taste of its readers. *The Times* is in possession of extensive influence: it forms the political creed, and is arbiter of the opinions of the many who must be led. I hold it therefore no unworthy antagonist.

Now, in any pretension to criticise a poetic work of internal unity, the first duty, plainly, is to comprehend the structure of it as a whole, and master the leading idea. It is to be regretted that this is precisely what English critics generally do not. Even with our own Shakspere, admiration or blame is usually confined to the beauties and blemishes of detached passages. For the significance of each play, as a whole, we had to look, in the first instance, to such foreigners as Augustus Schlegel to teach us.

Let us inquire what conception the critic of *The Times* has formed of this beautiful poem.

'Let the acknowledgment be made at once that the writer dedicated his thoughts to a most difficult task. He has written 200 pages upon one person – in other words, he has painted 120 miniatures of the same individual.'

Mr Tennyson has not painted 120 portraits of the same individual. He has written a poem in 120 divisions, illustrative of the manifold phases through which the soul passes from doubt through grief to faith. With so entire and radical a misconception of the scope of the poem, it is not wonderful if the whole examination of the details should be a failure.

The first general charge is one of irreverence. The special case selected is these verses which are called blasphemous –

> But brooding on the dear one dead,
>   And all he said of things divine,
> (And dear as sacramental wine
>   To dying lips is all he said –)

One would have thought that the holy tenderness of this passage would have made this charge impossible. However, as notions of reverence and irreverence in some minds are singularly vague, we will give the flippant objection rather more attention than it merits.

By a sacrament we understand a means of grace: an outward something through which pure and holy feelings are communicated to the soul. In the church of Christ there are two sacraments – the material of one is the commonest of all elements, water; the form of the other the commonest of all acts, a meal. Now there are two ways in which reverence may be manifested towards any thing or person: one, by exalting that thing or person by means of the depreciation of all others: another, by exalting all others through it. To some minds it appears an honoring of the sacraments to represent them as solitary things in their own kind, like nothing else, and all other things and acts profane in comparison of them. It is my own deep conviction that no greater dishonor can be done to them than by this conception, which degrades them to the rank of charms. The sacraments are honoured when they consecrate all the things and acts of life. The commonest of all materials was sanctified to us in order to vindicate the sacredness of all materialism, in protest against the false spiritualism which affects to despise the body, and the world whose impressions are made upon the senses; and in order to declare that visible world God's, and the organ of His manifestation. The simplest of all acts is sacramental, in order to vindicate God's claim to all acts, and to proclaim our common life sacred, in protest against the conception which cleaves so obstinately to the mind, that religion is the performance of certain stated acts, not necessarily of moral import, on certain days and in certain places. If there be anything in this life sacred, any remembrance filled with sanctifying power, any voice which symbolizes to us the voice of God, it is the recollection of the pure and holy ones that have been taken from us, and of their examples and sacred words—

> dear as sacramental wine
> To dying lips

In those lines Tennyson has deeply, no doubt unconsciously, that is, without dogmatic intention, entered into the power of the sacraments to diffuse their meaning beyond themselves. There is no irreverence in them: no blasphemy; nothing but delicate Christian truth.

The next definite charge is more difficult to deal with before a mixed society, because the shades of the feeling in question blend into each other with exceedingly fine gradation. The language of the friend towards the departed friend is represented as unfitted for any but amatory tenderness. In this blame the critic is compelled to include Shakspere: for we all know that his sonnets, dedicated either to the Earl of Southampton or the Earl of Pembroke, contain expressions which have left it a point of controversy whether they were addressed to a lady or a friend. Now in a matter which concerns the truthfulness of a human feeling, when the anonymous critic of *The Times* is on one side and Shakspere on the other, there are some who might be presumptuous enough to suppose *a priori* that the modest critic is possibly not the one in the right. However, let us examine the matter. There are two kinds of friendship: One is the affection of the greater for the less, the other that of the less for the greater. The greater and the less may be differences of rank, or intellect, or character, or power. These are the two opposites of feeling which respectively characterise the masculine and the feminine natures, the familiar symbols of which relationship are the oak and the ivy with its clinging tendrils. But though they are the masculine and feminine types, they are not confined to male and female. Most of us have gone through both these phases of friendship. Whoever remembers an attachment at school to a boy feebler than himself, will recollect the exulting pride of guardianship with which he shielded his friend from the oppression of some young tyrant of the play-ground. And whoever, at least in boyhood or youth, loved a man, to whose mental or moral qualities he looked up with young reverence, will recollect the devotion and the jealousies, and the almost passionate tenderness, and the costly gifts, and the desire of personal sacrifices, which characterise boyish friendship, and which certainly belong to the feminine, and not the masculine type of affection. Doubtless the language of *In Memoriam* is tender in the extreme, such as a sister might use to a brother deeply loved.

But it is to be remembered that it expresses the affection of the
spirit which rejoices to confess itself the feebler; and besides, that,
the man has passed into a spirit, and that time and distance have
thrown a hallowing haze of tenderness over the lineaments of the
friend of the past. It may be well also to recollect that there is a
precedent for this woman-like tenderness, against whose authority
one who condemns so severely the most distant approach to irreverence will scarcely venture to appeal. 'I am distressed for thee,
my brother Jonathan: very pleasant hast thou been to me. Thy
love to me was wonderful, *passing the love of women.*'

Again, the praise and the grief of the poem are enormously 'exaggerated'; and as an instance of the manner in which the '*poet* may
underline the moralist', and delicately omit the defects without
hyperbolical praise, Dr Johnson's lines on Levett are cited with
much fervour of admiration. Good, excellent Dr Johnson! sincerely pious; very bigoted and very superstitious, yet one, withal,
who fought the battle of life bravely out, in the teeth of disease
and poverty; a great lexicographer; of massive learning; the
author of innumerable prudential aphorisms, much quoted by
persons who season their conversation with proverbs and old
saws; the inditer of several thousand ponderous verses; a man
worthy of all respect. But it is indeed a surprising apparition
when the shade of Dr Johnson descends upon the Nineteenth
Century as the spirit of a poet, and we are asked to identify the
rugged portrait which Boswell painted with a model of delicate
forbearance.

After these general observations, the writer in *The Times* pro-
ceeds to criticise in detail; he awards some praise, and much blame.
You shall have a specimen of each. Let us test the value of his
praise. He selects for approbation, among others, these lines: –

> Or is it that the Past will win
> A glory from its being far;
> And orb into the perfect star
> We saw not when we moved therein?

The question has suggested itself as a misgiving to the poet's
mind, whether his past affection was really as full of blessedness

as memory paints it, or whether it be not the perspective of distance which conceals its imperfections, and throws purer hues upon it than it possessed while actual. In the rapid reading of the two last lines I may not have at once conveyed to you the meaning. So long as we remain upon any planet, this earth for instance, it would wear a common-place, earthy look: but if we could ascend from it into space, in proportion to the distance, it would assume a heavenly aspect, and orb or round itself into a star. This is a very simple and graceful illustration. Now hear the critic of *The Times* condescending to be an analyst of its beauties:

'There is something indeed striking and suggestive in comparing the gone by time to some luminous body rising like a red harvest moon behind us, lighting our path homeward.'

So that this beautiful simile of Tennyson's, of a distant star receding into pale and perfect loveliness, in the hands of *The Times* becomes *a great red harvest moon*!

So much for the praise. Now for the blame. The following passage is selected: –

> Oh, if indeed that eye foresee,
>   Or see (in Him is no before)
>   In more of life true love no more,
> And love the indifference to be,
>
> So might I find, ere yet the morn
>   Breaks hither over Indian seas,
>   That Shadow waiting with the keys
> To cloak me from my proper scorn.

That is, as you will see at once, after the thought of the transitoriness of human affection has occurred to him, the possibility is also suggested with it, that he himself may change; but he prays that before that day can come, he may find the Shadow waiting with the keys to cloak him from his own scorn. Now I will read the commentary: –

'Lately we have heard much of keys, both from the Flaminian Gate and Piccadilly, but we back this verse against Hobbs. We dare him to pick it. Mr Moxon may hang it up in his window, with a £200 prize attached, more safely than a Bramah. That a shadow

should hold keys at all, is a noticeable circumstance; but that it
should wait with a cloak, ready to be thrown over a gentleman
in difficulties, is absolutely amazing.'

The lock may be picked without any exertion of unfair force.

A few pages before he has spoken of the breaking up of a
happy friendship –

> There sat the Shadow, feared by man,
> Who broke our fair companionship.

Afterwards he calls it –

> The Shadow, cloaked from head to foot,
> Who keeps the key of all the creeds.

Take, at a venture, any charity-school boy, of ordinary intelligence; read to him these lines; and he will tell you that the
Shadow feared by man is death; that it is cloaked from head to
foot because death is mysterious, and its form not distinguishable;
and that he keeps the keys of all the creeds, because he alone can
unlock the secret of the grave, and shew which of all conflicting
human creeds is true.

'It is a noticeable thing', we are told, 'that a shadow should
hold keys at all.' It is a very noticeable thing that a skeleton should
hold a scythe and an hour-glass: very noticeable that a young
lady should hold scales when she is blindfold; yet it is not a particularly uncommon rule of symbolism so to represent Time and
Justice. Probably the writer in *The Times*, if he should chance to
read of 'riding on the wings of the wind', would consider it a very
noticeable method of locomotion; perhaps would enquire, with
dull facetiousness, what was the precise length of the primary,
secondary, and tertiary quills of the said wings; and if told of a
spirit clothing itself in light, he might triumphantly demand in
what loom light could be woven into a great coat.

Finally. The critique complains that a vast deal of poetic feeling
has been wasted on a lawyer; and much wit is spent upon the
tenderness which is given to 'Amaryllis of the Chancery bar'. A
barrister, it seems, is beyond the pale of excusable, because
poetical, sensibilities. So that, if my friend be a soldier, I may love

him, and celebrate him in poetry, because the profession of arms is by all conventional associations heroic: or if he bears on his escutcheon the red hand of knighthood, or wears a ducal coronet, or even be a shepherd, still there are poetic precedents for romance; but if he be a member of the Chancery bar, or only a cotton lord, then, because these are not yet grades accredited as heroic in song, worth is not worth, and honor is not honor, and nobleness is not nobility. O, if we wanted poets for nothing else, it would be for this, that they are the grand levellers, vindicating the sacredness of our common humanity, and in protest against such downright vulgarity of heart as this, reminding us that –

> For a' that, and a' that,
> A man's a man for a' that.

So much then for the critic of *The Times*: wrong when he praises and wrong when he blames: who finds Shakspere false to the facts of human nature, and quotes Dr Johnson as a model poet: who cannot believe in the Poetry of any expression unless it bear the mint-stamp of a precedent, and cannot understand either the exaggerations or the infinitude of genuine grief.

Let it serve to the members of this Institution as a comment on the opinion quoted at the outset that it is sufficient education for Working Men to read the newspapers. If they form no more living conception of what Poetry is than such as they get from the flippant criticism of a slashing article, they may learn satire, but not enthusiasm. If they limit their politics to the knowledge they may pick up from daily newspapers, which, with a few honorable exceptions, seem bound to pander to all the passions and prejudices of their respective factions, they will settle down into miserable partizans. And if Working-Men are to gain their notions of Christianity from the sneering, snarling gossip of the religious newspapers, I, for one, do not marvel that indignant infidelity is so common amongst them.

And let it be to us all a warning against that detracting, depreciating spirit which is the curse and bane both of the religion and the literature of our day – that spirit which has no sympathy with aught that is great beyond the pale of customary formalities, and sheds its blighting influence over all that is enthusiastic, and generous, and high-minded. It is possible for a sneer or a cavil to strike sometimes a superficial fact; I never knew the one or the other reach the deep heart and blessedness of truth.

(from *Two Lectures on the Influences of Poetry on the Working Classes* (1852))

Henry Sidgwick

AFTER thinking over the matter, it has seemed to me better to write to you a somewhat different kind of letter from that which I originally designed: a letter not primarily intended for publication, though I wish you to feel at liberty to print any part of it which you may find suitable, but primarily intended to serve rather as a 'document' on which you may base any statements you may wish to make as to the impression produced by *In Memoriam*. I have decided to adopt this course: because I want to write with rather more frank egotism than I should otherwise like to show. I want to do this, because in describing the impression made on me by the poem, I ought to make clear the point of view from which I approached it, and the attitude of thought which I retained under its influence. In what follows I shall be describing chiefly my own experiences: but I shall allow myself sometimes to say 'we' rather than 'I', meaning by 'we' my generation, as known to me, through converse with intimate friends.

To begin, then: our views on religious matters were not, at any rate after a year or two of the discussion started in 1860 by *Essays and Reviews*, really in harmony with those which we found suggested by *In Memoriam*. They were more sceptical and less Christian, in any strict sense of the word: certainly this was the case with myself: I remember feeling that Clough *represented* my individual habits of thought and sentiment more than your father, although as a poet he *moved* me less. And this more sceptical attitude has remained mine through life; while at the same time I feel that the beliefs in God and in immortality are vital to human well-being.

Hence the most important influence of *In Memoriam* on my thought, apart from its poetic charm as an expression of personal emotion, opened in a region, if I may so say, deeper down than the difference between Theism and Christianity: it lay in the unparalleled combination of intensity of feeling with comprehensiveness of view and balance of judgment, shown in presenting the *deepest* needs and perplexities of humanity. And this influence, I find, has increased rather than diminished as years have gone on, and as the great issues between Agnostic Science and Faith have become continually more prominent. In the sixties I should say that these deeper issues were somewhat obscured by the discussions on Christian dogma, and Inspiration of Scripture, etc. You may remember Browning's reference to this period –

> The Essays and Reviews debate
> Begins to tell on the public mind
> And Colenso's words have weight.

During these years we were absorbed in struggling for freedom of thought in the trammels of a historical religion: and perhaps what we sympathized with most in *In Memoriam* at this time, apart from the personal feeling, was the defence of 'honest doubt', the reconciliation of knowledge and faith in the introductory poem, and the hopeful trumpet-ring of the lines on the New Year –

> Ring out the thousand wars of old,
> Ring in the thousand years of peace,

and generally the *forward* movement of the thought.

Well, the years pass, the struggle with what Carlyle used to call 'Hebrew old clothes' is over, Freedom is won, and what does Freedom bring us to? It brings us face to face with atheistic science: the faith in God and Immortality, which we had been struggling to clear from superstition, suddenly seems to be *in the air*: and in seeking for a firm basis for this faith we find ourselves in the midst of the 'fight with death' which *In Memoriam* so powerfully presents.

What *In Memoriam* did for us, for me at least, in this struggle was to impress on us the ineffaceable and ineradicable conviction that *humanity* will not and cannot acquiesce in a godless world: the 'man in men' will not do this, whatever individual men may do, whatever they may temporarily feel themselves driven to do, by following methods which they cannot abandon to the conclusions to which these methods at present seem to lead.

The force with which it impressed this conviction was not due to the *mere intensity* of its expression of the feelings which Atheism outrages and Agnosticism ignores: but rather to its expression of them along with a reverent docility to the lessons of science which also belongs to the essence of the thought of our age.

I remember being struck with a note in *Nature*, at the time of your father's death, which dwelt on this last-mentioned aspect of his work, and regarded him as preeminently the Poet of Science. I have always felt this characteristic important in estimating his effect on his generation. Wordsworth's attitude towards Nature was one that, so to say, left Science unregarded: the Nature for which Wordsworth stirred our feelings was Nature as known by simple observation and interpreted by religious and sympathetic intuition. But for your father the physical world is always the world as known to us through physical science: the scientific view of it dominates his thoughts about it; and his general acceptance of this view is real and sincere, even when he utters the intensest feeling of its inadequacy to satisfy our deepest needs. Had it been otherwise, had he met the atheistic tendencies of modern Science with more confident defiance, more confident assertion of an Intuitive Faculty of theological knowledge, overriding the results laboriously reached by empirical science, I think his antagonism to these tendencies would have been far less impressive.

I always feel this strongly in reading the memorable lines: 'If e'er, when faith had fallen asleep' down to 'I have felt'.

At this point, if the stanzas had stopped here, we should have shaken our heads and said, 'Feeling must not usurp the function of Reason. Feeling is not knowing. It is the duty of a rational being to follow truth wherever it leads.'

But the poet's instinct knows this; he knows that this usurpation by Feeling of the function of Reason is too bold and confident; accordingly in the next stanza he gives the turn to humility in the protest of Feeling which is required (I think) to win the assent of the 'man in men' at this stage of human thought.

These lines I can never read without tears. I feel in them the indestructible and inalienable minimum of faith which humanity cannot give up because it is necessary for life; and which I know that I, at least so far as the man in me is deeper than the methodical thinker, cannot give up.

If the possibility of a 'godless world' is excluded, the faith thus restored is, for the poet, unquestionably a form of Christian faith: there seems to him then no reason for doubting that the

> Sinless years
> That breathed beneath the Syrian blue,

and the marvel of the life continued after the bodily death, were a manifestation of the 'immortal love' which by faith we embrace as the essence of the Divine nature. 'If the dead rise not, Christ is not risen': but if we may believe that they rise, then it seems to him, we may and must believe the main drift of the Gospel story; though we may transiently wonder why the risen Lord told his disciples only of life, and nothing of 'what it is to die' (see Browning's 'Epistle containing the Strange Medical Experience of Karshish').

From this point of view the note of Christian faith struck in the introductory stanzas is in harmony with all that follows. And yet I have always felt that in a certain sense the effect of the introduction does not quite represent the effect of the poem. Faith, in the introduction, is too completely triumphant. I think this is inevitable, because so far as the thought-debate presented by the poem is summed up, it must be summed up on the side of Faith. Faith must give the last word: but the last word is not the whole utterance of the truth: the whole truth is that assurance and doubt must alternate in the moral world in which we at present live, somewhat as night and day alternate in the physical world. The revealing visions come and go; when they come we *feel* that we *know*: but in the intervals we must pass through states in which all is dark, and in which we can only struggle to hold the conviction that

> Power is with us in the night
> Which makes the darkness and the light
> And dwells not in the light alone.

(letter to Hallam Tennyson)

PART THREE

Modern Criticism

T. S. Eliot

IN MEMORIAM (1936)

TENNYSON is a great poet, for reasons that are perfectly clear. He has three qualities which are seldom found together except in the greatest poets: abundance, variety, and complete competence. We therefore cannot appreciate his work unless we read a good deal of it. We may not admire his aims: but whatever he sets out to do, he succeeds in doing, with a mastery which gives us the sense of confidence that is one of the major pleasures of poetry. His variety of metrical accomplishment is astonishing. Without making the mistake of trying to write Latin verse in English, he knew everything about Latin versification that an English poet could use; and he said of himself that he thought he knew the quantity of the sounds of every English word except perhaps *scissors*. He had the finest ear of any English poet since Milton. He was the master of Swinburne; and the versification of Swinburne, himself a classical scholar, is often crude and sometimes cheap, in comparison with Tennyson's. Tennyson extended very widely the range of active metrical forms in English: in *Maud* alone the variety is prodigious. But innovation in metric is not to be measured solely by the width of the deviation from accepted practice. It is a matter of the historical situation: at some moments a more violent change may be necessary than at others. The problem differs at every period. At some times, a violent revolution may be neither possible nor desirable; at such times, a change which may appear very slight, is the change which the important poet will make. The innovation of Pope, after Dryden, may not seem very great; but it is the mark of the master to be able to make small changes which will be highly significant, as at another time to make radical changes, through which poetry will curve back again to its norm. . . .[1]

The reading of long poems is not nowadays much practised: in the age of Tennyson it appears to have been easier. For a good many long poems were not only written but widely circulated; and the level was high: even the second-rate long poems of that time, like *The Light of Asia*, are better worth reading than most long modern novels. But Tennyson's long poems are not long poems in quite the same sense as those of his contemporaries. They are very different in kind from *Sordello* or *The Ring and the Book*, to name the greatest by the greatest of his contemporary poets. *Maud* and *In Memoriam* are each a series of poems, given form by the greatest lyrical resourcefulness that a poet has ever shown. The *Idylls of the King* have merits and defects similar to those of *The Princess*. An *idyll* is a 'short poem descriptive of some picturesque scene or incident'; in choosing the name Tennyson perhaps showed an appreciation of his limitations. For his poems are always descriptive, and always picturesque; they are never really narrative. The *Idylls of the King* are no different in kind from some of his early poems; the 'Morte d'Arthur' is in fact an early poem. *The Princess* is still an idyll, but an idyll that is too long. Tennyson's versification in this poem is as masterly as elsewhere: it is a poem which we must read, but which we excuse ourselves from reading twice. And it is worth while recognizing the reason why we return again and again, and are always stirred by the lyrics which intersperse it, and which are among the greatest of all poetry of their kind, and yet avoid the poem itself. It is not, as we may think while reading, the out-moded attitude towards the relations of the sexes, the exaspera-ting views on the subjects of matrimony, celibacy, and female education, that make us recoil from *The Princess*.[2] We can swal-low the most antipathetic doctrines if we are given an exciting narrative. But for narrative Tennyson had no gift at all. For a static poem, and a moving poem, on the same subject, you have only to compare his 'Ulysses' with the condensed and intensely exciting narrative of that hero in the XXVIth Canto of Dante's *Inferno*. Dante is telling a story. Tennyson is only stating an elegiac mood. The very greatest poets set before you real men talking, carry you on in real events moving. Tennyson could not tell a story at all. It is not that in *The Princess* he tries to tell a story and failed: it is rather that an idyll protracted to such length becomes unreadable. So *The Princess* is a dull poem; one of the poems of which we may say, that they are beautiful but dull.

But in *Maud* and in *In Memoriam*, Tennyson is doing what every conscious artist does, turning his limitations to good purpose. Of the content of *Maud*, I cannot think so highly as does Mr Humbert Wolfe, in his interesting essay on Tennyson which is largely defence of the supremacy of that poem. For me, *Maud* consists of a few very beautiful lyrics, such as 'O let the solid ground', 'Birds in the high Hall-garden', and 'Go not, happy day', around which the semblance of a dramatic situation has been constructed with the greatest metrical virtuosity. The whole situation is unreal; the ravings of the lover on the edge of insanity sound false, and fail, as do the bellicose bellowings, to make one's flesh creep with sincerity. It would be foolish to suggest that Tennyson ought to have gone through some experience similar to that described: for a poet with dramatic gifts, a situation quite remote from his personal experience may release the strongest emotion. And I do not believe for a moment that Tennyson was a man of mild feelings or weak passions. There is no evidence in his poetry that he knew the experience of violent passion for a woman; but there is plenty of evidence of emotional intensity and violence – but of emotion so deeply suppressed, even from himself, as to tend rather towards the blackest melancholia than towards dramatic action. And it is emotion which, so far as my reading of the poems can discover, attained no ultimate clear purgation. I should reproach Tennyson not for mildness, or tepidity, but rather for lack of serenity.

> Of love that never found his earthly close,
> What sequel?

The fury of *Maud* is shrill rather than deep, though one feels in every passage what exquisite adaptation of metre to the mood Tennyson is attempting to express. I think that the effect of feeble violence, which the poem as a whole produces, is the result of a fundamental error of form. A poet can express his feelings as fully through a dramatic, as through a lyrical form; but *Maud* is neither one thing nor the other: just as *The Princess* is more than an idyll, and less than a narrative. In *Maud*, Tennyson neither identifies himself with the lover, nor identifies the lover with himself: consequently, the real feelings of Tennyson, profound and tumultuous as they are, never arrive at expression.

It is, in my opinion, in *In Memoriam*, that Tennyson finds full expression. Its technical merit alone is enough to ensure its perpetuity. While Tennyson's technical competence is everywhere masterly and satisfying, *In Memoriam* is the most unapproachable of all his poems. Here are one hundred and thirty-two passages, each of several quatrains in the same form, and never monotony or repetition. And the poem has to be comprehended as a whole. We may not memorize a few passages, we cannot find a 'fair sample'; we have to comprehend the whole of a poem which is essentially the length that it is. We may choose to remember:

> Dark house, by which once more I stand
>   Here in the long unlovely street,
>   Doors, where my heart was used to beat
> So quickly, waiting for a hand,
>
> A hand that can be clasp'd no more –
>   Behold me, for I cannot sleep,
>   And like a guilty thing I creep
> At earliest morning to the door.
>
> He is not here; but far away
>   The noise of life begins again,
>   And ghastly thro' the drizzling rain
> On the bald street breaks the blank day.

This is great poetry, economical of words, a universal emotion in what could only be an English town: and it gives me the shudder that I fail to get from anything in *Maud*. But such a passage, by itself, is not *In Memoriam*: *In Memoriam* is the whole poem. It is unique: it is a long poem made by putting together lyrics, which have only the unity and continuity of a diary, the concentrated diary of a man confessing himself. It is a diary of which we have to read every word.

Apparently Tennyson's contemporaries, once they had accepted *In Memoriam*, regarded it as a message of hope and reassurance to their rather fading Christian faith. It happens now
and then that a poet by some strange accident expresses the mood
of his generation, at the same time that he is expressing a mood of
his own which is quite remote from that of his generation. This is
not a question of insincerity: there is an amalgam of yielding and
opposition below the level of consciousness. Tennyson himself,
on the conscious level of the man who talks to reporters and poses
for photographers, to judge from remarks made in conversation
and recorded in his son's *Memoir*, consistently asserted a convinced, if somewhat sketchy, Christian belief. And he was a
friend of Frederick Denison Maurice – nothing seems odder about
that age than the respect which its eminent people felt for each
other. Nevertheless, I get a very different impression from *In
Memoriam* from that which Tennyson's contemporaries seem to
have got. It is of a very much more interesting and tragic Tennyson. His biographers have not failed to remark that he had a good
deal of the temperament of the mystic – certainly not at all the
mind of the theologian. He was desperately anxious to hold the
faith of the believer, without being very clear about what he
wanted to believe: he was capable of illumination which he was
incapable of understanding. The 'Strong Son of God, immortal
Love', with an invocation of whom the poem opens, has only a
hazy connection with the Logos, or the Incarnate God. Tennyson is distressed by the idea of a mechanical universe; he is naturally, in lamenting his friend, teased by the hope of immortality
and reunion beyond death. Yet the renewal craved for seems at
best but a continuance, or a substitute for the joys of friendship
upon earth. His desire for immortality never is quite the desire
for Eternal Life; his concern is for the loss of man rather than for
the gain of God.

> shall he,
>
> Man, her last work, who seem'd so fair,
>   Such splendid purpose in his eyes,
>   Who roll'd the psalm to wintry skies,
> Who built him fanes of fruitless prayer,

> Who trusted God was love indeed
>   And love Creation's final law –
>   Tho' Nature, red in tooth and claw
> With ravine, shriek'd against his creed –
>
> Who loved, who suffer'd countless ills,
>   Who battled for the True, the Just,
>   Be blown about the desert dust,
> Or seal'd within the iron hills?

That strange abstraction, 'Nature', becomes a real god or goddess, perhaps more real, at moments, to Tennyson than God ('Are God and Nature then at strife?'). The hope of immortality is confused (typically of the period) with the hope of the gradual and steady improvement of this world. Much has been said of Tennyson's interest in contemporary science, and of the impression of Darwin. *In Memoriam*, in any case, antedates *The Origin of Species* by several years, and the belief in social progress by democracy antedates it by many more; and I suspect that the faith of Tennyson's age in human progress would have been quite as strong even had the discoveries of Darwin been postponed by fifty years. And after all, there is no logical connection: the belief in progress being current already, the discoveries of Darwin were harnessed to it:

> No longer half-akin to brute,
>   For all we thought and loved and did,
>   And hoped, and suffer'd, is but seed
> Of what in them is flower and fruit;
>
> Whereof the man, that with me trod
>   This planet, was a noble type
>   Appearing ere the times were ripe,
> That friend of mine who lives in God,
>
> That God, which ever lives and loves,
>   One God, one law, one element,
>   And one far-off divine event,
> To which the whole creation moves.

These lines show an interesting compromise between the religious attitude and, what is quite a different thing, the belief in
human perfectibility; but the contrast was not so apparent to
Tennyson's contemporaries. They may have been taken in by it,
but I don't think that Tennyson himself was, quite: his feelings
were more honest than his mind. There is evidence elsewhere –
even in an early poem, 'Locksley Hall', for example – that Tennyson by no means regarded with complacency all the changes that
were going on about him in the progress of industrialism and the
rise of the mercantile and manufacturing and banking classes; and
he may have contemplated the future of England, as his years drew
out, with increasing gloom. Temperamentally, he was opposed to
the doctrine that he was moved to accept and to praise.

Tennyson's feelings, I have said, were honest; but they were
usually a good way below the surface. *In Memoriam* can, I think,
justly be called a religious poem, but for another reason than that
which made it seem religious to his contemporaries. It is not religious because of the quality of its faith, but because of the
quality of its doubt. Its faith is a poor thing, but its doubt is a very
intense experience. *In Memoriam* is a poem of despair, but of
despair of a religious kind. And to qualify its despair with the ad-
jective 'religious' is to elevate it above most of its derivatives.
For *The City of Dreadful Night*, and the *Shropshire Lad*, and
the poems of Thomas Hardy, are small work in comparison
with *In Memoriam*: it is greater than they and comprehends
them.[3]

In ending we must go back to the beginning and remember that
In Memoriam would not be a great poem, or Tennyson a great
poet, without the technical accomplishment. Tennyson is the
great master of metric as well as of melancholia; I do not think
any poet in English has ever had a finer ear for vowel sound, as
well as a subtler feeling for some moods of anguish:

> Dear as remember'd kisses after death,
> And sweet as those by hopeless fancy feign'd
> On lips that are for others; deep as love,
> Deep as first love, and wild with all regret.

And this technical gift of Tennyson's is no slight thing. Tennyson lived in a time which was already acutely time-conscious: a great many things seemed to be happening, railways were being built, discoveries were being made, the face of the world was changing. That was a time busy in keeping up to date. It had, for the most part, no hold on permanent things, on permanent truths about man and God and life and death. The surface of Tennyson stirred about with his time; and he had nothing to which to hold fast except his unique and unerring feeling for the sounds of words. But in this he had something that no one else had. Tennyson's surface, his technical accomplishment, is intimate with his depths: what we most quickly see about Tennyson is that which moves between the surface and the depths, that which is of slight importance. By looking innocently at the surface we are most likely to come to the depths, to the abyss of sorrow. Tennyson is not only a minor Virgil, he is also with Virgil as Dante saw him, a Virgil among the Shades, the saddest of all English poets, among the Great in Limbo, the most instinctive rebel against the society in which he was the most perfect conformist.

Tennyson seems to have reached the end of his spiritual development with *In Memoriam*; there followed no reconciliation, no resolution.

> And now no sacred staff shall break in blossom,
>   No choral salutation lure to light
>   A spirit sick with perfume and sweet night,

or rather with twilight, for Tennyson faced neither the darkness nor the light, in his later years. The genius, the technical power, persisted to the end, but the spirit had surrendered. A gloomier end than that of Baudelaire: Tennyson had no *singulier avertissement*. And having turned aside from the journey through the dark night, to become the surface flatterer of his own time, he has been rewarded with the despite of an age that succeeds his own in shallowness.

Source: *Selected Essays* (1932).

NOTES

1. [*Editor's note.*] Eliot here quotes from an early poem, 'The Hesperides', to illustrate Tennyson's classical learning and mastery of metre.

2. For a revelation of the Victorian mind on these matters, and of opinions to which Tennyson would probably have subscribed, see the Introduction by Sir Edward Strachey, Bt, to his emasculated edition of the *Morte D'Arthur* of Malory, still current. Sir Edward admired the *Idylls of the King*.

3. There are other kinds of despair. Davidson's great poem, *Thirty Bob a Week*, is not derivative from Tennyson. On the other hand, there are other things derivative from Tennyson besides *Atalanta in Calydon*. Compare the poems of William Morris with *The Voyage of Maeldune*, and *Barrack Room Ballads* with several of Tennyson's later poems.

Graham Hough

THE NATURAL THEOLOGY OF
IN MEMORIAM (1947)

THE reputation of *In Memoriam* as a philosophical poem, immensely high in its own day, dropped very rapidly in the early part of this century. It is now commonly assumed that its virtues are entirely those of a personal confession: and that, for the rest, it merely provided a slightly disreputable form of comfort for discomfited Victorians. It is true that its argument follows the course of an emotional, not a logical development. But Tennyson's aim was to make an emotionally satisfying synthesis of current scientific and religious thought. To do justice to *In Memoriam* it is necessary to find out what scientific and religious ideas were actually at his disposal. To look for the sources of Tennyson's thought is not, in this case, to disparage his originality, but simply to discover what he was trying to do.

The basis of eighteenth-century religious apologetic is the belief that the whole course of nature supports, if not revelation, at any rate the major hypotheses of natural religion. The pessimistic version of this creed is found in Butler's *Analogy*: if revelation is confusing and incomplete, so is nature: those who find that nature leads them to belief in a God should logically find no difficulty in being led by revelation to a belief in the Christian God. The argument is a curious one: the point of interest to us is that Butler assumes throughout that nature *will* lead men to God, even if unaided it takes them no farther than Deism. A far more optimistic (and also more commonplace) line of argument is found in Paley's *Natural Theology*: it is the familiar argument from design. If we found a watch lying on the ground it would be immediately evident to us that it must have had a maker, and the more we studied its workings the clearer this would become. So it is with the universe: study of the admirable constitution of the natural world and of the many ingenious devices with which it is filled can only lead us back to the hypothesis of an intelligent and benevolent Creator. Paley is an unfailing optimist; he is quite convinced of the substantial happiness of the universe: and, strong in the knowledge that he is only summing up a whole body of contemporary opinion, he is quite confident of having sufficient weight to settle the freethinkers and sceptics. This was in 1802.

The trend of liberal religious opinion changed very rapidly in the next generation. By the time *In Memoriam* appeared in 1850 the whole line of argument is different. In some places in the poem there is a vague optimism about the progress of nature: but its general tenor is to show that nature cannot lead men to God: even if natural appearances are sometimes in conformity with faith (and more often they are not) they cannot form the real basis on which faith rests: its only sure foundation is inner experience: belief must be based on what men feel.

> I found Him not in world or sun
>   Or eagle's wing, or insect's eye;
>   Nor thro' the questions men may try,
> The petty cobwebs we have spun:
>
> If e'er when faith had fall'n asleep
>   I heard a voice 'believe no more'
>   And heard an ever-breaking shore
> That tumbled in the Godless deep;
>
> A warmth within the breast would melt
>   The freezing reason's colder part,
>   And like a man in wrath the heart
> Stood up and answer'd 'I have felt'. [cxxiv]

Hallam Tennyson quotes his father as saying almost the same thing in 1892: 'Yet God is love, transcendent, all-pervading! We do not get this faith from Nature or the world. If we look at Nature alone, full of perfection and imperfection, she tells us that God is disease, murder and rapine. We get this faith from ourselves, from what is highest within us, which recognises that there is not one fruitless pang, just as there is not one lost good.'¹

If we ask what has happened to change the apparent relations between God and Nature in the fifty years since Paley wrote, we are usually told, somewhat vaguely, evolution. This is partly true, but it is usually misleading. The reader almost inevitably begins to think in terms of the post-Darwinian evolution controversy. It is perhaps as well to repeat once more that the ideas in *In Memoriam* have not, and could not have had, anything to do with Darwinism. *In Memoriam* appeared in 1850, but it was mostly written long before. The sections which are, or which appear to be, about evolution were written before 1844.² The *Origin of Species* did not appear till 1859: in any case it says nothing whatever about the descent of man. But, of course, evolutionary ideas were current in England before Darwin. The book which popularized them in the pre-Darwinian period and which could have influenced *In Memoriam* was Robert Chambers's *Vestiges of the Natural History of Creation*, It came out in 1844 and Tennyson sent to Moxon for it in 1845.³ But he also says 'it seems to contain many speculations with which I have been familiar for years, and on which I have written more than one poem'. In fact the idea that species were not immutable, but had developed from one another, is as old as Buffon, though he does little more than throw out the suggestion. The earliest writer to give anything like a developed view of the matter is Lamarck: but in England, at any rate, Lamarck was not very much read. His views were, however, very fully presented to the English public in a book which was very much read – Lyell's *Principles of Geology* – of which the first edition appeared in 1830. The influence of the book was immense: it was the principal means by which pre-Darwinian scientific thought on the history of the earth and of living matter was diffused. Because of its implied refutation of the Mosaic cosmogony it aroused violent opposition: a glance at the entries under Lyell's name in the British Museum catalogue will show the number of books and pamphlets written to refute it. Tennyson was busy studying it in 1837,⁴ and it is much the most likely source of his early scientific ideas.

It should be noted that at this stage Lyell was not an evolutionist. (In later editions of the book the ideas were fundamentally modified.) He gives a detailed analysis of Lamarck expressly in order to refute the theory of the mutability of species.[5] Nor were most English scientists about this time at all disposed to accept the evolutionary hypothesis. Thus, although Tennyson was, as he says, familiar with this line of speculation, it is quite possible that at this time he did not accept it. It has indeed been argued by Mr G. Potter[6] that there is no evidence at all that Tennyson believed in the mutability of species before the appearance of Darwin's work. He suggests that the sections of *In Memoriam* which appear to be about evolution really refer to something else, to a theory which was at this time widely held, the theory of the successive separate creation of first lower, then higher, forms of life, in an ascending scale of complexity. Perhaps we may add to this, as almost equal in influence, the evidence, very prominent in Lyell, for the extinction of species. Mr Potter, I believe, shows quite conclusively that the passage in the Epilogue about consciousness moving through 'life of lower phase', resulting in man, who himself leads on to 'the crowning race', refers not, as is commonly supposed, to the mutability of species, but to this other theory of successive separate creations. I think we can see the consequences that Tennyson deduced from this view in other places in *In Memoriam*: that man is but 'the herald of a higher race' [CXVIII]; that he 'but subserves another's gain' [LIV]; that instead of being the end and purpose of creation, he is only a member of a series and is destined to be extinguished like the rest. Tyndall records that Tennyson was 'by no means content to accept our present existence as a mere preparation for the life of more perfect beings. He had once asked John Sterling whether he would be content with such an arrangement, and Sterling had replied that he would. "I would not," added Tennyson emphatically; "I should consider that a liberty had been taken with me if I were made simply a means of ushering in something higher than myself." '[7] It was this belief that the individual is only an instrument in the perfection of a total scheme, far more than the belief in the mutability of species, that made Tennyson doubt the benevolence of the order of the universe. Indeed there is no evidence, if Tennyson did believe in the mutability of species at this period, that it greatly worried him. Twenty years later, when he certainly did believe in it, Darwin called at Farringford and Tennyson said to him, 'Your theory of Evolution does not make against Christianity.' To which Darwin replied, 'No, certainly not.'[8] Throughout the Darwinian controversy Tennyson showed no unwillingness to accept the Darwinian theory in the sense that the physical nature of man was derived from the lower animals. In a conversation with Tyndall he actually appears to welcome the view of the 'Life of Nature as a lower stage in the manifestation of a principle which is more fully manifested in the spiritual life of man'.[9] What did trouble him was the fear that the spiritual life of man might be only a lower stage in the evolution of something else.

His attitude towards this is ambiguous. Sometimes, as in the Epilogue, he contrives a measure of optimism out of it; sometimes he tries above all to attain some assurance that, in spite of appearances, there is no created being which 'but subserves another's gain'. But there is no ground whatever for the view that Tennyson wrote *In Memoriam* in some sort of panic about monkeys.

Other reflections which helped to upset his belief in the benevolent ordering of the universe were the amount of pain in the world and the blind profusion of nature. 'An omnipotent Creator who could make such a painful world is to me sometimes as hard to believe in as blind matter behind everything. The lavish profusion too in the natural world appals me, from the growths of the tropical forest to the capacity of man to multiply, the torrent of babies.'[10] There is nothing remarkable in being troubled by the amount of pain in the world: what is far more remarkable is the ease with which apologists of Paley's type have explained it away. To Tennyson it remained real, and his scientific reading did nothing to mitigate the impression. Why the profusion of the natural world should have appalled him is less clear. To many people it has seemed a striking evidence of the power and benevolence of the Creator. We can find the answer, I think, in section LV of *In Memoriam*:

> Are God and Nature then at strife,
>   That Nature lends such evil dreams?
>   So careful of the type she seems,
> So careless of the single life;
>
> That I, considering everywhere
>   Her secret meaning in her deeds,
>   And finding that of fifty seeds
> She often brings but one to bear . . .

The profusion of nature is only an effort to keep the type in being, and Tennyson hates it because it implies a carelessness about the individual. For the purpose of *In Memoriam* is above all to assert the transcendent importance of the individual soul.

On all this the influence of Lyell was profound. Quite apart from Lyell's own beliefs and conclusions, the *Principles of Geology* is important as a mere compendium of the biological theories which were affecting Tennyson at this time. They are all to be found in the book – the progressive creation of species in an ascending scale of complexity; Lamarckian evolution; the extinction of species. Lyell does not, as a matter of fact, accept either of the first two. The general argument of his book is that the world as we know it has not been produced by catastrophic divine intervention, but by the regular operation of natural causes. He does not at this stage accept evolution, and does not regard the appearance of man as part of the uniform series of causes. 'We may easily conceive that there was a considerable departure from the succession of phenomena previously exhibited in the organic world, when so new and extraordinary circumstances arose, as the union, for the first time, of moral and intellectual faculties capable of indefinite improvement, with the animal nature.'[11] But he is not, he says, contending for 'absolute uniformity throughout all time of the succession of sublunary events':[12] and suggests that in any case man has made little difference to the physical order of nature. He argues that the effects of man on his environment are perhaps greater than, but similar to, the effects of other species of animals:

The larger carnivorous species give way before us, but other quadrupeds of smaller size, and innumerable birds, insects and plants which are inimical to our interests increase in spite of us, some attacking our food, others our raiment and persons, and others interfering with our agricultural and horticultural labours. We force the ox and the horse to labour for our advantage, and we deprive the bee of his store; we raise the rich harvest with the sweat of our brow, and behold it devoured by myriads of insects, and we are often as incapable of arresting their depredations as of staying the shock of an earthquake, or the course of a stream of burning lava. The changes caused by other species, as they gradually diffuse themselves over the globe, are inferior probably in magnitude, but are yet extremely analogous to those which we occasion. The lion, for instance, and the migratory locust, must necessarily, when first they made their way into districts now occupied by them, have committed immense havoc amongst the animals and plants which became their prey.[13]

The implied comparison of man to the lion and the migratory locust is not encouraging to one who, like Tennyson, seeks support for a belief in the special destiny of the human soul. The effect of a succession of such passages is to suggest (although this may have formed no part of Lyell's intention) that, though the appearance of man in the universe was extraordinary, it was not really very relevant to the universal scheme. And it is this, far more than any consideration of man's origins, that made cosmic optimism difficult for Tennyson.

It is possible to hope

> That nothing walks with aimless feet;
>   That not one life shall be destroy'd,
>   Or cast as rubbish to the void,
> When God has made the pile complete;
>
> That not a worm is cloven in vain;
>   That not a moth with vain desire
>   Is shrivell'd in a fruitless fire,
> Or but subserves another's gain. [LIV]

But nature gives little support for the belief. 'So careful of the type she seems, so careless of the single life . . .' [LV]. On examination, we find that she is not even careful of the type.

> 'So careful of the type?' but no.
> From scarped cliff and quarried stone
> She cries, 'A thousand types are gone:
> I care for nothing, all shall go.' [LVI]

The testimony of the rocks shows that multitudes of whole species have gone, have been created apparently only in order to disappear. The evidence for this is prominently displayed in Lyell's chapters on the extinction of species. The lines a little farther on, about man cherishing his belief in love,

> Tho' Nature, red in tooth and claw
> With ravine, shriek'd against his creed,

spring, I believe, from the same source. They are often read as if they referred to Darwinian natural selection and the survival of the fittest. This, of course, is not possible. But there are many passages in the chapters of Lyell just referred to which paint a sort of Hobbesian state of nature among organic forms:

> All the plants of a given country are at war with one another. [14]
> Every plant, observes Welcke, has its proper insect allotted to it to curb its luxuriancy, and to prevent it multiplying to the exclusion of others. [15]
> Entomologists enumerate many parallel cases where insects, appropriated to certain plants, are kept down by other insects, and these again by parasites especially appointed to prey on them. [15]

This is Malthusianism applied to the natural world: and it was, in fact, the speculations of Malthus on the natural limitation of human population that provided one of the starting-points of Darwin's argument. Darwin was concerned with the mechanism, Tennyson with the moral and theological consequences: but they are, quite independently, following the same movement of thought.

Before leaving Lyell, it is also necessary to emphasize the tone of his writing. The layman reading a scientific treatise is often more affected by its emotional colouring than by the actual

evidence produced: this was particularly likely to happen with one
so sensitive to mood and feeling as Tennyson. It is difficult for
the untechnical reader to separate the operations of nature from
the attitude of the particular natural philosopher he is studying.
There is a certain undertone of sombre relish in Lyell's writing
on these topics that I believe has had its effect on Tennyson's
gloomier conceptions of the natural order.

But there is another aspect to the natural philosophy of *In
Memoriam*. Side by side with the passages where God and Nature
are seen in blank opposition we find passages where the process
of nature is given an optimistic interpretation, and one even com-
patible with Theism.

> They say,
> The solid earth whereon we tread
>
> In tracts of fluent heat began,
>   And grew to seeming-random forms,
>   The seeming prey of cyclic storms,
> Till at the last arose the man;
>
> Who throve and branch'd from clime to clime,
>   The herald of a higher race,
>   And of himself in higher place,
> If so he type this work of time
>
> Within himself, from more to more;
>   Or, crown'd with attributes of woe
>   Like glories, move his course, and show
> That life is not as idle ore,
>
> But iron dug from central gloom,
>   And heated hot with burning fears,
>   And dipt, in baths of hissing tears,
> And batter'd with the shocks of doom
>
> To shape and use. Arise and fly
>   The reeling Faun, the sensual feast;
>   Move upward, working out the beast,
> And let the ape and tiger die. [CXVIII]

And the Epilogue contains a similar idea. Here I think that it is reasonable to suspect the influence of Chambers's *Vestiges of Creation*. We are told that the evolution poems were written before it appeared; but Hallam Tennyson's note is vague and does not necessarily include all the evolution poems. The contrast between the ideas of LIV, LV, and LVI and those of CXVIII and the Epilogue is so marked that it is extremely unlikely that both were composed at the same time. LIV, LV, and LVI come earlier in the time-scheme of the poem by over a year; and though the poem as it stands is an artificial arrangement and not a diary, it does in a general way represent the actual progress of Tennyson's thought. It is possible to connect this progress with the transition of Tennyson's reading from Lyell to Chambers. The two books are of very different kinds. Lyell's *Principles of Geology* is an objective contribution to science, which only accidentally affected religious thought. The *Vestiges of Creation* is almost the worst kind of scientific popularizing. Chambers had no first-hand knowledge of his subject, the book has no pretensions to accuracy, produces little evidence for its speculations, and goes far beyond what any available facts could possibly have warranted. But it is clearly and attractively written, and did perform a considerable service merely by introducing the British public to the general trend of evolutionary thought. Its most striking feature is that it steadily interprets evolution in terms of progress, and gives the whole argument a strongly theistic cast:

It has pleased Providence to arrange that species should give birth to one another, until the second highest gave birth to man: be it so, it is our part to admire and to submit. The very faintest notion of there being anything ridiculous or degrading in the theory – how absurd does it appear, when we remember that every individual amongst us, actually passes through the stages of the insect, the fish, the reptile (to speak nothing of others) before he is permitted to breathe the breath of life![16]

With much of this line of speculation Tennyson was, as he says, familiar before the *Vestiges of Creation* came out. What he may have derived from it is the realization that it was possible to

view natural development in a more complacent light, and that it
was not necessarily incompatible with religious faith.

This appears, in a somewhat confused way, in the Epilogue:

> A soul shall draw from out the vast
> And strike his being into bounds,
>
> And, moved thro' life of lower phase,
>   Result in man, be born and think,
>   And act and love, a closer link
> Betwixt us and the crowning race
>
> Of those that, eye to eye, shall look
>   On knowledge; under whose command
>   Is Earth and Earth's, and in their hand
> Is Nature like an open book;
>
> No longer half-akin to brute,
>   For all we thought and loved and did,
>   And hoped, and suffer'd, is but seed
> Of what in them is flower and fruit;
>
> Whereof the man, that with me trod
>   This planet, was a noble type
>   Appearing ere the times were ripe,
> This friend of mine who lives in God,
>
> That God, which ever lives and loves,
>   One God, one law, one element,
>   And one far-off divine event,
> To which the whole creation moves.

It is not clear whether the lines describing the soul moved through
life of lower phase, resulting at last in man, refer to the evolution
of man from the lower animals, or, as I think Mr Potter has shown,
to the doctrine of successive separate creations. In either case,
Tennyson now seems content to regard man as a step in the
development of the crowning race, which is presumably something different from man. Yet it remains sufficiently human for
Arthur Hallam to be a 'type' of it. And though it was generally

agreed that Hallam was an exceptionally talented young man, I do not think that anyone, even Tennyson, could really suggest that he was a biological advance on *homo sapiens*. It is not clear, either, what the 'one far-off divine event, To which the whole creation moves' actually is. It is evidently something to do with the reconciliation of God and Nature: but it is not plain how Tennyson in this mood of evolutionary optimism supposed that it would come about. As we have seen in our own day, those who seek in the doctrines of science a support for a religious faith are apt to find it, but at the cost of considerable confusion of thought.

To attempt to distinguish different levels of sincerity in a poem is always an uncertain business: but I do not believe that in these lines Tennyson is expressing any very deep conviction, or indeed doing anything but manufacturing a conclusion to the poem which will at least appear to draw the scattered threads together. Many of the religious difficulties in the poem are caused by the new scientific world-view, and Tennyson wishes to provide an answer in scientific terms. But the real answer, the one that really satisfied him, is not in those terms at all. It is a thorough-going subjectivism which does not meet the difficulties raised by science, but simply bypasses them:

> If e'er when faith had fall'n asleep,
>   I heard a voice 'believe no more'
>   And heard an ever-breaking shore
> That tumbled in the Godless deep;
>
> A warmth within the breast would melt
>   The freezing reason's colder part,
>   And like a man in wrath the heart
> Stood up and answer'd 'I have felt'. [CXXIV]

This seems both honest and extremely moving; but it is this subjectivist attitude in *In Memoriam* that has received the severest criticism: and it does indeed give rise to some of the weakest passages in the poem, section cxx, for instance, which is merely peevish. The struggle to interpret the biological and geological evidence optimistically shows how anxious Tennyson was to find a reason outside his own heart for believing in a benevolent

Providence. Yet the total effect of the poem is to make the reader feel that for Tennyson the only sure basis of religious belief is in interior experience.

It is commonly supposed that Tennyson adopted this position as a *pis aller* because he had failed to make anything satisfactory out of the argument from natural philosophy. I do not think this is so. Here, too, Tennyson is showing exactly the same sensitiveness to contemporary opinion as he does in the scientific field. The philosophy of religious experience had already been set up against the demonstration of God from nature, by Coleridge. And Coleridge was one of the most powerful religious influences in the mid-nineteenth century. Although Tennyson is alleged not to have cared much for Coleridge's prose,[17] his early career was passed in an environment steeped in Coleridgian influence. F. D. Maurice, the founder and inspiring spirit of the 'Apostles', was a lifelong disciple of Coleridge: to the *Aids to Reflection* especially he acknowledges a 'solemn obligation'. His influence on Tennyson's generation at Cambridge is sufficiently attested by Arthur Hallam. 'The effects which he has produced on the minds of many at Cambridge by the single creation of that society of "Apostles" (for the spirit though not the form was created by him) is far greater than I can dare to calculate, and will be felt, both directly and indirectly, in the age that is upon us.'[18] John Sterling, another 'Apostle' and friend of Tennyson, according to Hallam Tennyson 'the typical intellectual undergraduate of his day',[19] was a strong Coleridgian. Fitzgerald, recalling his undergraduate days, remarks, 'The German school, with Coleridge, Julius Hare, etc. to expound, came to reform all our notions.'[20]

Aids to Reflection has not, one supposes, many readers now: but this clotted and somewhat unctuous work was nevertheless the one through which Coleridge made his most powerful effect on the generation that followed him. It would be difficult to analyse anything so confused, but its general tendency is to take religious apologetic out of the Paley realm of reasoning from natural phenomena, into the domain of inner experience. Coleridge devotes some pages of his conclusion to an attack on

Paley's line of argument, and refers with disgust to the 'prevailing taste for books of Natural Theology, Physico-theology, Demonstrations of God from Nature, Evidences of Christianity, &c.'[21] A very few passages will show how closely Tennyson follows Coleridge's line of thought –

As far, at least, as I dare judge from the goings-on in my own mind ... I should say that the full and life-like conviction of a gracious Creator is the Proof (at all events, performs the office and answers all the purposes of a Proof) of the wisdom and benevolence in the construction of the creature.[22]

In order to non-suit the infidel Plaintiff, we must remove the cause from the Faculty that judges according to Sense, and whose judgments therefore avail only on Objects of Sense, to the superior courts of Conscience and Intuitive Reason.[22]

This last is paralleled in Tennyson's lines on Knowledge:

> Let her know her place;
> She is the second, not the first.

> A higher hand must make her mild,
>   If all be not in vain; and guide
>   Her footsteps, moving side by side
> With wisdom, like the younger child:

> For she is earthly of the mind,
>   But wisdom heavenly of the soul. [CXIV]

Of a future life, Coleridge says that he has become convinced that the *consensus gentium* applies even more strongly to the 'continuance of a personal being after death' than to the existence of God:

Throughout animated Nature, of each characteristic Organ and Faculty there exists a pre-assurance, an instinctive and practical Anticipation: and no pre-assurance common to a whole species does in any instance prove delusive. All other prophecies of Nature have their exact fulfilment – in every other 'ingrafted word' of promise Nature is found true to her word, and is it in her noblest Creature that she tells her first Lie?[23]

An argument more than once echoed by Tennyson in conversation: 'If you allow a God, and God allows this strong instinct and universal yearning for another life, surely that is in a measure a presumption of its truth.'[24] In the passages on immortality in *In Memoriam* the same idea is repeated in several forms:

> Thou wilt not leave us in the dust:
>   Thou madest man, he knows not why;
>   He thinks he was not made to die;
> And thou hast made him: thou art just. [Prologue]

It is probable, however, that when 'the heart Stood up and answer'd "I have felt"', Tennyson is referring to something other than idealist metaphysics as interpreted by Coleridge, and something more than mere emotion or desire. More than once in the *Memoir* a kind of mystical experience to which he was subject is referred to. It is best described in a conversation recorded by Tyndall:

With great earnestness Tennyson described to me a state of consciousness into which he could throw himself by thinking intently of his own name. It was impossible to give anything that could be called a description of the state, for language seemed incompetent to touch it. It was an apparent isolation of the spirit from the body. Wishing doubtless to impress upon me the reality of the phenomenon, he exclaimed, 'By God Almighty, there is no delusion in the matter! It is no nebulous ecstasy, but a state of transcendent wonder, associated with absolute clearness of mind.' ... The condition here referred to appears to be similar to that 'union with God' which was described by Plotinus and Porphyry.[25]

Tyndall then calls attention to the fact[26] that this very experience is made the ground of an argument against materialism and a proof of immortality in 'The Ancient Sage':

> And more, my son! for more than once when I
> Sat all alone, revolving in myself
> The word that is the symbol of myself,
> The mortal limit of the self was loosed,

And passed into the Nameless, as a cloud
Melts into Heaven. I touched my limbs, the limbs
Were strange not mine – and yet no shade of doubt,
But utter clearness, and thro' loss of self
The gain of such large life as match'd with ours
Were sun to spark – unshadowable in words,
Themselves but shadows of a shadow-world.

I have not discussed at all the personal side of *In Memoriam* as an elegy, but have tried to trace its religious argument to its origins. We find three important elements – the influence of science, transmitted especially through Lyell's *Geology*; the influence of Coleridge, experienced at Cambridge; and Tennyson's own religious intuitions, based ultimately on an unanalysable but completely cogent mystical experience. Tennyson was trying to make a synthesis of the living thought of his time, in the light of a strong personal conviction. The elements are not completely unified, and the balance between them is unstable. But he opened up to his generation a possible way of thinking and feeling about these conflicting notions: and it is difficult to see how, in that climate of opinion, he could have done more.

SOURCE: *Review of English Studies*, XXIII (1947).

NOTES

1. Hallam Tennyson, *Alfred Lord Tennyson, a Memoir*, I 314.
2. Ibid. p. 223 n. 'The sections of *In Memoriam* about Evolution had been read by his friends some years before the publication of *Vestiges of Creation*.'
3. Ibid. p. 223. [*Editor's note*.] More about Tennyson's interest in Chambers's book and the review that probably drew his attention to it may be found in John Killham, *Tennyson and 'The Princess': Reflections of an Age* (1958), especially chapter eleven and the appendix. A recent book on Chambers might also supplement and perhaps correct Hough's chastening remarks on *Vestiges of Creation*; it is Milton Millhauser's *Just Before Darwin: Robert Chambers and 'Vestiges'* (Wesleyan U.P., 1959).
4. *Memoir*, I 162.
5. A. Lyell, *Principles of Geology* (1830) II, chs II, III, IV.

6. 'Tennyson and the Biological Theory of the Mutability of Species', *Philological Quarterly*, XVI (1937).

7. *Memoir*, II 474.

8. Ibid. p. 57.

9. Ibid. I 323.

10. Ibid. p. 314.

11. Lyell, I 156.

12. Ibid. p. 157

13. Ibid.

14. Lyell, II 130.

15. Ibid. p. 132.

16. R. Chambers, *Vestiges of the Natural History of Creation* (1844) p. 233.

17. *Memoir*, I 50.

18. Arthur Hallam in a letter to Gladstone, quoted in ibid. p. 43.

19. Ibid. p. 42.

20. Ibid. p. 36.

21. Coleridge, *Aids to Reflection*, Conclusion.

22. Ibid. Aphorism CVII.

23. Ibid. Aphorism CXXIII (*c*).

24. *Memoir*, I 321.

25. *Memoir*, II 473.

26. Ibid. p. 478.

Arthur J. Carr

TENNYSON AS A
MODERN POET (1950)

THE theme of *In Memoriam* is loss and the subjective crisis it provokes. For this reason, the poem recapitulates much of Tennyson's previous development: the moods of frustration and longing, the strategy of the mask of age, the issues of sceptical doubt, the question of the poet's involvement in the world of affairs, and the issues of social disorder and social inertia encountered in the political songs. Tennyson was fully aware that his private grief for Arthur Hallam involved his 'passion of the past' and worked its way through all his being:

> Likewise the imaginative woe,
>   That loved to handle spiritual strife,
>   Diffused the shock thro' all my life,
> But in the present broke the blow.

The melancholic temperament upon which Tennyson had boldly erected the structure of his art was now baptized in the experience of real grief. Freud theorized 'that melancholia is in some way related to an unconscious loss of love-object, in contradistinction to mourning, in which there is nothing unconscious about the loss'.[1] Freud's insight would reveal the nature of Tennyson's fixed response to 'the picture and the past', that he idealized in 'Tears, Idle Tears' and stated more explicitly, long afterwards, in 'The Ancient Sage'.

>   ... for oft
> On me, when boy, there came what then I call'd,
> Who knew no books and no philosophies,
> In my boy-phrase, 'The Passion of the Past'.
> The first gray streak of earliest summer-dawn,
> The last long stripe of waning crimson gloom,
> As if the late and early were but one –

A height, a broken grange, a grove, a flower
Had murmurs, 'Lost and gone, and lost and gone!'
A breath, a whisper – some divine farewell –
Desolate sweetness – far and far away –
What had he loved, what had he lost, the boy?
I know not, and I speak of what has been.

This passage leads at once to a description of such a mystical trance as takes the centre of 'Armageddon'. If there is a definitive Tennysonian theme, this is it – a reiterated and dreamlike sense of loss that becomes idyllic self-assurance.

If we suppose such a loss or alienation, Arthur Hallam's role in Tennyson's development would be to clarify the motive in Tennyson's remarkably dependent nature that rendered his mind sluggish in freeing itself from supporting ideas and habits and that made him lean heavily upon his friends, his wife, and his son. It is a supposition that lets us see in Arthur, the symbolic figure of *In Memoriam* and of the *Idylls of the King*, the means by which Tennyson gained some conscious control over his divided nature. The conscious loss of Arthur Hallam enables Tennyson to confront the demon of his temperament. If we are to see in Arthur Hallam a possible surrogate for Tennyson's father,[2] we may better understand what the friendship meant to Tennyson and why the loss of Hallam seemed more than the death of a friend. Hallam's death would re-enact the father's death and would arouse again the sense of guilt that springs from the repression of aggressive impulses, 'the blindfold sense of wrong' that Tennyson finds alien to his love for Hallam and that yet marks the anniversary of his death 'as with some hideous crime'. Later, the imaginative reunion with Hallam might also touch some thrilling overtones of reconciliation with the father. To the degree that the unconscious elements of melancholia are not entirely resolved in conscious grief, *In Memoriam* would remain somewhat asymmetrical and strange:

But there is more than I can see,
    And what I see I leave unsaid,
    Nor speak it, knowing Death has made
His darkness beautiful with thee.

Because the death of Arthur Hallam is both a real and a symbolic loss that radiates from the centre of Tennyson's art, the tone of amatory affection which suffuses *In Memoriam* cannot be read as simple evidence of an erotic relationship in fact between Tennyson and his friend. It is enough that the loss of Hallam touches Tennyson at every nerve and that the demand for reunion is expressed with an energy that will not forgo the connotations of physical bereavement. Hallam himself had emphasized the intimate connection between intense spiritual devotion and erotic expression in his 'Remarks on Professor Rossetti's "Disquisizione sullo spirito antipapale" ': 'What is the distinguishing character of Hebrew literature, which separates it by so broad a line of demarcation from that of every ancient people? Undoubtedly, the sentiment of *erotic devotion* that pervades it.' Whatever we may choose to call the bond between Tennyson and Hallam, the crisis of *In Memoriam* would not have been induced by the rupture of feelings less complex and profound.

The stages and the achievement of *In Memoriam* are in some respects more clearly visible in those other poems that the death of Hallam almost immediately called forth. 'The Two Voices' (at first called 'Thoughts of a Suicide') bears in the *Poems* of 1842 the significant date '1833'. In J. M. Heath's *Commonplace Book* 'Ulysses' is dated 'Oct: 20 1833', and 'Tithonus', which Tennyson called a 'pendant' to 'Ulysses', was drafted at about the same time, although not published until 1860. 'Morte d'Arthur' was in hand before the end of 1833. Considered together, these poems strongly suggest that Tennyson rapidly passed through the stages projected across a longer scheme of time in *In Memoriam*.

The theme of all these poems that cluster together is loss, frustration, and the need to explore,

> How much of act at human hands
> The sense of human will demands
> By which we dare to live or die.

'The Two Voices', a diffuse debate between Self and Soul, turns on the question of whether life can be endured. The affirmative not easily gained, rests upon 'the heat of inward evidence', like that cry of 'I have felt', in section CXXIV of *In Memoriam*. The poet then passes into the vernal woods that symbolize his reborn existence. Characteristically, the impulse towards 'suicide' is more fully objectified in the imaginative sympathy that Tennyson shows for the legend of Tithonus. The poem 'Tithonus' is an elaborate and beautiful ritual for release from frustration. If love is withheld, death is desired. Tithonus, caught in the web of memory and desire, appeals for a release no less idyllic than the erotic vision of Aurora that motivates his plea.

'There is more about myself in "Ulysses",' said Tennyson. 'It was more written with the feeling of his loss upon me than many poems in *In Memoriam*.' As in 'The Lotos-Eaters', the Ithaca of responsibilities is renounced, this time explicitly, in favour of a voyage into ever-widening 'experience'. But this is not mere experience and it is not true that 'the margin fades, Forever and forever when I move'. Ulysses moves towards a possible reunion, as in the dream-voyage described in *In Memoriam*, section CIII, towards the Happy Isles and a meeting with 'the great Achilles, whom we knew'. In small compass, Tennyson forecasts the dual answer of *In Memoriam*: life and nature are a continuum extending uninterruptedly towards a spiritual climax; yet at some point the 'lower' material world passes over into the 'higher' spiritual world. The continuum belongs to the world of nature and history; in the subjective vision of reunion with Hallam the poet crosses the bar between two separate spheres.

'Morte d'Arthur' unites the themes of all these poems in Sir Bedivere who must 'go forth companionless', and in the death of King Arthur. Defeated in the material world, he voyages without abrupt transition to the happy island-valley of Avilion. A vision of his return and a dream of reunion with him close the lines which frame the epic fragment.

The theme of reunion is the personal core of *In Memoriam*. It develops in a series of fairly distinct approaches that culminate in the trance-vision in section XCV and the dream of the future in section CIII. In these two lyrics Tennyson contrives to knit the past to the present and the present to the future. The stages of approach to reunion are most clearly defined in sections XLI–

XLVII, which discuss death as a barrier to reunion, sections LX–
LXV, which suggest that friendship may cross the barrier, and the
series of dreams, sections LXVII–LXXI. These advance painfully,
through imagery recalling the ominous preludes of 'Armageddon'
and 'A Dream of Fair Women', to a sleep, akin 'To death and
trance And madness', in which there is 'forged at last'

> A night-long Present of the Past
> In which we went thro' summer France.

After a pause quickened only by the lyrics of spring (LXXXIII and
LXXXVI), the forward movement begins again with vivid re-
collections of Hallam's presence at Cambridge and at Somersby (LXXXVII and LXXXIX).

Sections XC–XCV achieve reunion with Hallam in the present.
The ritual preparation is fastidious. It begins (XC) with a passionate invocation – 'Ah dear, but come thou back to me' – that is
qualified (XCI) by a rejection of mere dreams of the past – 'Come:
not in watches of the night.' Sections XCII and XCIII refuse to invoke a stage-phantom, 'a wind Of memory murmuring the past'.
Tennyson thus invites the return of a mystical disclosure, and
section XCIV is symbolic lustration. Then, in the moonlight on
the lawn of Somersby (XCV), in the midst of images from memory,

> The dead man touch'd me from the past,
> And all at once it seem'd at last
> The living soul was flash'd on mine . . .

> . . . At length my trance
> Was cancell'd, stricken thro' with doubt.

In 'the doubtful dusk' of dawn, the breeze that had trembled in
'In Deep and Solemn Dreams' shakes sycamore and elms, and
dies away at the talismanic hour when

> East and West, without a breath,
> Mixt their dim lights, like life and death. . . .

The lyrics concerning Tennyson's departure from Somersby

are crowned by the dream (CIII) that blends many elements of Tennyson's poetry and merges the present in the future. The Hall with a river flowing past recalls 'The Lady of Shalott' and 'The Palace of Art'. The 'summons from the sea' and the poet's voyage with maidens down the river towards the sea have affinities with 'Ulysses', 'Morte d'Arthur', 'Locksley Hall', and 'Crossing the Bar'. The magic of the dream increases,

> Until the forward-creeping tides
>> Began to foam, and we to draw
>> From deep to deep, to where we saw
> A great ship lift her shining sides.

> The man we loved was there on deck,
>> But thrice as large as man he bent
>> To greet us. Up the side I went,
> And fell in silence on his neck . . .

Although the reunion with Hallam's spirit is imperfect and consequently demands renewal (for example, in section CXXII), Hallam becomes the symbolic thread that knits Tennyson's world of experience together again. Section CIII is followed at once by the 'third Christmas' lyrics (CIV, CV) that renounce the observance of 'an ancient form Thro' which the spirit breathes no more'. The New Year song (section CVI) celebrates instead 'the Christ that is to be'; and section CVII ('It is the day when he was born') establishes the observance of Hallam's nativity. The remaining lyrics of *In Memoriam* are the apotheosis of Hallam as 'herald of a higher race' who redeems from doubt and pain the intellectual difficulties that had joined in the train of personal grief.

If the nature of Tennyson's subjective crisis had made him unusually sensitive to the moral implications of the revolution that was occurring in art, in society, in science, and in history, the loss of Hallam had quickened that awareness. He perceived the approach of Darwinian materialism and the rising class struggle as outward manifestations of that loss of values which he had suffered in his own life. Unsanctified by tradition and lacking 'objective foundations' in common morality, the scientific view of nature and the liberal position in politics resolve the conflict

between good and evil into a mere struggle for existence and cast
the artist to the mercy of his impressions:

> This round of green, this orb of flame,
>> Fantastic beauty; such as lurks
>> In some wild Poet, when he works
> Without a conscience or an aim.

The full weight of modern knowledge, 'Submitting all things to
desire', seemed cast into the balance on the side of sense. In the
dialectic of his poetry, Tennyson had rendered himself fully responsive to the attractions of materialism and of a monistic
ontology, most visibly in 'The Lotos-Eaters', to which he could
not commit himself. If art, nature, and history are empty of a
higher will,

> 'Twere best at once to sink to peace,
>> Like birds the charming serpent draws,
>> To drop head-foremost in the jaws
> Of vacant darkness and to cease.

But when he finds darkness 'made beautiful' by reunion with
Hallam, that friend becomes the 'higher hand' that frees knowledge from the bonds of sense.

Yet, as 'Ulysses' showed, Tennyson's answer to the intellectual difficulties that he faced is paradoxical. He tries to accept the
materialist-monistic continuum of nature and of history as a scale
upon which evil is merely historical process. Ends justify the
means, and evil is redeemed in the evolutionary faith,

> That all, as in some piece of art,
> Is toil coöperant to an end.

At some point the material cosmos is to sail smoothly and imper-
ceptibly across into the realm of spirit. The presence of spiritual
and 'higher' values renders the materialist continuum tolerable,
yet at times unendurable. A thoroughly material progress was not
the answer to Tennyson's needs, and he spurns a purely evolutionary faith in 'the greater ape', whose scheme of values gave no
room to the qualities that endeared Arthur Hallam to his friend.

The 'far-off divine event' could not happen in the Malthusian world of Huxley and Darwin.

The material world must be, at length, defeated; the great result of time must be negated. The Battle in the West and the defeat of Arthur herald his departure into the happy island of Avilion. The way to transcendental values lies through loss, death, and defeat. No accumulation of material advances can leap the transcendental barrier. Tennyson is tossed between the wealthy attractions of materialistic monism and the dualistic demands of his subjective strife and system of values. The world of nature can be sanctified only by another and a higher. At least once, he got the paradox fully stated:

> Dear friend, far off, my lost desire,
> So far, so near in woe and weal;
> O loved the most, when most I feel
> There is a lower and a higher;
>
> Known and unknown; human, divine;
> Sweet human hand and lips and eye;
> Dear heavenly friend that canst not die,
> Mine, mine, for ever, ever mine;
>
> Strange friend, past, present, and to be;
> Loved deeplier, darklier understood;
> Behold, I dream a dream of good,
> And mingle all the world with thee.

The irredeemable flaw of Tennyson's poetry is that he habitually weakens and dulls his perception of this paradox. Because he could sometimes make the transcendental leap in his own experience, he is bemused into regarding it as an objective truth common to all men. Thus he inclines to further in his art the idyllic mood rather than the tragic perspectives that a genuine dualism might have afforded. Nevertheless, the tragic view develops, almost surreptitiously, in the themes of defeat and disaster that dominate *Idylls of the King* and even the plays. Without the constant support of any traditional systems of value, Tennyson contrived to face, and in part to comprehend, the problem of tragedy in modern art. No English poet explored more widely the range of possibilities that had closed.

Tennyson is a modern poet, also, in his attempt to provide the personal themes of *In Memoriam* with a formal structure responsive to both private instinct and the elegiac traditions. His attempt embodies in practical form the question of the artist's involvement or non-involvement in the life of his culture. Tennyson withholds himself from the objective form of the pastoral elegy and at the same time he draws upon its inherent strength. *In Memoriam* was undertaken 'for his own relief and private satisfaction', and was anonymously published. Yet it is, of course, an enormously ambitious work, and imbedded in its discursive and informal manner are many of the traditional elegiac conventions. It opens with a formal invocation to a higher power and closes with an epithalamium. It describes the funeral procession (the voyage of the ship returning Hallam's body to England) and the mourning of nature, which is a kind of death. The poet himself represents the mourners. In accordance with the sophisticated tradition of the elegy, Tennyson launches forth on sober and noble themes, both personal and general, concerning the meaning of history, the nature of nature, and his personal destiny as man and as poet. The poem draws to a close with a lengthy apotheosis that dismisses the mood of grief, settles the perplexities, and issues upon a higher plane.

The presence of these traditional elements helps Tennyson in playing out the ritual of his private grief and in giving it objective form. Under the personal theme lie the ancient elegiac conventions, and through them the poem observes a simple, pastoral ritual of the cycle of the year: the death and reawakening of nature. This 'natural piety' underlies the comparatively superficial time-scheme of three years and is organically related to the theme of loss and reunion. It is adumbrated rather than announced. The death of nature is symbolized by the autumn and winter imagery dominating the allusions to nature in the poem as far as section LXXXIII, by the mournful observances of Christ's nativity (sections XXVIII–XXX, LXXVIII), and by the commemoration (section LXXII) of the 'disastrous day' of Hallam's death. Section

LXXXIII, a sudden invocation of spring, initiates the series of springtime poems (sections LXXXVI, LXXXVIII, LXXXIX, CXV, CXVI) that light the way towards reunion with Hallam and his apotheosis. As the statesman that he might have become, Hallam symbolizes that 'life in civic action warm' that may turn society from its wavering course. He also represents that wisdom of a 'higher hand' that must control the results of scientific and practical 'Knowledge'. Hallam's efficacy as a symbol that 'touches into leaf' the issues that had been filled with pain and death depends on the subjective experiences which revivified Tennyson's universe of values. The experience of loss itself became endeared as the prelude to reunion:

> That out of distance might ensue
> 　Desire of nearness doubly sweet,
> 　And unto meeting, when we meet,
> Delight a hundredfold accrue . . .

The cycle of nature is completed, and into the future is projected the passion of the past. The marriage-song that finishes the poem can welcome again the imagery of living nature and the conception of a child whose birth is the rebirth of Hallam and of Tennyson.

SOURCE: abridged from an essay in *University of Toronto Quarterly*, XIX (1950).

NOTES

1. *Collected Papers* (1925) IV 155.

2. Dr George Clayton Tennyson died in March 1831. W. D. Paden [in *Tennyson in Egypt*] thinks it probable that the death of Dr Tennyson rather than that of Hallam is the personal theme of 'Morte d'Arthur', because it deals with 'the end, not the beginning, of an epoch'. Certainly Hallam's death felt to Tennyson like the end of an epoch. But it is not necessary to make a simple choice between the father and the friend.

Freud's hypothesis would also intimate why *In Memoriam* opens with what may be a covert allusion to the grave of Tennyson's father (section 11) and ends not simply with a marriage-song but with the rebirth of a being like Hallam. And it would clarify the otherwise clouded theme of section CII, in which 'Two spirits of a diverse love Contend for loving masterdom' as Tennyson is on the point of leaving the Somersby home. In the face of his father's ambiguous comment, Hallam Tennyson plainly identified the two spirits as Alfred's father and Arthur Hallam (*Memoir*, I 72).

To see the function of melancholic sensibility in Tennyson's poetry does not require, however, that we disentangle the subtle skein of biography, interesting though it is to try.

Humphry House

POETRY AND PHILOSOPHY IN
IN MEMORIAM (1950)

I HAVE chosen to talk on *In Memoriam*, not because it is primarily a philosophical poem in any strict sense of the term – in fact Tennyson himself made it quite clear that he did not intend it to be so; but because it represents so very clearly the mood of its time in relation to some great problems which border on philosophy; because that mood gave it a popularity which few long English poems have ever had; and because I think it is a poem which many modern readers find it very difficult to be clear-headed about.

In Memoriam was not originally planned as a single long poem at all; it was a series of short poems in the same metre, which gradually grew in bulk over a long period. Up to quite late Tennyson was speaking of his 'Elegies' in the plural. Some were certainly written to form short groups with others; some ran straight on from the one preceding. But the idea of working them all into a sequence under a single title was strictly an afterthought. This fact is a main cause of the difficulty we now have in reading the poem; it is impossible to apprehend it as a unified whole; for it is not a whole; and it fluctuates waywardly. It *is* possible, of course, with the aid of Bradley's famous *Commentary* to see that the poem does fall into four main Parts, divided by the Christmas Poems; to see that each of three of the Parts does have a predominant mood; and to see that there *is* a development of mood and thought from beginning to end. But at the same time all readers would agree that within each Part, in the slow process of reading as poetry ought to be read, it is often impossible to see a genuine poetic unity. Especially in Bradley's Part III, that is sections LXXVIII to CIII, the movement is often wayward and inconsequential.

The poem then was never planned as a whole, and its composition was spread over a long period; and also its theme was never properly *apprehended* as a whole. I say its theme; but part of the problem is to be sure whether there was a single theme. Is the theme the personal sorrow for Arthur Hallam's death? Is the theme the whole question of human immortality? Is the theme the interplay of the personal sorrow with the general doubt about survival?

I think we should agree now that, if we are to talk in terms of a single theme at all, then the theme is the interplay of the personal sorrow with the general doubting and debating. But even when so much is said, the matter is not finally defined; for the interplay is complex; and a part of what I have to say will be an attempt to unravel it.

The attempt can only be made with the facts about the friendship with Arthur Hallam and about his death in mind. Tennyson first came to know Hallam well in 1829 when they were both undergraduates at Trinity, and both members of the famous group of young men called the 'Apostles':

> we held debate, a band
> Of youthful friends, on mind and art,
> And labour, and the changing mart,
> And all the framework of the land;

They were serious young men, in fact, who talked about psychology, aesthetics, economics and politics – unlike the later

> boys
> That crash'd the glass and beat the floor.

They shared each others' hopes and ideals; they went abroad together; Hallam stayed with the Tennyson family at Somersby; and a more special kind of link was formed when he got engaged to Tennyson's sister Emily. This friendship grew in intimacy and in mutual admiration for rather more than four years. In the summer of 1833 Arthur Hallam went abroad with his father, Henry Hallam the historian; on 15 September he died with complete suddenness of a burst blood-vessel in Vienna. His body was

brought to England by sea, and was buried on 3 January 1834 at
Clevedon, on the Bristol Channel:

> The Danube to the Severn gave
> The darken'd heart that beat no more;
> They laid him by the pleasant shore,
> And in the hearing of the wave.

To try to estimate the quality of Tennyson's first sorrow at this
appalling loss, is the first step in trying to appreciate the relationship between the elegiac and the philosophical elements in the
final poem.

There is little doubt, especially from the evidence in the
biography by Sir Charles Tennyson published in 1949, that not
only Alfred but the whole family had come to look on Arthur
Hallam as a centre of stability. Emily, of course, had lost a lover;
but, as Sir Charles writes,

the melancholy state of the whole family made a deep impression
on their cousins. . . . Even Frederick's spirit was broken. He felt
that the family had lost its sheet anchor. 'Never', he wrote, 'was
there a human being better calculated to sympathise with and
make allowances for those peculiarities of temperament and those
feelings to which we are liable.'

This is valuable in redressing the common view that the grief
expressed in *In Memoriam* is grossly exaggerated. For if Frederick and other members of the family felt like this, they must have
further tended to increase a sorrow in Alfred which we may
fairly suppose to have been already greater than theirs. It is curious to find them also sharing a sense of loss which became almost
a feeling of desertion, a feeling which has been noted as underlying a number of Tennyson's best poems. It does not seem possible to doubt that his first grief was immediate, genuine and
overwhelming. Its first poetic expression was in 'Break, break,
break' and in 'The Two Voices'.

> A still small voice spake unto me,
> 'Thou art so full of misery,
> Were it not better not to be?'

'The Two Voices' is a poem about the temptation to suicide, the possible valuelessness of human life, and the doubt of immortality. Much of the matter of *In Memoriam* is already there; it was written under the first impact of grief; but it is no elegy and Hallam is not mentioned. The question then is, did Hallam's death bring on doubt for the first time, or did it intensify in new and terrible forms an already existing doubt about the whole status and future of human personality?

There is scarcely time to develop all the reasons for thinking that the doubt was already there; but, broadly, they are of two kinds –first, Tennyson's own preoccupation from childhood with questions about his own identity, and, second, the general, current speculations in the early thirties about the nature of the world and of man. In particular, the publication of Lyell's *Principles of Geology* coincided with the last years of Arthur Hallam's life. In a poem called 'Parnassus', written very many years later, Tennyson called Astronomy and Geology 'terrible Muses'; the word 'terrible' has its full force; they were causes of terror. They overthrew the traditional cosmology and the traditional time-scheme of history; they made impossible the literal acceptance of the account of creation given in the book of Genesis; and they forced the imagination to dwell, both in time and in space, on vistas of unprecedented vastness. I have argued elsewhere that the early Victorians in general, in the face of these new terrors, turned for comfort and reassurance to an intensification of their personal relationships; Matthew Arnold's poem 'Dover Beach' is a clear expression of this development. And in Tennyson's case there is explicit evidence that he regarded his friendship as a safeguard against fear; he wrote in an early sonnet:

> If I were loved, as I desire to be,
> What is there in the great sphere of the earth,
> And range of evil between death and birth,
> That I should fear, – if I were loved by thee?

and

> 'Twere joy, not fear, claspt hand-in-hand with thee,
> To wait for death.

Thus the intensity of affection for Hallam, even in his lifetime, was linked to the terrors of speculation. I think that we can even go further and suggest that the affection increased posthumously, in proportion as his death increased the doubts and fears about human life. For *In Memoriam* most plainly shows the *fostering* of an affection after the loved person was lost; what has been called the exaggeration of the sorrow and the exaggeration of the love can be better explained, I believe, as the building up of a progressively more and more idealised friendship in retrospect, as a rallying-point when so much else was uncertain. Thus the memorial purpose of the poem and the speculative purpose each worked on the other from the beginning, because the friendship itself had so much of its peculiar value only in the context of the speculation.

How deeply Tennyson's feelings for Hallam were tinged with fear even after his death can be seen from the ending to *In Memoriam* section XLI; the dread of desertion persists even into an imagined immortality:

> For tho' my nature rarely yields
>   To that vague fear implied in death;
>   Nor shudders at the gulfs beneath,
> The howlings from forgotten fields;
>
> Yet oft when sundown skirts the moor
>   An inner trouble I behold,
>   A spectral doubt which makes me cold,
> That I shall be thy mate no more,
>
> Tho' following with an upward mind
>   The wonders that have come to thee,
>   Thro' all the secular to-be,
> But evermore a life behind.

It is, you see, an elaboration of the desertion theme; even though both friends should enjoy personal immortality, yet there would still be an eternal separation; for Hallam would have by then advanced too far in the 'grades' of the future life for Tennyson to overtake him.

I have purposely so far stressed the fears and terrors of the speculative parts of *In Memoriam*, because I think most modern readers agree in finding that it is exactly those parts which come from the deepest experience and have achieved the most satisfying poetic expression. The corollary of this view is that the optimistic, progressive view of the world and of life, that in the poem ultimately triumphs, is correspondingly shallow, even emotionally dishonest, and so produces inferior poetry.

There is no doubt that for his contemporaries Tennyson's salvation of hope was his greatest achievement; this was a great poem of spiritual and emotional victory. Bradley, writing at the turn of the century, said that parts of the poem

come home to readers who never cared for a poem before, and were never conscious of feeling poetically till sorrow opened their souls. . . . 'This', they say to themselves as they read, 'is what I dumbly feel. This man, so much greater than I, has suffered like me and has told me how he won his way to peace. Like me, he has been forced by his own disaster to meditate on "the riddle of the painful earth", and to ask whether the world can really be governed by a law of love, and is not rather the work of blind forces, indifferent to the value of all that they produce and destroy.'

Only a few weeks ago I was talking about this to an American poet and teacher, a man now in later middle age, who said he thought that younger readers now disliked *In Memoriam* because they thought that a mood of 'honest doubt', tinged with a strong hope, was an untenable or disreputable position; whereas he himself thought it was both tenable and quite honourable. I answered him then that I thought the real objection lay, not in the tenableness or not of the ultimate residuary doctrine, but in the poetic presentation of it. An expansion of that answer is what I now want to attempt.

If you boil out the ultimate residuary doctrine of *In Memoriam* in some such phrase as 'Love conquers Death', the result is of no more interest than the wording of a Wayside Pulpit or a poem by Wilhelmina Stitch or Patience Strong; and it makes no difference if you say the ultimate doctrine ought rather to be 'On the whole I hope Love conquers Death'. The trouble with the last part of

In Memoriam is that at times Tennyson himself seems to be under
the illusion that he can in some such way as this present his case in
a nutshell. The 'honest doubt' passage – section xcvi – is a case in
point:

> one indeed I knew
> In many a subtle question versed,
> Who touch'd a jarring lyre at first,
> But ever strove to make it true:
>
> Perplext in faith, but pure in deeds,
> At last he beat his music out.
> There lives more faith in honest doubt,
> Believe me, than in half the creeds.
>
> He fought his doubts and gather'd strength,
> He would not make his judgment blind,
> He faced the spectres of the mind
> And laid them: thus he came at length
>
> To find a stronger faith his own;
> And Power was with him in the night.

I could go on for a whole twenty-five minutes saying nothing else
but why I think that passage fails as poetry; the specious wording
of the central paradox, based on equivocations, is the main objection; and it is made worse by the button-holing 'Believe me';
which is as good as saying 'Don't really believe me.' But beyond
this there is a coarseness in the metaphors used to describe what
should appear as a highly complex and delicate process – I mean
such phrases as 'a jarring lyre', 'beat his music out' and 'fought
his doubts'; they are crude and inexpressive.

Another example of this tendency to rely on a too slick near-
epigram or a catch-phrase at a critical moment is to be seen in
section cxxiv: it also is concerned with the vital question of the
resolution of doubt:

> If e'er when faith had fall'n asleep,
> I heard a voice 'believe no more'
> And heard an ever-breaking shore
> That tumbled in the Godless deep;

> A warmth within the breast would melt
> The freezing reason's colder part,
> And like a man in wrath the heart
> Stood up and answer'd 'I have felt'.

The matter cannot, least of all for poetic purposes, be so drastically simplified. Such over-simplification is one of the forms of bathos, least of all tolerable at such a crucial point. It is, I think, literary faults of this kind that have led so many readers to think that all Tennyson's recovered faith is factitious and shallow.

One great strength of *In Memoriam* as a quasi-philosophical poem is in the images of the various stages of evolution. In this Tennyson not only caught the mind of his time, but even anticipated it; his knowledge of the details of Astronomy and Geology combined here with his descriptive skill to produce physical images of a kind that had scarcely been possible in an earlier age. Consider this, of geological change:

> There rolls the deep where grew the tree.
> Oh earth, what changes hast thou seen!
> There where the long street roars, hath been
> The stillness of the central sea.

and

> The moanings of the homeless sea,
> The sound of streams that swift or slow
> Draw down Aeonian hills, and sow
> The dust of continents to be.

Sections LIV to LVI are the central passages dealing with biological evolution, where a sanguine belief that *somehow* all will ultimately turn to good is wrung out of the despondent contemplation of Nature's wastefulness. But I think that the use of the scientific and evolutionary images – though very effective there – is not most effective in those passages which are explicitly dealing with questions of belief about man and the universe; they have their greatest force when used not for exposition, but as part of the matter apprehended in the emotional moments on which the development of the poem most truly depends. Such a moment is

that presented in section XCV, when Tennyson had a kind of
trance one evening while re-reading Hallam's letters:

> A hunger seized my heart; I read
>   Of that glad year which once had been,
>   In those fall'n leaves which kept their green,
> The noble letters of the dead:
>
> And strangely on the silence broke
>   The silent-speaking words, and strange
>   Was love's dumb cry defying change
> To test his worth; and strangely spoke
>
> The faith, the vigour, bold to dwell
>   On doubts that drive the coward back,
>   And keen thro' wordy snares to track
> Suggestion to her inmost cell.
>
> So word by word, and line by line,
>   The dead man touch'd me from the past,
>   And all at once it seem'd at last
> His living soul was flash'd on mine,
>
> And mine in his was wound, and whirl'd
>   About empyreal heights of thought,
>   And came on that which is, and caught
> The deep pulsations of the world,
>
> Aeonian music measuring out
>   The steps of Time – the shocks of Chance –
>   The blows of Death.

Here the imagery which he commonly uses for the vastness of
astronomical and geological time, and still belonging properly to
that, gives a peculiar greatness to this momentary spiritual touch
with Hallam.

I think the true development in the later part of *In Memoriam*
lies less in the *explicit* conquests of doubt; less in the assertions of
the power of love; less in the sentinel

> Who moves about from place to place,
> And whispers to the worlds of space,
> In the deep night, that all is well.

less in the statement that

> all is well, tho' faith and form
> Be sunder'd in the night of fear.

The true development of the poem lies less in these passages, than in those moments of achieved happiness and hope, in which the optimistic evolutionary philosophy is not described, but simply taken for granted, as providing the setting and the mode of thought. There is no doubt that the poem does contain the record of a deep and genuine transposition of mood from despair to acceptance and hope. We can let all the over-simplified argument go, and the facile political optimism, and all the sillinesses and mannerisms with which the poem certainly abounds, and hold to such passages as the ending of section CXII:

> For what wert thou? some novel power
>   Sprang up for ever at a touch,
>   And hope could never hope too much
> In watching thee from hour to hour,
>
> Large elements in order brought,
>   And tracts of calm from tempest made,
>   And world-wide fluctuation sway'd
> In vassal tides that follow'd thought.

or in the last part of the Epithalamium for Cecilia Tennyson, in the epilogue in which the bridal night and the conception of a child are seen in all their local beauty against the vastness of star and system rolling past.

SOURCE: Originally broadcast in a B.B.C. Third Programme series on 'Poetry and Philosophy', and published in *All in Due Time* (1955).

Walker Gibson

BEHIND THE VEIL

A DISTINCTION BETWEEN POETIC AND SCIENTIFIC LANGUAGE IN TENNYSON, LYELL, AND DARWIN (1956)

No doubt Huxley was over-enthusiastic in his remark that 'Tennyson was the first poet since Lucretius who understood the drift of science'.[1] Still, Tennyson's confronting of the new science was real and to some degree successful, if by that we mean at least that he expressed in poetry a crucial Victorian intellectual dilemma. The fashion today of deploring the philosophical Tennyson in favor of the melancholic or the technically graceful Tennyson should not obscure for us the experience of reading lines that carry the most detailed response in nineteenth-century poetry to the great challenge of science. Indeed, the reader who depreciates Tennyson's mid-century cries of alarm had better have some better answers ready, for his own mid-century, to questions that remain not essentially different for us than they were for the Victorians.

'Tennyson was Darwin's exact contemporary,' a recent writer points out, 'and when *The Origin of Species* appeared at the end of 1859, the poet had been pondering the subject of Evolution as deeply and as long as the biologist himself, if not exactly from the same angle.'[2] It will be the purpose of this paper to begin to lay out, in literary terms, the 'angle' from which Tennyson pondered some of the new nineteenth-century science, and to distinguish this angle from that of the scientist.

We all know of Tennyson's wide reading and early interest in science. His progressive enthusiasms for the various scientific branches have frequently been summarized,[3] and his solemn list

of subjects to be studied during a single week in 1833 has often
been quoted:

> Monday. History, German.
> Tuesday. Chemistry, German.
> Wednesday. Botany, German.
> Thursday. Electricity, German.
> Friday. Animal Physiology, German.
> Saturday. Mechanics.
> Sunday. Theology.[4]

When the notorious *Vestiges of Creation* appeared in 1844 with
its heady popularizations of recent discoveries, Tennyson had
already been a reader and indeed a writer on scientific subjects for several years. 'I want you', he wrote Edward Moxon
immediately on the publication of *Vestiges*, 'to get me a book
which I see advertised in the *Examiner*; it seems to contain many
speculations with which I have been familiar for years, and on
which I have written more than one poem.'[5] His 'more than
one poem' evidently refers to, among other things, the scientific
sections of *In Memoriam*, which was certainly well launched
during the late thirties. 'The sections of *In Memoriam* about
Evolution', stated his son, 'had been read by his friends some
years before the publication of *Vestiges of Creation* in 1844.'[6] 'Unfortunately,' A. C. Bradley has commented, 'the sections are not
specified; but CXVIII and CXXIII are presumably among them.'[7]

Let us inspect, then, one of these Evolutionary sections Bradley
mentions, composed – 'presumably' – some time before 1844.
Our purpose will be to define the stance or 'angle' from which the
poet approached the experience of science:

> There rolls the deep where grew the tree.
>   O earth, what changes hast thou seen!
>   There where the long street roars hath been
> The stillness of the central sea.
>
> The hills are shadows, and they flow
>   From form to form, and nothing stands;
>   They melt like mist, the solid lands,
> Like clouds they shape themselves and go.

But in my spirit will I dwell,
    And dream my dream, and hold it true;
    For tho' my lips may breathe adieu,
I cannot think the thing farewell. [CXXIII]

This is a poem about change in the earth's surface, and it clearly
owes its origin to Tennyson's reading in the contemporary
literature of geology. It is no great task to find passages from
scientific writing of the time that suggest just this notion of geologic change. It is possible even to find appropriate passages that
are known actually to have been read by Tennyson. The great
Principles of Geology of Charles Lyell, for example, which
appeared in 1830–3 and was read by Tennyson in 1837,[8] contains the following paragraph:

I may here conclude my remarks on deltas, observing that,
imperfect as is our information of the changes which they have
undergone within the last 3000 years, they are sufficient to show
how constant an interchange of sea and land is taking place on
the face of our globe. In the Mediterranean alone, many flourishing inland towns, and a still greater number of ports, now stand
where the sea rolled its waves since the era of the early civilization
of Europe. If we could compare with equal accuracy the ancient
and actual state of all the islands and continents, we should
probably discover that millions of our race are now supported by
lands situated where deep seas prevailed in earlier ages. In many
districts not yet occupied by man, land animals and forests now
abound where ships once sailed, and, on the other hand, we shall
find, on inquiry, that inroads of the ocean have been no less
considerable. When to these revolutions, produced by aqueous
causes, we add analogous changes wrought by igneous agency
we shall, perhaps, acknowledge the justice of the conclusion of
Aristotle, who declared that the whole land and sea on our globe
periodically change places.[9]

What bears literary interest here is not so much that Tennyson
should have responded to passages like this in order to write
poems, but that his response included or accompanied or neces-
sitated a shift in dramatic position, in 'angle'. We may understand

this shift most easily if we first locate the position of the speaking voice in Lyell by examining some grammatical structures in his sentences. Who is this geological speaker – what does he do?

One test of who a speaker is and what he does is surely his choice of verbs. There are six main verbs in the five sentences of the paragraph, and four of these verbs point to the intellectual activity of human beings, with 'I' or 'we' as their subjects. I *may conclude.* We *should discover.* We *shall find.* We *shall acknowledge.* (The remaining two main verbs – towns *stand* and forests *abound* – appear in the second and fourth sentences, and have the effect of a kind of elegant variation in a context which perhaps might otherwise seem monotonously structured.) Several of the dependent verbs in the subordinate clauses similarly dramatize the speaker and his reader as intellectual observers of evidence and commentators thereon. 'I may conclude my remarks, *observing.*' 'The changes *are sufficient to show* how.' 'If we *could compare.*' 'When we *add* analogous changes.' This speaker, then, is consistently conscious of himself and his reader as engaged in an activity (observing present evidences of past change) which by its very nature separates him from the actual movement of the earth's surface. The tentative, cautious, distant quality of his voice may be illustrated by a slow reading of the third sentence: 'If we could compare [which we can't] with equal accuracy the ancient and actual state of all the islands and continents, we *should* probably *discover* [main verb] that millions of our race *are* now *supported* [dependent verb to main clause] by lands situated where deep seas *prevailed* [dependent verb within dependent clause] in earlier ages.' The description of the earlier ages in this sentence occurs, then, in the most subordinate position possible, a long way from the main activity of the sentence, the *should discover* conditional on the *if* clause. (And even that main activity was modified by a modest 'probably'.) Our separation from and our scientific caution about those deep seas *prevailing* in earlier ages are dramatized here by a perfectly appropriate organization of clauses. The speaker is a long way, both in time and space, *and grammar*, from those deep seas. Rather, he is

at a desk, let us say, or on a lecturer's platform, concluding his
careful remarks on deltas.

> There rolls the deep where grew the tree.
> O earth, what changes hast thou seen!
> There where the long street roars hath been
> The stillness of the central sea.

> The hills are shadows, and they flow
> From form to form, and nothing stands;
> They melt like mist, the solid lands,
> Like clouds they shape themselves and go.

The astonishing difference here will be plain to any reader. It is
not a difference in 'subject matter'; indeed some of the very same
words are used: 'there rolls the deep' and Lyell's 'the sea rolled its
waves'. But though the two speakers are concerned with the
same phenomena in nature, how different is their 'angle'! 'There
rolls the deep' – a speaker at a desk? on a platform? Not at all: he
is on a beach, perhaps, or a seaside cliff, and he points – 'there!'
Then he turns and addresses the whole world (O earth) and
speculates on the changes the earth has witnessed. Then he glides,
as if by magic carpet, off to a city where again he points (there)
to the long street roaring. In the second stanza this extraordinary speaker, who has been able to shift his physical position so
abruptly, now actually becomes almost timeless as he assumes a
state of being from which he can see hills as shadows: they *flow*,
melt, *shape* themselves, and *go* through eons of geological time. All
this activity takes place in main verbs and independent clauses;
the activity described is not the speaker's, but the hills', the
lands'. If Lyell had permitted himself a verb like 'flow', he would
hardly have placed it in an independent position, at least in his
characteristic sentence. We can imagine him more moderately
asserting that 'we can perhaps observe from this evidence that the
hills might be said to *flow* through unknown periods of geological change'. The difference in grammar is crucial. The subjects of
the verbs for Tennyson are not 'I' and 'we' – they are the very
objects in nature that act before him: the deep, the street, the hills,
the solid lands. There is no human intellectual activity expressed

here at all, and the speaker is not observing evidences of change: he is *there*, and change takes place before his very eyes. With no effort at caution, no deliberate placing of these changes at a grammatical distance through a series of dependent clauses, Tennyson can utter sentences that are notable (in this instance) for their brevity and simplicity of structure. But finally, after his dizzy flights through time and space in the first eight lines, he can – he must – soar back into himself in the third stanza:

> But in my spirit will I dwell,
>> And dream my dream, and hold it true;
>> For tho' my lips may breathe adieu,
> I cannot think the thing farewell.

A consciousness of the self as a talker does enter into the expression here at the end, as Tennyson seems to dismiss his former stand as a kind of lip-service. He cannot (after all) think the thing farewell. But the damage has surely been done. As so often in Tennyson, it is ironic that the most memorable passages are those expressing the very wild unrest that he later seeks to repudiate.

If we attempt to apply the description outlined here to other 'scientific' passages in *In Memoriam*, we discover a similar characteristic grammatical structure supporting the directness of a speaker who is on the spot. This is not to suggest that I am proposing a rigorous rule to distinguish Tennyson's voice from the scientist's at all times and places: obviously Tennyson (like all poets) occasionally *sees signs* that are interpreted intellectually in dependent clauses;[10] obviously scientists occasionally take grammatical flyers. But there are variations of the poetic stance I have described again and again in *In Memoriam* – for example, in the famous Evolutionary section, cxviii, where he begins:

> Contemplate all this work of Time,
>> The giant laboring in his youth;
>> Nor dream of human love and truth
> As dying Nature's earth and lime.

Here the speaker is urging us to adopt the very dramatic posture he has elsewhere demonstrated himself. 'Contemplate' here surely means more than simply 'reflect on' – it means look upon, and if what we look upon is a giant laboring in his youth, we possess, of course, pretty extraordinary eyes, in which a metaphor for the whole progress of Time becomes for us a real event occurring in a form to be physically observed. The second stanza of this section begins the long sentence in which Tennyson summarizes conclusions of the scientists; it is amusing to notice how he has translated their manner of talk into his own manner of talk.

> They say
> The solid earth whereon we tread
>
> In tracts of fluent heat began,
>   And grew to seeming-random forms,
>   The seeming prey of cyclic storms,
> Till at the last arose the man;
>
> Who throve and branch'd from clime to clime,
>   The herald of a higher race . . .

They – surely scientists – say what? The solid earth whereon we tread *began*, *grew*, etc., till man *arose*, *throve*, *branch'd*, etc. The grammatical structure of the scientists' statements (all, to be sure, dependent on 'say') reflects, though in past tense, very much the sort of rhetoric that Tennyson himself uses when he waxes scientific in CXXIII. As a matter of fact (we might argue, after our reading of Lyell), *that*'s not what scientists 'say' at all. What they say is something like this: 'We might conclude from the examination of certain geological evidence as well as from recent solar observations that the earth was originally composed of fluid material at a high temperature.' After all, this was the nebular *hypothesis* Tennyson was referring to, not statements of fact. The distinction, of course, is one that scientists have sometimes been guilty of ignoring as blithely as if they were poets.

Section CXVIII and its central sentence proceed with a complexity of grammar that could equal the dependent clauses of any scientist, but in the great conclusion we return to the imperative mood and an invitation to the reader to assume again with the speaker his magical position:

> Arise and fly
> The reeling Faun, the sensual feast;
> Move upward, working out the beast,
> And let the ape and tiger die.

Here of course is science made moral: recapitulate Evolution
within yourself and improve on it. The flight of imagination required for the reader to obey these precepts is obvious. To move
upward working out the beast is to become virtually immortal,
like the speaker who watched the solid lands shape themselves
and go. It is to be not a man, but Man.

In LV, another well-known scientific section, the speaker does
actually observe signs and draw conclusions, seemingly like a
scientist, and the subject of the verbs is 'I'. But the sentence
structure is crucially different from what I take to be the 'standard'
sentence of the scientist:

> Are God and Nature then at strife
>   That Nature lends such evil dreams?
>   So careful of the type she seems,
> So careless of the single life,
>
> That I, *considering* everywhere
>   Her secret meaning in her deeds,
>   And *finding* that of fifty seeds
> She often brings but one to bear,
>
> I falter where I firmly trod,
>   And falling with my weight of cares
>   Upon the great world's altar-stairs
> That slope thro' darkness up to God,
>
> I stretch lame hands of faith, and grope,
>   And gather dust and chaff, and call
>   To what I feel is Lord of all,
> And faintly trust the larger hope.

The italicized verbs – or are they merely adjectives? – do point
of course to intellectual activity not unlike that in the talk of
scientists, but their grammatical subordination is plain. What the
'I' does more importantly, once those intellectual participles are

over and done with, is *falter*, *stretch* lame hands, *grope*, etc. These verbs, which technically speaking are dependent on 'seems' two or three stanzas earlier, have by this time virtually acquired the force of independent verbs, and they certainly express the speaker's main activity. The point seems to be that when Tennyson does give us a locution in which 'I' is the subject of a verb, that verb is less likely to be one of observing, concluding, or analyzing, and more likely to be a verb of action suggesting intense emotional response.

The speaker in *In Memoriam*, I have been arguing, is not a man who observes signs and makes conclusions about Nature therefrom; he is instead a spectator as Nature acts before his very eyes. Sometimes he simply has to listen while Nature obligingly makes a statement for him, as in the section following the one we have just been considering (LVI):

> 'So careful of the type?' but no.
> From scarped cliff and quarried stone
> She cries, 'A thousand types are gone;
> I care for nothing, all shall go.'

The speaker responds by asking if Man, 'who roll'd the psalm to wintry skies', shall 'Be blown about the desert dust, / Or seal'd within the iron hills?' And he concludes the section with one of the most extreme confessions of mystification in the poem: 'What hope of answer, or redress? / Behind the veil, behind the veil.' But we must remember that even here, where the speaker seems to be as far from answers as any mere mortal or modest scientist, his dramatic stance has actually taken him a long way from any such humble position. He has, after all, just been carrying on a conversation with Nature, and it is from Nature's own mouth that he has learned to take the view he presents to us. The information he gives us – namely, that further information is 'behind the veil' – is conclusive, straight from the source, absolute. In the poem, we are taken right up to the veil, we almost see it; no scientist, I suppose, would want to claim even that there is any such thing as a 'veil'.

If one were to ask which of the two, the scientist or the poet, approaches the mysteries of Nature with the surer foot, the more positive voice, the more knowledgeable air, I think most of us might offhand answer the scientist. But if we consider their statements as dramatic expressions, expecially in relation to their grammar, the answer might well be the other way around. Here are two kinds of statement: (1) I measure and relate these skeletons; I suggest that a number of forms of life have passed out of existence; the next step must await further study; (2) O Nature, you cry to me, 'A thousand types are gone, I care for nothing, all shall go.' The poet is far closer to penetrating 'behind the veil' than the scientist is; he is in a position to get his information first-hand. It is the poet who *knows*, even when what he knows is a certainty of absolute ignorance; the scientist proposes (as indeed does the author of this paper). These are two ways of looking at the world, to repeat a platitude, and every one has his choice, from moment to moment. What I have offered here is an attempt to relate their differences to grammatical relations of words in sentences as actually composed by two great Victorian practitioners.

Tennyson, then, read Lyell in 1837 and may well have written cxxiii, more or less consciously, out of the experience of that very passage in the *Principles of Geology*. There seems to be no evidence that he read Darwin, however, before *The Origin of Species* appeared in 1859, nine years after the publication of *In Memoriam*. But there is a passage in *The Voyage of the Beagle* (1839) that expresses in the vividest terms a scientist's recognition of geological change, and whether it was ever seen by Tennyson or not, it displays for us once again the voice that a scientist can assume. At this point in the *Voyage*, Darwin was travelling through that part of mountainous South America called the Cordillera when he came upon a group of petrified trees embedded in volcanic sandstone. Immediately he went to work, reading the signs before him:

It *required* little geological practice to *interpret* the marvellous story which this scene at once *unfolded*: though I *confess* I *was* at first so much *astonished*, that I *could* scarcely *believe* the plainest evidence. I *saw* the spot where a cluster of fine trees once *waved* their branches on the shores of the Atlantic, when that ocean (now driven back 700 miles) *came* to the foot of the Andes. I *saw* that they *had sprung* from a volcanic soil which *had been raised* above the level of the sea, and that subsequently this dry land, with its upright trees, had been let down into the depths of the ocean.... Vast, and scarcely comprehensible as such changes must ever appear, yet they have all occurred within a period, recent when compared with the history of the Cordillera; and the Cordillera itself is absolutely modern as compared with many of the fossiliferous strata of Europe and America.[11]

In this wonderful piece of writing (which I have cut severely) we can see a scientist again facing a realization of change in the earth's surface. And it is not 'feeling' or 'emotion' that defines the difference between scientist and poet, for surely Darwin is moved here as he interprets 'the marvellous story'. The point is that he does dramatize himself *as* an interpreter, and again the verbs demonstrate his role. 'The scene unfolded its story'; 'I confess I was astonished'; 'I could scarcely believe'; 'I saw.' The repeated main verb 'saw' is followed in both second and third sentences by a description of past events in *dependent* constructions: 'I saw where trees once waved', 'I saw that they had sprung', etc. This is a speaker whose main activity is the observation of signs, *which* he interprets as signifying a story of change *that* took place in the past, and *that* is relegated accordingly to a clause *which* is dependent.

I submit, then, that Tennyson's 'poetic imagination' can sometimes be examined in terms of his grammar. The poet reads a scientist's sentence, and *imagines himself,* not in the role of the scientist (I saw), but in the role of some magical mind who can experience directly the activity of the dependent clause. He renders the scientist's dependent verb independently, and lo! the hills flow. He approaches the absolute ultimate limits of knowledge as no scientist would pretend to do: he sees the veil, and he knows when he has reached the end. To do this, he projects himself into a position of observation that is, strictly speaking, impossible: he stands where no one can stand, unrestrained by space or time, and he watches things happen that no one can watch. The magic carpet of this rhetoric floats a good many poets besides Tennyson, of course, and indeed it may suggest another way of distinguishing what we mean by prose from what we mean by verse. But more immediately, it seems to suggest one method by which a great Victorian poet was able to use for his own purposes the disquieting new world of science.

SOURCE: *Victorian Studies*, II (1958).

NOTES

1. Letter to John Tyndall dated 15 Oct 1892, quoted in Leonard Huxley, *Life and Letters of Thomas Henry Huxley* (New York, 1901) II 359.

2. William R. Rutland, 'Tennyson and the Theory of Evolution', *Essays and Studies by Members of the English Association*, XXVI (1940) 8.

3. For example in Rutland, or in Lionel Stevenson, *Darwin Among the Poets* (Chicago, 1932) ch. 2.

4. Hallam, Lord Tennyson, *Alfred Lord Tennyson: A Memoir* (New York, 1897) I 124.

5. *Memoir*, I 222–3.

6. Ibid. p. 223.

7. A. C. Bradley, *A Commentary on Tennyson's 'In Memoriam'* (1901) p. 15.

8. According to Stevenson, *Darwin*, p. 60.

9. Charles Lyell, *Principles of Geology* (Philadelphia, 1837) I 236–7.

10. An example of such *seeing* may occur at the end of CXXVIII: 'I see in part / That all, as in some piece of art, / Is toil coöperant to an end.' Here it is most interesting to observe how an effort to be modest or 'scientific' in the main clause ('I see in part') creates a logical difficulty in the dependent clause. How can one see *in part* that *all* is coöperant to an end is a poser: it has come about, one might say, because the speaker has uttered scientific and poetical language inside the same sentence. They do not easily mix. Note too that the simile – 'as in some piece of art' – is peculiarly inappropriate to the main clause, though not to the dependent clause. The very significance of a piece of art is that we do *not* see it 'in part' – we see it whole. That is what art is; that is why it is not life.

11. Charles Darwin, *Journal of Researches into the Natural History and Geology of the Countries Visited during the Voyage of the H. M. S. Beagle Round the World* (New York, 1846) II 85–6.

E. D. H. Johnson

THE WAY OF THE POET (1958)

THE tendency to regard *In Memoriam* exclusively as spiritual autobiography has obscured the importance of this work as a record of Tennyson's artistic development during the formative years between 1833 and 1850. Yet among the components of the ordeal through which the poet passed in his journey to faith was the search for an aesthetic creed answerable alike to his creative needs and to the literary demands of the age. Of the lyrics making up *In Memoriam*, approximately one quarter[1] relates to this concern; and when taken together, they constitute an index to Victorian poetic theory and practice as suggestive in its way as the testimony of *The Prelude* with reference to the poetry of the Romantic generation.

In tracing the stages through which Tennyson came to an awareness of his mission as a poet, there is no need to get involved in the perplexing problem of dating the sections of *In Memoriam*.[2] A. C. Bradley's *Commentary* has demonstrated the organic unity of the elegy in its published form. With three Christmas seasons as chronological points of division, it falls into four parts, the dominant mood progressing from an initial reaction of despair over Hallam's death (I–XXVII), through a period of philosophic doubt (XXVIII–LXXVII), to nascent hope (LXXVIII–CIII), and finally, to a confident assertion of faith (CIV–CXXXI). This paper will undertake to show, first, that Bradley's schematization lends itself equally well to a formal analysis of the evolution of the Tennysonian poetic, and secondly, that the processes of philosophic and aesthetic growth exhibited in the poem are so interrelated in their successive phases as ultimately to be inseparable.

Shattered by grief during the early months of his bereavement,

Tennyson found in poetry an anodyne bringing temporary release from obsessive introspection:

> But, for the unquiet heart and brain,
>   A use in measured language lies;
>   The sad mechanic exercise,
> Like dull narcotics, numbing pain.   (v)

At this time he makes of art a private ceremony, a votive offering to the friend on whose sympathetic encouragement he had been accustomed to rely (VIII). Vacillating between 'calm despair' and 'wild unrest', he senses the want of emotional perspective necessary to sustained and disciplined creativity. So crippled seems the shaping power of the imagination that the poet is even provoked to surmise whether the shock of sorrow has not alienated 'all knowledge of myself':

> And made me that delirious man
>   Whose fancy fuses old and new,
>   And flashes into false and true,
> And mingles all without a plan?   (xvi)

Yet this very impulse toward self-scrutiny had begun to knit 'the firmer mind' which Tennyson attributes in the eighteenth lyric to the purgative effect of suffering. The important grouping which follows (XIX–XXI) shows the poet at a provisional resting-place affording respite to assess the essentially lyric quality of his response to the experience which he is undergoing. His poetic faculties, incapable of dealing with the full impact of this experience are commensurate only with the 'lighter moods . . . / That out of words a comfort win.' Nevertheless, as though perfection of manner might serve to compensate for superficiality of content, the elaborately wrought metaphors of the nineteenth and twentieth poems point in their deliberate artifice to a notable increase in artistic detachment. Despite the fact that he continues to describe his method of compensation as 'breaking into song by fits' (XXIII), Tennyson must by now have begun to entertain thoughts of future publication; for the twenty-first lyric introduces a new element of anxiety over the poet's responsibility to his audience. The slighting comments of a chorus of imaginary interlocutors anticipate the kind of criticism which may be expected to greet a work so subjective in mode. The first speaker condemns the unabashed display of feeling as a eulogy of weakness, while to the second it seems that the poet's inclination 'to make parade of pain' originates from an egoistic motive. The third speaker, in drawing attention to the encroachments of democracy on established institutions and to the challenge to received opinions made by science, asks more weightily: 'Is this an hour / For private sorrow's barren song?' To which objections Tennyson, unable as yet to surmount his sense of personal deprivation, can only reply by again pleading that he writes solely in order to give vent to emotions that spontaneously well up; 'I do but sing because I must, / And pipe but as the linnets sing.'

The passing of the first Christmastide left Tennyson in a more stable frame of mind and disposed, in consequence, to try to come to intellectual terms with the fact of Hallam's death. As the second part of *In Memoriam* shows, however, the search for a meaning in the experience, at least in its initial stages, had no other effect than to involve the mind in the heart's distress. The lyrics relating to poetic theory in this part of the elegy occur in clusters, as follows: XXXVI–XXXVIII, XLVIII–XLIX (with which LII belongs), LVII–LIX, and LXXV–LXXVII. It is significant that each of these groups follows on a section of philosophic inquiry in which speculations precipitated by the irresolvable problems of death and change culminate in a paroxysm of doubt. Whereas the poet had previously looked to art to provide a release from emotional despair, he now discovers its further efficacy in allaying the tormenting 'dialogue of the mind with itself'.

Tennyson's increasing uneasiness over the limited scope of his work is implied in the derogatory reference of the thirty-fourth lyric to 'some wild poet, when he works / Without a conscience or an aim.' Yet, what message can be derived from the bleakly materialistic findings of modern historical and scientific knowledge hopeful enough to set beside the homely truths embodied in Christ's parables? In an age of unfaith art perforce abdicates its ethical function in favor of the kinds of teaching that issue in action, 'In loveliness of perfect deeds, / More strong than all poetic thought' (XXXVI). Guiltily aware of the shaky foundations of his own belief in the Christian revelation, the poet cries: 'I am not worthy ev'n to speak / Of thy prevailing mysteries' (XXXVII). By so much as daring to trespass on such matters he stands convinced of having 'loiter'd in the master's field, / And darken'd sanctities with song.' In dismay at the presumption of this first venture beyond the confines of immediate sensation, he falls back on the consolation offered by his 'earthly Muse' with her

> little art
> To lull with song an aching heart,
> And render human love his dues . . .

For all the continuing modesty of his pretensions, Tennyson could take additional gratification from the sense that each poem of *In Memoriam* had the truth of fidelity to the mood which had inspired it. Thus, in the sequence preceding the forty-eighth poem, the author's inconclusive brooding, this time over the related enigmas of individual identity and personal immortality, again results in a disavowal of any higher significance for his lyrics than as 'Short swallow-flights of song, that dip / Their wings in tears, and skim away.' In this very diffidence, however, he recognizes subservience to 'a wholesome law', not unlike the Keatsian Negative Capability. And, if his songs leave unplumbed the deeps of human experience, it can at least be asserted in their defense that by giving voice to whatever fancy is uppermost at the moment they register the full range of the poet's sensibility: 'From art, from nature, from the schools, / Let random influences glance' (XLIX).

The note of pessimism sounded in the thirty-fifth lyric recurs in the famous fifty-fourth, -fifth, and -sixth poems, formidably reinforced by Tennyson's reading in evolutionary doctrine. Before the blank futility of the view of life here revealed he recoils in horror, conscious of the indignity to Hallam's memory in further pursuing so wild a train of thought (LVII). At the same time, by forcing him out of purely subjective involvement in his grief, this crisis of doubt leaves in its wake newly won reliance on the capacity of the mind under trial not just to endure, but to grow in dignity. 'Wherefore grieve / Thy brethren with a fruitless tear?' the spirit of poetry inquires: 'Abide a little longer here, / And thou shalt take a nobler leave' (LVIII). In a still more confident mood the ensuing lyric, which first appeared in the fourth edition of *In Memoriam* (1851), testifies to Tennyson's satisfaction in the discovery that he has gained the power to sublimate private feelings, and as a result to display his sorrow

> With so much hope for years to come,
>   That, howsoe'er I know thee, some
>   Could hardly tell what name were thine.

Furthermore, just as he has experienced the humanizing effect of suffering (LXVI), so the poet is brought to realize that his constant endeavor to give artistic expression to his ordeal has been a cathartic exercise:

> And in that solace can I sing,
>   Till out of painful phases wrought
>   There flutters up a happy thought,
>   Self-balanced on a lightsome wing ...   (LXV)

His philosophic misgivings momentarily dormant, Tennyson undertakes in the lyrics immediately preceding the seventy-fifth to memorialize Hallam's brilliant promise and the loss to the age resulting from his untimely death. This subject is deemed too taxing for 'verse that brings myself relief'; but there has occurred a significant shift in the reasons which the poet gives for his reluctance to tackle themes of high seriousness. The burden of the blame is now laid on the unpoetic temper of the time, rather than on the writer's own lack of endowment: 'I care not in these fading days / To raise a cry that lasts not long.' And although, admittedly, no work of art can withstand the erosion of time (LXXVI), Tennyson, like Arnold, feels that the hope for modern poetry is nullified from the outset by a hostile *Zeitgeist*. Counteracting this pessimism, however, is the creative self-fulfillment which he increasingly derives from the writing of his elegy; and the tone on which the second part ends is anything but apologetic in the earlier manner:

> My darken'd ways
> Shall ring with music all the same;
> To breathe my loss is more than fame,
> To utter love more sweet than praise.   (LXXVII)

The attitude of stoic resignation with which Tennyson greets the second Christmas season is prelude to the recovery of hope in the third part of the poem. Concurrently, art ceases to be valued so much as a distraction from the central conflict in which the writer's deeper thoughts and emotions are involved. The process of spiritual regeneration thus has its aesthetic analogue in the closer identification of artistic considerations with the main themes of the elegy. For example, the coming of spring in the eighty-third lyric is made an image not only for the healing principle of growth, but also for the reawakening of the creative impulse which, too long sorrow-bound, now 'longs to burst a frozen bud / And flood a fresher throat with song'.

That Tennyson remained distrustful of the promptings of the poetic imagination is evident from the long retrospective eighty-fifth lyric in which he considers whether his pretended communion with Hallam's spirit is not willful self-deception: 'so shall grief with symbols play / And pining life be fancy-fed.' Yet, there is no disposition to discount the importance of artistic endeavor as a means of assimilating experience:

> Likewise the imaginative woe,
>   That loved to handle spiritual strife,
>   Diffused the shock thro' all my life,
> But in the present broke the blow.

As if poetry were, indeed, the spontaneous voice of hope reborn, Tennyson is more and more inclined to trust its directive power. Significant in this respect is his changing response to nature. In the first part of *In Memoriam* the phenomenal world had been invoked more often than not to mirror and hence to intensify subjective moods. In the second part the natural order had been questioned in more impersonal terms in a vain attempt to establish some sanction for human values. The eighty-eighth lyric, however, takes the form of a transcendental paean in praise of the beauty and vitality inherent in nature:

> And I – my harp would prelude woe –
> I cannot all command the strings;
> The glory of the sum of things
> Will flash along the chords and go.

The series of poems beginning with ninety is climaxed by the mystical revelation of the ninety-fifth, in which Tennyson fleetingly achieves union in the spirit with Hallam. Although his friend's own search for faith is ostensibly the subject of the following lyric, the moral that 'There lives more faith in honest doubt, / Believe me, than in half the creeds' is unmistakably derived from the writer's own experience. And by the same token, it is his own poetic progress that Tennyson has in mind when he equates the struggle for intellectual certitude with artistic growth:

> one indeed I knew
> In many a subtle question versed,
> Who touch'd a jarring lyre at first,
> But ever strove to make it true:
>
> Perplext in faith, but pure in deeds,
> At last he beat his music out.

The departure from Somersby, now first announced, is symbolic in more senses than one; and the allegorical one hundred and third poem fittingly brings the third part of *In Memoriam* to a conclusion with Tennyson's resolve to rededicate his poetry to more ambitious goals. The interpretation of this lyric offers no special difficulties, but its theme becomes more meaningful if viewed in relation to the stages through which the poet had passed in attaining the conception of his role here set forth. The opening four stanzas rehearse the elements of the first part of the elegy when Tennyson had devoted his art ritualistically to the private image of Hallam enshrined in his heart. The summons from the sea, here as in 'Ulysses' and elsewhere a metaphor for the life of active commitment in pursuit of transmundane goals, suggests through the device of the river journey the severe struggle with doubt in the second part of the poem, a struggle now looked back on as integral to the attainment of artistic as well as spiritual maturity. The quest is consummated in the final stanzas where the poet is reunited with Hallam – but a Hallam transubstantiated into the type of ideal humanity to the service of which the writer will henceforth exert his talents.

The third Christmas, observed in a new abode, ushers in the great New Year's hymn (CVI) with its exultant proclamation of progress toward the earthly paradise. His vision cleared and his purpose steadied by the perception of a goal which will enlist the altruistic devotion enjoined on him by Hallam's example, Tennyson is now ready to don the bardic mantle: 'Ring out, ring out my mournful rhymes, / But ring the fuller minstrel in.' No longer will he embrace isolation out of a refusal to connect the life of the imagination with the general life:

> I will not shut me from my kind,
> And, lest I stiffen into stone,
> I will not eat my heart alone,
> Nor feed with sighs a passing wind ...   (CVIII)

No longer will he make the mistake of seeking the meaning of his experience in the cloudlands of subjective consciousness amidst the delusions of 'vacant yearning': 'What find I in the highest place, / But mine own phantom chanting hymns?' For in the wisdom sprung from associating his loss with the common lot, he can now perceive that all along 'a *human* face' had shone on him from the 'depths of death' within a landscape of sorrow overarched by '*human* skies' (italics added).

As the group of lyrics extending from one hundred and twenty to one hundred and twenty-five makes clear, the assumption of the Carlylean role of poetic sage paradoxically provided Tennyson with an argument in final vindication of the subjective mode of his elegy. Like the confessional writings of his great contemporaries, Carlyle's *Sartor Resartus*, Mill's *Autobiography*, and Newman's *Apologia*, the message of *In Memoriam*

was addressed to the age; but the persuasiveness of the message
in each of these works resided precisely in the essentially private
nature of the experiential evidence which backed it up. The Victorian autobiographers thought of themselves as representative
figures within the context of their times; and however intimate
the circumstances from their lives selected for narration, they ad-
mitted nothing in which the particular could not be subsumed
under the guise of the typical. Thus, when Tennyson declares, 'I
trust I have not wasted breath' (CXX), it is in the hope that the
record of his own victory over doubt will guide others, similarly
beset, along the road to faith.

The mood of affirmation which characterizes the concluding
poems of *In Memoriam* is expressive not only of the poet's
acceptance of love as the pervasive cosmological principle, but
also of renewed delight in creative activity as an aspect of this
faith. The boon conferred by willed belief has been

> To feel once more, in placid awe,
>   The strong imagination roll
>   A sphere of stars about my soul,
> In all her motion one with law.   (CXXII)

And so Tennyson can invoke Hallam's genius to sustain poetic
utterance which, no longer shadowed by grief, will joyfully sing
once more its author's responsiveness to the beauty of the world:

> be with me now,
> And enter in at breast and brow,
> Till all my blood, a fuller wave,
>
> Be quicken'd with a livelier breath,
>   And like an inconsiderate boy,
>   As in the former flash of joy,
> I slip the thoughts of life and death;
>
> And all the breeze of Fancy blows,
>   And every dew-drop paints a bow,
>   The wizard lightnings deeply glow,
> And every thought breaks out a rose.

In the end, then, Tennyson turns back to the life of the imagination, rediscovering in its resources confirmation of the intuitions which formed the basis of his religious faith: 'But in my spirit will I dwell, / And dream my dream, and hold it true' (cxxiii).[3] The one hundred and twenty-fifth lyric develops in more straightforward terms the quest motif embodied in the allegory of the one hundred and third. In casting a backward glance over the stages of his spiritual pilgrimage, the poet explicitly identifies with each a distinguishing aesthetic manifestation:

> Whatever I have said or sung,
>   Some bitter notes my harp would give,
>   Yea, tho' there often seem'd to live
> A contradiction on the tongue,
>
> Yet Hope had never lost her youth,
>   She did but look through dimmer eyes;
>   Or Love but play'd with gracious lies,
> Because he felt so fix'd in truth;
>
> And if the song were full of care,
>   He breathed the spirit of the song;
>   And if the words were sweet and strong
> He set his royal signet there;
>
> Abiding with me till I sail
>   To seek thee on the mystic deeps,
>   And this electric force, that keeps
> A thousand pulses dancing, fail.

And when, three poems later, he seeks a figure to encompass the organic totality of his experience, it is the process of artistic creation that comes to mind:

> I see in part
>   That all, as in some piece of art,
>   Is toil coöperant to an end.

Tennyson's emergence from his long night of sorrow over Hallam's death into the light of living faith is dramatized through the bold device of appending an epithalamion as epilogue to the elegy. He here takes final leave of the threnodic vein in which his suffering had found voice, 'No longer caring to embalm / In dying songs a dead regret.' The poetry born of subjective striving with private emotion no longer suffices the artist to whom the passing years have brought knowledge of the transcendent power of love:

> For I myself with these have grown
> To something greater than before;
>
> Which makes appear the songs I made
> As echoes out of weaker times,
> As half but idle brawling rhymes,
> The sport of random sun and shade.

The Prologue to *In Memoriam*, dated 1849, seven years later than the Epilogue, was clearly conceived as a set-piece to introduce the elegy; and this fact explains the deprecatory tone of its final stanza. The rather formal and perfunctory ring of these lines simply reemphasizes the poet's intention, foreshadowed in the Epilogue, to devote himself henceforth to more public themes:

> Forgive these wild and wandering cries,
> Confusions of a wasted youth;
> Forgive them where they fail in truth,
> And in thy wisdom make me wise.

In the opening lyric of *In Memoriam* Tennyson had adumbrated the view of evolutionary progress which controls his method in the elegy and furnishes the key to the poem's structure: 'men may rise on stepping-stones / Of their dead selves to higher things.' These 'stepping-stones', as psychologically distinguished by the author, ascend through three orders of consciousness: the emotional, identified with man's sensory being; the intellectual, identified with the human mind; and the intuitive, identified with the realm of spirit. Following Bradley's quadripartite arrangement, the consecutive stages of growth recorded in the poem may be roughly diagrammed as follows:

Part One: Despair (ungoverned sense)
Part Two: Doubt (mind governing sense, i.e. despair)
Part Three: Hope (spirit governing mind, i.e. doubt)
Part Four: Faith (spirit harmonizing sense and mind)

If now a corresponding diagram is constructed to illustrate the stages of aesthetic growth in the elegy, it will appear that the demands which Tennyson made on his art in each of the four parts were directly responsive to the psychological needs of the phase through which he was passing:

> Part One: Poetry as release from emotion
> Part Two: Poetry as escape from thought
> Part Three: Poetry as self-realization
> Part Four: Poetry as mission

In Memoriam, as a poem of spiritual quest, represents the Way of the Soul. It is not less surely a poem of aesthetic quest, which sets forth the Way of the Poet. Tennyson came to the writing of his elegy fresh from such compositions as 'The Lady of Shalott', 'Oenone', 'The Palace of Art', and 'The Lotos-Eaters'. With its publication he was to attain the laureateship and to go on to the planning of *Maud* and the early *Idylls of the King*. Bridging, as it does, the earlier and later work, *In Memoriam* is quite as much a testament to artistic as to philosophic growth.

SOURCE: *Victorian Studies*, II (1958).

NOTES

1. The elegy consists of 133 separate poems, of which the following bear on the present discussion: Prologue, V, VIII, XVI, XIX, XX, XXI, XXIII, XXXIV, XXXVI, XXXVII, XXXVIII, XLVIII, XLIX, LII, LVII, LVIII, LIX, LXV, LXXV, LXXVI, LXXVII, LXXXIII, LXXXV, LXXXVIII, XCVI, CIII, CVI, CVIII, CXX, CXXII, CXXIII, CXXV, CXXVIII, Epilogue.

2. [*Editor's note.*] See Select Bibliography, 1.

3. The one hundred and twenty-ninth lyric defines the substance of this dream, love being conceived as the harmonizing force which unites the poet's adulation of all that Hallam had stood for with his concern for human welfare in general: 'Behold, I dream a dream of good, / And mingle all the world with thee.'

John D. Rosenberg

THE TWO KINGDOMS OF
IN MEMORIAM (1959)

I

THE praise of Tennyson's ear is sometimes a prelude to the damning of his mind. Thus when Auden, who conceives of Tennyson as a kind of disembodied ear, mindless and melancholy, tells us that he had 'the finest ear, perhaps, of any English poet', he at once adds that 'he was also undoubtedly the stupidest'.[1] But can we so simply dissociate the use of language from the use of reason? Surely the stupid poet is a bad poet. Perhaps if Tennyson's contemporaries had less eagerly encumbered their laureate with the mantles of the philosopher and prophet, we might not now be so sceptical of his intelligence.

Yet it is more than the image of the unsmiling, bearded, public bard which inhibits our response to Tennyson. We react to Victorian poetry with an incapacitating sense that too much of it is, in Morris' phrase, the idle singing of an empty day. Thus in a perceptive analysis Cleanth Brooks expresses surprise on finding ambiguities in 'Tears, Idle Tears'. The tears are not idle, he points out, but limpid with the virtues we associate with seventeenth-century verse. He concludes that Tennyson has unwittingly *blundered* into ambiguity.

Our notion of Tennyson's perfect but mindless craftsmanship blinds us to his remarkably poised handling (especially evident in *In Memoriam*) of symbols and their associated movements of passion and idea. Perhaps symbol seems too sophisticated, passion too violent, a term for Tennyson. But do we deny the terms to, say, Emily Dickinson because, like Tennyson in one of his many styles, she also clothes energy of idea and emotion in the sparsest of diction? Are we instantly certain which of the two wrote:

> For this alone on Death I wreak
> The wrath that garners in my heart:
> He put our lives so far apart
> We cannot hear each other speak.[2]

II

In Memoriam was composed over a seventeen-year period, from 1833, when Arthur Hallam died, to 1849, the year before Tennyson published the elegy dedicated to his friend. The poem was widely read as an orthodox testament of Victorian faith, and as such it has been reread and misread in our own century.[3] Yet the opening lines (among the last to be composed), in which the tone of affirmation is struck after years of the doubter's agony, betray an astonishing uncertainty. The Prologue is clogged with qualifications working antiphonally against the statement of faith, which is most vigorously offered in the first line but then retracted, celebrated, denied, and asserted through not only the Prologue but the entire poem. Admittedly only a poet with a great ear is capable of such counterpoint, but the mindless poet would be equally incapable of handling the subtler modulations of Tennyson's theme. The ear itself is here an intellectual instrument used not to rouse our admiration for a variation in vowel but to initiate the reader to the contrasting tones and rhythms by which Tennyson is later to reveal his agonized or exultant soul.

Thus, although the first line of the Prologue invokes the 'Strong Son of God, immortal Love', the poet admits that 'We have but faith: we cannot know' (l. 21): he can only '*trust*' (l. 39) that Hallam lives eternally with the Strong Son of God. This final admission is extraordinary, for it climaxes seventeen years of obsessive meditation on the death and after-life of the poet's friend. It epitomizes the energetic conflict between doubt and the will to believe which makes *In Memoriam* the most dramatic as well as the most religious of English elegies. This is the point of T. S. Eliot's important comment on the poem: 'It is not religious

because of the quality of its faith, but because of the quality of its
doubt.'4

In the early sections of *In Memoriam*, when the sudden pain of
loss is at its keenest, images of darkness and death are forced
upon us. The Strong Son of God, embraced by faith in the Prologue, gives way to Tennyson's clasping of Death in the raven
blackness and *danse macabre* of Section I. Death's predominance
is further symbolized in Section II by the old yew tree, whose
roots grasp at the headstones of the dead and whose branches are
without bloom. Sorrow, Priestess of Death in Section III, tells
the poet that the sun is dying and that nature herself is a lifeless
phantom. With Section VI we come upon a series of domestic
idylls, 'little pictures' of Victorian life which are, unhappily,
interspersed throughout the poem. Each of the idylls depicts a
miniature of humanity suffering under the weight of mortality.
The last, with its overtones of romantic love, prepares us for the
great seventh section:

> Dark house, by which once more I stand
>   Here in the long unlovely street,
>   Doors, where my heart was used to beat
> So quickly, waiting for a hand,
>
> A hand that can be clasp'd no more —5
>   Behold me, for I cannot sleep,
>   And like a guilty thing I creep
> At earliest morning to the door.
>
> He is not here; but far away
>   The noise of life begins again,
>   And ghastly thro' the drizzling rain
> On the bald street breaks the blank day.

In making this pained visitation, the poet has become a noc-
turnal creature ('I cannot sleep'), the darkness shrouding him
'like a guilty thing' and severing him from the normal waking
world. With the self-evident opening of the third stanza – 'He
is not here' – Tennyson is forced to recognize anew his first
shocked astonishment at Hallam's death. That shock is heightened

by a probable allusion to the Gospels, in all of which, save that of St John, the angel announces before the empty sepulcher, 'He is not here' but has risen in immortal glory. Yet Tennyson, standing before the darkened, empty house – itself an image of the tomb – is nowhere more conscious of Hallam's *mortality*, a consciousness painfully intensified by the contrast between the dead friend and the risen God.

We feel ourselves closer to Hallam's death in the opening sections of *In Memoriam* than at any other point. That event clouds all of nature and grates against the harmony of life itself. Before the dark house, as the 'blank day' breaks, Tennyson hears the waking sounds of the city as a *'noise* of life', a distant cacophony from which, in the hostility of his isolation, he is utterly apart. The dawn, symbol of rebirth, is without light – merely a lesser darkness looming through the rain. The poem has reached a point analogous to the heavy close of the eighth stanza of Wordsworth's Immortality Ode:

> Full soon thy Soul shall have her earthly freight,
> And custom lie upon thee with a weight,
> Heavy as frost, and deep almost as life!

The note must change or Tennyson will lapse into inaudibility, chilled into silence by those tears of Section III which grief 'hath shaken into frost'.

III

The poem now moves to a series of lyrics (Sections IX through XVII) about the 'fair ship' which bears the 'lost Arthur's loved remains' home to England. Hallam, who died on land, dies once more as Tennyson pictures him engulfed 'fathom-deep in brine', the 'hands so often clasp'd' in his, now tossing 'with tangle and with shells' (x, ll. 17–19). The clasping of hands is weighted, as it was in Section VII, with the sense of impossibility; it has yet to become Tennyson's symbol of reunion in the shared immortal life. Still, there has been a change. The tears once shaken to frost have thawed, as the poet tells us in Section XIII that his eyes now 'have leisure for their tears'.

On the first joyless Christmas after Hallam's death (XXX) Tennyson prays that 'The light that shone when Hope was born' – the hope of immortal life – be lit again. Without that hope he is convinced that 'earth is darkness at the core' (XXXIV), a vast dark house from which the human race is doomed never to arise. He asserts the immortality of the soul not as a religious dogma but as a personal necessity. The argument recalls Arnold's claim in the preface to *God and the Bible* that one of the two evident facts about Christianity is 'that men cannot do without it'. *In Memoriam* is Tennyson's assertion that *he* could not do without its promise of personal immortality. 'The cardinal point of Christianity', his son quotes him as saying, 'is the Life after Death.'[6]

Tennyson's obsession with that life makes much of *In Memoriam* inaccessible to the modern reader. Our own obsessions have become secularized and we are at a loss to follow a poet who through some thirty-seven stanzas (XL–XLVII) pursues such questions as, Do the dead remain inactive until some general awakening (XLIII), or do they at once begin a new life, forgetting us entirely (XLIV)? It would seem that the problem of a poet's beliefs embarrasses us in direct proportion as they approach us in time. We know all about the ghost in *Hamlet*, scrupulously suspending our disbelief in him so that we may believe in the exigencies of Hamlet's dilemma. But the 'ghost' of *In Memoriam* eludes us completely. Because he eludes us, we conclude in our secret hearts that Tennyson, if not the stupidest, is certainly the most naïve of poets. Yet to overlook Tennyson's passionate quest for Hallam's 'ghost' is to fail to see that *In Memoriam* is one of the great love poems in English.

For Hallam when alive was very nearly the center of Tennyson's life, and Hallam dead was the focal point of his life during the poem's composition. Despite its overlay of conventional pastoral elegy,[7] *In Memoriam* is deeply, in places almost obnoxiously, personal. Herein lies its uniqueness and distressing modernity among the major English elegies. Edward King is irrelevant to *Lycidas*; Keats is only the occasion for *Adonais*; but Arthur Hallam – above all Tennyson's love for Hallam – is the overriding subject of *In Memoriam*. Indeed, Tennyson's unending speculation on immortality is rooted in his inexhaustible impulse to visualize and to *touch* Hallam. Hence the ubiquitous image of the hand.

After the victorious affirmation concluding the immortality group – 'And I shall know him when we meet' (XLVII) – Tennyson plunges into the panic despair of Section L:

> Be near me when my light is low,
>   When the blood creeps, and the nerves prick
>   And tingle; and the heart is sick,
> And all the wheels of being slow. . . .

The regressive movement culminates in Sections LIV–LVI. The poet compares himself to

>   An infant crying in the night;
>   An infant crying for the light,
>   And with no language but a cry. (LIV, ll. 18–20)

The primitive fear of 'Be near me . . .' here becomes a plea for release from the animal terror of extinction. Without assurance of that release, Nature herself is a hostile goddess, a shrieking Fury 'red in tooth and claw' (LVI, l. 15). 'I bring to life, I bring to death' (LVI, l. 6), she cries, usurping the work of the Prologue's Strong Son of God who 'madest Life' and 'madest Death' (ll. 6–7). Shall man, Nature's final creation, who 'trusted God was love indeed',

>   Who loved, who suffer'd countless ills,
>   Who battled for the True, the Just,
>   Be blown about the desert dust,
> Or seal'd within the iron hills?   (LVI, ll. 17–20)

We are at the opposite pole from the confident assertion of Section XLVII – 'And I shall know him when we meet.' Hallam's death, first felt by Tennyson alone, has here been generalized to include the whole of living nature in one arid, iron negation.

Nature retains her hostility in the great lyric marking the first anniversary of Hallam's death (LXXII), a day which rises howling, blasts the poplar and the rose, and is 'mark'd as with some hideous crime' – the slaying of Hallam. Only with the second Christmas after his death is there a clear release from the paralyzing preoccupation with loss. 'O last regret,' Tennyson exclaims, 'regret can die!' (LXXVIII). He can now grace his theme with paradox, marking that detachment from the past necessary for the full growth of his faith in Hallam's immortality.

Death, the dark-handed criminal of the anniversary poem, becomes 'holy Death' in LXXX, sanctified by contact with Hallam. In LXXXIV Tennyson feels 'The low beginnings of content'. In LXXXVII, lingering outside Hallam's former rooms at Cambridge, he is for the first time capable of recollection in tranquility (st. 6–10), a tranquility which becames absolute in LXXXIX as he recalls his friend's idyllic visits to the Tennyson home at Somersby. But after these calm retrospects Tennyson's desire for the sight and touch of Hallam returns with increased intensity. In XCIII he cries to Hallam, 'Descend, and touch, and enter,' a desire gratified in XCV, one of the four or five climactic lyrics of *In Memoriam*.

It opens in the calm of evening with the poet and his family together on the lawn. The trees lay their 'dark arms' about the fields, and as night falls the family departs, symbolizing the larger society from which Tennyson's grief has isolated him. He reads Hallam's letters written during the period of friendship (the 'glad year' of l. 22) and finds that the dead leaves still retain their life. Then the dead man himself becomes a living spirit which 'touches' Tennyson's own, their souls now intertwined as were once their hands:

> So word by word, and line by line,
>   The dead man touch'd me from the past,
>   And all at once it seem'd at last
> The living soul was flash'd on mine,[8]
>
> And mine in this was wound, and whirl'd
>   About empyreal heights of thought . . .

The two souls 'come on that which is' and feel 'the deep

pulsations of the world'. But Tennyson's 'trance' is at length 'stricken thro' with doubt' (l. 44), and the blinding flash of his vision fades into the less revealing light of the visible world:

> And suck'd from out the distant gloom
> A breeze began to tremble o'er
> The large leaves of the sycamore,
> And fluctuate all the still perfume,
>
> And gathering freshlier overhead,
> Rock'd the full-foliaged elms, and swung
> The heavy-folded rose, and flung
> The lilies to and fro, and said,
>
> 'The dawn, the dawn', and died away;
> And East and West, without a breath,
> Mixt their dim lights, like life and death,
> To broaden into boundless day.

The breeze speaks only four words, which Tennyson translates into a parable interpreting much of *In Memoriam*. Light and dark, day and night – *'like life and death'* – are dual aspects of that single reality to which the poet aspires, the eternal life-after-death in which Hallam will not appear in a moment's flash but abide with Tennyson in the lasting light of 'boundless day'.

IV

Section xcv reveals the symbolic structure of *In Memoriam* with unusual clarity. That structure at times parallels and at times is independent of the poem's formal division into seasons. Within this section Tennyson achieves the transition from images of darkness and death to light and the promise of reunion with Hallam. The parallel movement in the formal organization of the poem is marked by Section cvi ('Ring out, wild bells, to the wild sky'), which celebrates the third Christmas after Hallam's death. Although it contains irrelevancies and its manner is forced, the dramatic success of this set-piece is unquestionable. The *tone* is

right, for the wild ringing of the bells to the wild sky counter-
balances the earlier hysteria of grief and the high-pitched shrieking of nature red in tooth and claw. Tennyson now rings out his
'mournful rhymes' and rings in 'the Christ that is to be' (l. 32).
When in quieter voice, he simply tells us that his regret has blos-
somed into an April violet (cxv, l. 19).

Yet *In Memoriam* demands a more articulate response to the
angry questions of Sections LV and LVI than the mere ringing of
bells. How can we be certain that God and Nature are not at
strife, that immortal Love does in fact govern all creation? Tennyson never attains absolute assurance; instead he attempts something perhaps braver and certainly more difficult – the synthesis
of a nightmare with a vision of felicity. For that synthesis he
draws on two great myths, the myth of Progress and the Christian vision of the Kingdom of Heaven on Earth. With these he
slays the dragon of doubt first shocked into formidable being with
Hallam's death in 1833 and later grown to monstrous proportions
with Tennyson's reading of Lyell's *Principles of Geology* in 1837.
From geological evidence Lyell argued that 'species cannot be
immortal, but must perish one after the other, like the individuals
which compose them'.[9] Thus man, the creation of immortal
Love in the Prologue, appears in Sections LV and LVI neither to
share his maker's immortality nor to inhabit an earth guided by
any conceivable laws of love: 'A thousand types are gone,' Nature
cries, 'I care for nothing, all shall go' (LVI, ll. 3–4).

This, then, is the nightmare. Whence the vision of felicity, of
faith rather than extinction? Tennyson points to the answer in
Section cxvIII, in which man, 'Who throve and branch'd from
clime to clime', becomes at last 'The herald of a higher race'
(ll. 13–14). Geology had revealed life as an 'idle ore' (l. 20), a
desert dust sealed within the iron hills of an earth darkened to the
core. But evolution speaks to us of the living forms which may
perpetuate the dead.

With increased confidence Tennyson asserts in Section cxxIv
that if doubt had ever shaken faith, his heart had stood firm and
answered 'I have felt.' He had once been like 'a child in doubt and
fear . . . a child that cries' (ll. 17, 19), a conscious echo of the in-

fant of Section LIV, 'An infant crying in the night . . . And with no language but a cry.' He had then extended lame hands of faith to God but gathered only dust and chaff (LV, ll. 17–18). Now, as when Hallam's soul had flashed on his in Section XCV, he again beholds 'What is',

> And out of darkness came the hands
> That reach thro' nature, moulding men.

Yet these hands, which Tennyson has sought throughout the poem, are not Hallam's but those of the immortal Love of the Prologue which 'madest Life' and 'madest man' and here shape and animate mankind.

The metamorphosis of Hallam's hands into those of the divinity would be more startling, were it not that in the latter part of *In Memoriam* Tennyson annihilates the distinction between the human and the divine. And with that annihilation Tennyson achieves the synthesis earlier alluded to, drawing at once on the assumptions of nineteenth-century science and orthodox Christianity. The evolutionary argument of Section CXVIII (man thriving from clime to clime) answered adequately to Tennyson's fears of racial extinction in Sections LV and LVI. Yet it failed to guarantee the personal immortality of Hallam. God, reaching hands through nature, might be Love indeed; but for Tennyson it was a feeble love which could not preside over the placing of his own immortal hand in Hallam's. Evolution offered no such union; Christianity did. Thus in the closing lyrics Tennyson joins the promise of the one – Progress – to the promise of the other – Immortality. Evolution's proffered 'higher race' becomes interchangeable with Christianity's promised Kingdom of Heaven on Earth. Hallam himself is a citizen of both realms, of the heavenly city which is to be manifested on earth and of the earthly city which is to evolve into the divine.[10]

It is not surprising, then, that as the poem draws to its close we find Tennyson simultaneously employing the language of religion and of Victorian science. Section CXXVII is especially pertinent, for it contains linguistic strata of Geology and the Apocalypse. Mountains tremble, sheets of ice topple from their peaks

> And molten up, and roar in flood;
> The fortress crashes from on high,
> The brute earth lightens to the sky,
> And the great Aeon sinks in blood.

Earlier (xxxv) Tennyson had described, with geological accuracy, streams which slowly 'Draw down Aeonian hills, and sow / The dust of continents to be.' Now he deliberately abandons Lyell's hypothesis that the present configuration of the earth is the product of wholly natural forces such as erosion. He reverts to the discredited concept of cataclysmic upheavals and in place of 'continents to be' we read of the great Aeon sinking in blood, 'compass'd by the *fires of hell*' (l. 17). The language, no longer scientific, recalls that of the destruction of the Great Babylon, of 'fire come down from heaven . . . and thunders, and lightnings; and . . . a great earthquake, such as was not since men were upon the earth'.[11]

Hallam, witness to this incandescent holocaust, '*smil*[*eth*], knowing all is well' (l. 20). The line is very nearly incredible. The smile is diabolic or divine, expressing either pyromaniacal joy or sublime content in the knowledge that the flaming of the earth is prelude to a finer order and a higher race. From the vantage point of the gods Hallam now sees what Tennyson (at the conclusion of cxxviii) sees only in part:

> That all, as in some piece of art,
> Is toil coöperant to an end.

The cataclysm is subsumed in the cosmic work of art.

Throughout the later poems Hallam has been progressively depersonalized, assuming many of the attributes of the Prologue's Strong Son of God. As human he anticipates evolutionary progress; as divine he fulfills the Gospel's promise of everlasting life. Thus the paradoxical address to Hallam in Section cxxix: he is 'Known and unknown, *human, divine*'. Uncertain of Hallam's identity in Section cxxx – 'What art thou then? I cannot guess' – he can nonetheless assert, 'I shall not lose thee tho' I die.' With the promise of that final possession Tennyson concludes the poem proper:

> O living will that shalt endure
>   When all that seems shall suffer shock,
>   Rise in the spiritual rock,
> Flow thro' our deeds and make them pure . . .
>
>   Until we close with all we loved,
>   And all we flow from, soul in soul.

Tennyson himself glossed 'living will' as 'Free will in man'.[12] Yet in the Prologue he writes 'Our wills are ours, to make them thine.' This transfer of will enables us to accept the cataclysm of CXXVII as that which only 'seems [to] suffer shock', a flaming instant of destruction in the eternity of rebirth, just as the loss of Hallam was a long moment's darkness preceding boundless day. The progression from death to life is again implicit in the reference to the 'spiritual rock'[13] from which Moses struck water in the desert and which Paul called the rock that 'was Christ' – the same rock from which man partakes of the baptismal waters of rebirth and on which Tennyson bases his faith that we shall '*close with all we loved . . . . soul in soul*'. The image, appropriately, is of an embrace; the clasping of hands has led to the union of souls.

V

Had Tennyson concluded *In Memoriam* without appending the Epilogue, he would have spared us the longest and most damaging of the poem's domestic idylls. There is much bad verse in another great long poem of the nineteenth century, *The Prelude*. But Wordsworth's ineptitudes are rarely offensive; they are merely unfortunate lapses into prose. Tennyson never deviates into prose but occasionally postures himself into verse. That posture in much of the closing epithalamium is mannered and false, although it is true that the marriage Tennyson celebrates has its symbolic relation to the whole poem: 'It begins', he said, 'with a funeral and ends with a marriage – begins with death and ends in promise of a new life – a sort of Divine Comedy, cheerful at the close.'[14]

Precisely as 'cheerful' is grossly inadequate to the tone of the *Paradiso*, so it is disastrously inadequate to the conclusion of *In*

Memoriam. Wrapped in a spell of wedding cheer, Tennyson can
refer to the preceding lyrics as 'echoes' of a weaker past, as 'half
but idle brawling rhymes' (ll. 22–3). He here rejects the larger
grief and the larger joy of *In Memoriam* in favor of the lesser
pleasantries of Celia Tennyson's marriage, on a bright Victorian
forenoon, to Edmund Lushington. A greater poet, or one less
responsive to the demands of his contemporaries, would have embraced both experiences, felt no compulsion to disparage the
earlier part of the poem in order to exalt the 'cheer' of its conclusion.

Fortunately, however, Tennyson is the master of many styles.
Nowhere are they called upon to accomplish more than in the
closing verses of the Epilogue. The wedded pair depart; the feast
draws to an end and the poet retires in darkness, withdrawing
into that isolation from the family group which preceded the
flashing of Hallam's soul on his in Section xcv. From the language of polite conversation he moves to that of resolution and
prophecy. The twenty-seventh stanza clearly marks the transition:

> Again the feast, the speech, the glee,
>   The shade of passing thought, the wealth
>   Of words and wit, the double health,
> The crowning cup, the three-times-three,   (26)
>
> And last the dance; – till I retire.
>   Dumb is that tower which spake so loud,
>   And high in heaven the streaming cloud,
> And on the downs a rising fire: (27)
>
> And rise, O moon, from yonder down,
>   Till over down and over dale
>   All night the shining vapor sail
> And pass the silent-lighted town,   (28)
>
> The white-faced halls, the glancing rills,
>   And catch at every mountain head . . .

I have begun to quote a sentence – one of the longest in English poetry – which extends through ten stanzas and thirty-nine

lines. Yet it is a compact unity which gathers into its imagery and statement the longer statement of the entire poem. It transports us from the lesser 'noise of life' in society to the enfolding quiet of nature. We move from microcosm to macrocosm, the moonlight serving Tennyson's lyric and symbolic intention precisely as the snow, falling faintly through the universe upon all the living and the nonliving, serves Joyce's intention at the close of *The Dead*.

The moonlight, playing on mountain and star, touches the 'bridal doors' behind which 'A soul shall . . . strike his being into bounds',

> And, moved thro' life of lower phase,
>   Result in man, be born and think,
>   And act and love, a closer link
> Betwixt us and the crowning race

> Of those that, eye to eye, shall look
>   On knowledge; under whose command
>   Is Earth and Earth's, and in their hand
> Is Nature like an open book.

The foetus, recapitulating the 'lower phases' of evolution, will develop, as had Hallam, into a closer link with the crowning race of perfected mankind, whose advent had been 'heralded' in Section CXVIII. That race will look on knowledge not as 'A beam in darkness' (Prologue, l. 24) but 'eye to eye', just as Hallam in the penultimate stanza 'lives in God', seeing Him not through a glass darkly but 'face to face':

> Whereof the man that with me trod
>   This planet was a noble type
>   Appearing ere the times were ripe,
> That friend of mine who lives in God,

> That God, which ever lives and loves,
>   One God, one law, one element,
>   And one far-off divine event,
> To which the whole creation moves.

Hallam is at once the noble type of evolution's crowning race and forerunner of 'the Christ that is to be'. The Strong Son of God of the Prologue again emerges, long after Nature's discordant shriek, as *immortal Love* – the God which 'ever lives and loves'. His creation, one element, resolves under one law the antitheses of life and death, darkness and light, destruction and rebirth.

With the 'one far-off divine event' we confront Tennyson's final effort at uniting evolutionary science and Christian faith. For that event holds out the promise both of the Kingdom of Heaven, when all shall 'live in God', and the Kingdom of Earth, when all shall have evolved into gods. The nineteenth century's conviction of man's perfectibility and Christianity's conviction of man's redemption become interchangeable. The synthesis is not without its inconsistencies, perhaps its absurdities; but it is the more remarkable in that the hundred years which followed the publication of *In Memoriam* have produced no like attempt more daring, persuasive, or eloquent.

SOURCE: *Journal of English and Germanic Philology*, LVIII, no. 2 (April 1959).

NOTES

1. *A Selection from the Poems of Alfred, Lord Tennyson*, ed. W. H. Auden (Garden City, 1944) p. x.

2. *In Memoriam*, LXXXII, stanza 4.

3. In Hugh I'Anson Fausset's *Tennyson: A Modern Portrait* (1923) p. 154, the poem is characterized as a rehash of the 'old belief in a Divine Providence, blindly held by the simple'.

4. Supra, p. 135.

5. Compare the companion poem, CXIX, l. 12: 'I take the pressure of thine hand'. I am indebted to Professor Jerome H. Buckley for having suggested to me the importance of the image of the hand throughout *In Memoriam*.

6. Hallam Tennyson, *Alfred Lord Tennyson: A Memoir by His Son* (New York, 1897) I 314.

7. This element of *In Memoriam* is generally overlooked, largely because it occurs in 'quiet' passages deliberately spaced as moments of rest between the climactic sections. But despite Tennyson's personalization of the traditional elegy, he was too resourceful a poet not to use its conventions to mute the louder notes of his anguish. Thus we

find references to 'The murmur of a happy Pan', to singing on 'Argive heights', and 'To many a flute of Arcady'. One quatrain is given to the conceit of the poet as a shepherd making 'pipes' of the grass on Hallam's grave; another depicts the 'bitter notes' he sings upon his 'harp'; and a third presents the familiar floral catalogue of the pastoral elegy. References might be multiplied, but see especially XXI 1; XXIII 3 and 6; LXXXIII 3; CXXV 1.

8. A. C. Bradley (*A Commentary on Tennyson's 'In Memoriam'* (1929) p. 90) observes that until *ca.* 1878 '*The* living soul' read '*His* living soul' and 'mine in *this*' read 'mine in *his*'. If 'The living soul' is not Hallam's, the lines are without meaning. For the remarkable impression Hallam left with his contemporaries, see Gladstone's eulogy quoted in the *Memoir*, I 299.

9. Quoted from Eleanor Bustin Mattes, *In Memoriam: The Way of a Soul* (New York, 1951) p. 59.

10. Tennyson suggests that the race will be reborn by evolution or divine grace through some sixty-five sections before man becomes the 'herald of a higher race' in CXVIII. In LV, for example, he 'faintly trusts' in the 'larger hope' of man's salvation. The *Memoir* (I 321) justifies this reading: 'He means by "the larger hope" that the whole human race would through, perhaps, ages of suffering, be at length purified and saved.' In CIII he writes of 'that great race which is to be', a clear anticipation of the higher race of CXVIII; and in CVI he rings in 'the Christ that is to be'.

11. Revelation 13:13; 16:18.

12. ' "O living will that shalt endure" he explained as that which we know as Free-will, the higher and enduring part of Man' (*Memoir*, I 319).

13. See 1 Corinthians 10:4: 'for they drank of that spiritual Rock that followed them: and that Rock was Christ'.

14. A remark made by Tennyson when reading the poem to Knowles. See *The Poetic and Dramatic Works of Alfred Lord Tennyson*, ed. W. J. Rolfe (Cambridge, 1898) p. 832.

Jerome H. Buckley

THE WAY OF THE SOUL (1960)

It is irrelevant to object that *In Memoriam*, published nine years before *The Origin of Species* and more than twenty before *The Descent of Man*, is not proto-Darwinian insofar as it does not present the doctrine of natural selection and transmutation. For the elegist is concerned with the purpose and quality of human life rather than the means by which mankind reached its present state. His great question arises out of the precise intellectual atmosphere in which the Darwinian hypothesis was to be born, and it anticipates the serious debate that Darwinism in particular and Victorian science in general would provoke. Man, 'who *seemed* so fair' under the older idealistic dispensation, now seems debased by a monistic naturalism which denies the soul and insists, with a dogged literalness, that 'The spirit does but mean the breath.' The fundamental conflict of the poem thus turns on an epistemological problem: the extent to which the old appearance did correspond with the reality, or to which the new 'knowledge' (or 'science') does give an adequate account of the human condition. The poet professes a deep devotion to knowledge and looks forward to its wide extension:

> Who loves not Knowledge? Who shall rail
> Against her beauty? May she mix
> With men and prosper! Who shall fix
> Her pillars? Let her work prevail.

But he demands that knowledge 'know her place', submit to the guidance of wisdom, learn that 'reverence' must interpret and supplement the known and the knowable:

> Let knowledge grow from more to more,
> But more of reverence in us dwell;
> That mind and soul according well,
> May make one music as before.

When it lacks due reverence for the claims of the soul, knowledge forfeits its right to command the allegiance or respect of mankind; having regained his assent, the poet rather truculently declares suicide preferable to life in a world of 'magnetic mockeries':

> Let Science prove we are, and then
> What matters Science unto men,
> At least to me? I would not stay.

He does not, of course, at the last believe knowledge capable of such proof; for he has once again warmed to the same 'heat of inward evidence' that conquered the cold reason in 'The Two Voices'; he has found life's necessary sanction quite beyond the things we see, altogether beyond knowing.

Concern with the mode of perception and the reality of the perceiving self turns the essential 'action' of *In Memoriam* toward the inner experience. As in Tennyson's earliest verse, the dream and the vision are called upon to explore and at last to validate the wavering personality. In the night of despair, 'Nature lends such evil dreams' to the frail ego; and in hours of hope 'So runs my dream, but what am I?' Dreaming, the poet wanders across a wasteland and through a dark city, where all men scoff at his sorrow, until 'an angel of the night' reaches out a reassuring hand. Half-waking, he tries to recall the features of the dead Hallam, but these 'mix with hollow masks of night' and the nightmare images of Dante's hell:

> Cloud-towers by ghostly masons wrought,
> A gulf that ever shuts and gapes,
> A hand that points, and palled shapes
> In shadowy thoroughfares of thought;
>
> And crowds that stream from yawning doors,
> And shoals of pucker'd faces drive;
> Dark bulks that tumble half alive,
> And lazy lengths on boundless shores.

Only when 'the nerve of sense is numb' and the self yields to the calm of the hushed summer night does the moment of full apprehension come, the 'epiphany' that reveals the continuous life for

which his whole heart hungers; as he reads Hallam's letters, the
past suddenly asserts its persistence and its infinite extension:

> And strangely on the silence broke
>   The silent-speaking words, and strange
>   Was love's dumb cry defying change
> To test his worth; and strangely spoke
>
> The faith, the vigour, bold to dwell
>   On doubts that drive the coward back,
>   And keen thro' wordy snares to track
> Suggestion to her inmost cell.
>
> So word by word, and line by line,
>   The dead man touch'd me from the past,
>   And all at once it seem'd at last
> His living soul was flash'd on mine,
>
> And mine in his was wound, and whirl'd
>   About empyreal heights of thought,
>   And came on that which is, and caught
> The deep pulsations of the world,
>
> Aeonian music measuring out
>   The steps of Time – the shocks of Chance –
>   The blows of Death. . . .[1]

Eventually the trance is 'stricken thro' with doubt'; the appearances of the world in all its 'doubtful dusk' obscure the vision,
and the poet returns to awareness of simple physical sensation.
Yet he brings with him renewed purpose and composure; his
experience has given him the certitude that 'science' could not
establish and therefore cannot destroy.

Though unable to sustain his vision, the 'I' of the poem finds
in his mystical insight the surest warrant for spiritual recovery.
Tennyson, as we have seen, had been familiar with such 'spots of
time' from his childhood, and there was, of course, ample literary
precedent for his use of 'mystical' materials. In the Confessions of
St Augustine – to cite but one striking example – he might have
found a remarkably similar passage recounting the ascent of the

mind by degrees from the physical and transitory to the unchangeable until 'with the flash of a trembling glance, it arrived at *that which is*'.[2] Yet he was perplexed as always by the difficulty of communicating what was essentially private and, in sensuous terms, incommunicable. The poet accordingly, having described his trance, at once recognizes an inadequacy in the description:

> Vague words! but ah, how hard to frame
>   In matter-moulded forms of speech,
>   Or ev'n for intellect to reach
> Thro' memory that which I became.

The mystical vision is assuredly the sanction of his faith, but he does not choose to seek fulfillment in a sustained and conscious pursuit of the mystic's isolation. Having found faith, he must assume his place in society and 'take what fruit may be / Of sorrow under human skies.' And as poet, aware of his mission, he must work in his fallible yet inexhaustible medium, the 'matter-moulded forms of speech'.

But whether or not it defies translation into poetic language, the trance has for the poet a profound religious implication. Lifted through and beyond self-consciousness, his individual spirit attains a brief communion with universal Spirit; 'what I am' for the moment beholds 'What is.' Yet Tennyson at no time insists that his private vision is representative or even that some way of 'mysticism' is open to all others. He assumes only that each man will feel the necessity of believing where he cannot prove; and only insofar as he makes this assumption does he think of his voice in the poem as 'the voice of the human race speaking through him'. For his own part, he rejects the standard 'proofs' of God's existence, especially Paley's argument from design, which the Cambridge Apostles had attacked and which a later evolutionary science seemed further to discredit:

> That which we dare invoke to bless;
>   Our dearest faith; our ghastliest doubt;
>   He, They, One, All; within, without;
> The Power in darkness whom we guess;

> I found him not in world or sun,
>   Or eagle's wing, or insect's eye;
>   Nor thro' the questions men may try,
> The petty cobwebs we have spun.

By intuition alone, the cry of his believing heart, can he answer the negations of an apparently 'Godless' nature. His faith, which thus rests on the premise of feeling, resembles that of Pascal, who likewise trusted the reasons of the heart which reason could not know. Its source, like the ground of Newman's assent, is psychological rather than logical, the will of the whole man rather a postulate of the rational faculty. And in its development, it is frequently not far removed from Kierkegaardian 'existentialism', which similarly balances the demands of the inner life against the claims of nineteenth-century 'knowledge'.

In his *Concluding Unscientific Postscript*, which may serve as an unexpected yet oddly apposite gloss on the faith of *In Memoriam*, Kierkegaard describes his own inability to find God in the design of the objective world:

I contemplate the order of nature in the hope of finding God, and I see omnipotence and wisdom; but I also see much else that disturbs my mind and excites anxiety. The sum of all this is an objective uncertainty. But it is for this very reason that the inwardness becomes as intense as it is, for it embraces this objective uncertainty with the entire passion of the infinite.

And to Kierkegaard '*an objective uncertainty held fast in an appropriation-process of the most passionate inwardness is the truth*, the highest truth attainable for an *existing* individual'.[3] Such truth is apparently close to the faith that lives in 'honest doubt', doubt that the physical order can in itself provide spiritual certainty. In a prose paraphrase of his poetic statement, Tennyson affirms the position even more emphatically than the philosopher:

God *is* love, transcendent, all-pervading! We do not get *this* faith from nature or the world. If we look at Nature alone, full of perfection and imperfection, she tells us that God is disease, murder and rapine. We get this faith from ourselves, from what is highest within us. . . .[4]

Believing that all 'retreat to eternity *via* recollection is barred by the fact of sin',[5] Kierkegaard questions the possibility of a complete mystical communion. Yet his faith requires 'the moment of passion' comparable to the trance experience of *In Memoriam*, for 'it is only momentarily that the particular individual is able to realize existentially a unity of the infinite and the finite which transcends existence'.[6] Through passionate feeling, he maintains, and not by logical processes, the individual man may unify his life and achieve the dignity of selfhood. True self-awareness, as *The Sickness unto Death* tells us,[7] is born, paradoxically, of man's despair, the possibility of which is his 'advantage over the beast', since in the deepest despair the soul faces its fear of imminent annihilation, 'struggles with death' but comes to know the agonizing life-in-death, the torment of 'not to be able to die' as prelude to acceptance of its indestructible obligation. Having also 'fought with Death' and reached the level of total or metaphysical anxiety, the poet likewise finds his acute self-consciousness an essential element in his final self-realization. Such similarities are inevitable: for Tennyson, though he differs sharply from the philosopher in his estimate of the aesthetic and moral components of life, is ultimately, according to Kierkegaard's definition, 'the subjective thinker': he is one who 'seeks to understand the abstract determination of being human in terms of this particular existing human being'.[8]

Fortified by his personal intuition, the elegist may at last give his sorrow positive resolution. He may assimilate the apparent confusions of history; he may trust that, though all political institutions are shaken in 'the night of fear' and 'the great Aeon sinks in blood', 'social truth' nonetheless shall not be utterly destroyed; for

> The love that rose on stronger wings,
> Unpalsied when he met with Death,
> Is comrade of the lesser faith
> That sees the course of human things.

Subjectively reappraised, natural evolution itself may now be seen as the dimly understood analogue of a possible spiritual progress;

and God, whom faith has apprehended, may be construed as the origin and the end of all change, the 'one far-off divine event, / To which the whole creation moves'. Though the prologue addresses the son of God as the principle of immortal Love, and thus as the warranty of the worth of human love, *In Memoriam* is seldom specifically Christian. Tennyson goes behind the dogmas of his own broad Anglicanism to discover the avail-ability of any religious faith at all and finally to establish sub-jective experience as sufficient ground for a full assent to the reality of God and the value of the human enterprise. His poem accordingly is not a defense of any formal creed but an apology for a general 'Faith beyond the forms of Faith'. And as such it is at once universal in its implication and directly relevant to a Victorian England which was finding all dogmatic positions increasingly vulnerable.

SOURCE: *Tennyson: The Growth of a Poet* (Cambridge, Mass., 1960).

NOTES

1. Editions after 1880 were revised so that 'His living soul' read 'The living soul', and 'mine in his' became 'mine in this'. The change was apparently intended to facilitate the transition from the awareness of the individual dead man to the perception of the One, the ultimate reality.

2. Confessions, Book VII, ch. xvii, sec. 23, *Confessions and Enchiri-dion*, trans. and ed. Albert C. Outler (Philadelphia, 1955) p. 151. Tennyson's trance is compared to St Augustine's vision by Percy H. Osmond, *The Mystical Poets of the English Church* (1919) pp. 309–10. The passage in the Confessions continues: 'But I was not able to sus-tain my gaze. My weakness was dashed back, and I lapsed again into my accustomed ways.' The ecstatic experience, in other words, took place some time before Augustine's conversion and had no direct relation to his decision to become a Christian.

3. Søren Kierkegaard, *Concluding Unscientific Postscript*, trans. David F. Swenson and Walter Lowrie (Princeton, 1944) p. 182; these passages are reprinted with an excellent brief introduction by Henry D. Aiken, *The Age of Ideology* (New York, 1956) p. 239. I have quoted them from the 1944 edition with the kind permission of Princeton University Press.

4. *Memoir*, I 314.

5. Kierkegaard, paraphrased by Howard Albert Johnson, 'The Deity in Time', pamphlet published by the College of Preachers, Washington Cathedral, Washington, D.C., reprinted from *Theology Today* (Jan 1945). Cf Tennyson's comment on the mists of sin and the far planet, quoted in *The Growth of a Poet*, ch. IV.

6. *Concluding Unscientific Postscript*, p. 176.

7. See *The Sickness unto Death*, trans. Walter Lowrie (New York, 1954) pp. 148–54.

8. *Concluding Unscientific Postscript*, p. 315.

Jonathan Bishop

THE UNITY OF
IN MEMORIAM (1962)

'THE unity of *In Memoriam*', says an introduction to the poem in the best of the current Victorian anthologies, 'is not immediately apparent.'[1] This agreeable understatement, addressed to the inexperienced student, will sum up the predicament of the shrewdest of us. My reader will say in his heart, *I* know how *In Memoriam* hangs together – and this paper is proof I share his belief. But do not our public dealings with the poem contradict us? When we teach *In Memoriam*, we affirm, of course, that it makes a whole, and adduce, if the notes don't anticipate us, the traditional evidence: the concentration of fifteen years of thought and feeling into a ritual three, the recurrent Christmases and anniversaries, and so on. But when we come down to poetic cases, are we not inclined to focus upon favorite lyrics? The 'Dark House' or the 'Old Yew' are teachable for their beauty as separate poems. The lyric beginning 'There rolls the deep where grows the tree' will neatly exemplify Tennyson's ability to turn geology into poetry. The equivocal tone of the opening prayer, with its tremulous equilibrium of faith and doubt, is a handy instance of the religious predicament of the poet and his age. As we demonstrate these useful truths, we go on calling *In Memoriam* 'Tennyson's masterpiece'; but I should guess we teach it not as a self-sufficient and entire creation (which a genuine masterpiece should minimally be) but as a quarry from which to extract good examples of Tennysonianism. And the anthologies we use in the survey courses where Tennyson is most frequently brought to the light of pedagogic day encourage this practice, for they often omit the 'less interesting' portions of the poem altogether.

This practical disbelief in the unity of the poem can find some support in Tennyson's admission that the separate sections were composed over a long period of time. Their present order, we know, was made later, and may therefore attract an imputation of artificiality. The poet's inspiration, like his reader's pleasure, was sporadic, fragmentary, and lyric. How *seriously* then need we take such continuities and developments as critical tradition tells us we can find? Scepticism can find additional support in the first book-length study of Tennyson to appear after the war, in which *In Memoriam* was compared to an opera 'which has lost everything but its overture and a few good tunes';[2] though scepticism ought to view sceptically a judgment emanating from an embarrassingly evident hostility to poetry in general and Tennyson in particular.

But the critical voices who speak with better authority agree that the unity of the poem is not factitious or arbitrary. There is Bradley's wonderful, unsupersedable *Commentary*;[3] there is Mr Eliot, who directly rebukes our classroom tendency to focus narrowly on selected lyrics, even such lyrics as the 'Dark House'. These isolated excellencies, he says, are not *In Memoriam*; '*In Memoriam* is the whole poem.'[4] More recently other students have begun to fill out the argument for unity by tracing significant recurrences of topics, theme, and image.[5] These efforts to rationalize the careful reader's persistent faith that the poem does somehow make a whole might all take as a common motto a sentence from Mr Buckley's study of the poet's development: '*In Memoriam* itself, as a finished "piece of art", is designed so that its many parts may subserve a single meaningful "end", a distinct if rather diffuse pattern of movement from death to life, from dark to light.'[6] My reader may consider what follows as an extended footnote to this remark.

I have just glanced at some of the familiar larger signposts of order, poetic elements of a kind stark enough to attract the notice of anthology introductions. Other, lesser, connectables strike the attention as one moves forward slowly or rapidly over the plain of the poem, some distinct enough to be worth registering in a conscientious footnote, some arcane enough to justify more deliberate scholarly reportage. The two yew tree poems, the two visits to Hallam's house, the two renderings of the image of the

child crying at night, are familiar resting places for the mind in
search of order. Thumbing through Bradley's *Commentary*, we
come into possession of definite regions within the poem where
single problems prevail through a chord of complementary lyrics.
We locate topics, and in the light of some central lyric arrange the
miniature idylls which re-express the major themes in terms of
domestic or social or natural analogies. Around such distinct
comparables and contrastables there remains a fine cloud of notice-
ably repeated elements, descending in dignity from consciously
paired incidents to apparently unconscious harmonies of image,
word, or even sound. These tease us with the hope of a still
larger synthesis, always just beyond the corner of our mental eye.

But the question is still alive to us, how far even the most
definite sequences and contrasts make a satisfactory whole. At
this stage in our reading we may be tempted to return to our
private anthology of striking lyrics. Yet we need not, I think,
give up. Nor need we settle for an abstract paraphrase. Our best
resource is to fall back on a Tennysonian trust in the potential
meaningfulness of the partial combinations we have succeeded in
noticing. We can re-examine these not at first as parts of some unknown whole, but as miniature statements whose implications
ramify outwards towards a general theme. If *In Memoriam* is
alive as a poem of momentary pleasures and evanescent combinations, we can look for the larger whole by dwelling upon the
general import of the isolated scenes and linkages that most attract us. The entirety of which we are in search may then begin
to appear as an overtone, echoes of which may be re-discovered
in some other context, and then in another, until we are ready to
generalize and talk about a plot for the whole. This tactic is
sanctioned by Romantic theory from Blake to Goethe; in an
organic entity, the smallest part should not merely contribute to
the whole, but reproduce its principle in miniature.

When we attend to the implications of the most interesting
particulars, we will become aware almost immediately of an
omnipresent theme. This is, to state it baldly, the theme of change.
It is change, natural, moral, psychological, and artistic, that we
locate within the separately memorable images as the secret of

their general relevance. *In Memoriam* grows into a whole, I believe, by virtue of the organic elaboration of this single principle.

Let me quickly try to make this proposal something more than a self-evident generality. The opening sequence of lyrics, you will recollect, shows the speaker – one might as well call him 'Tennyson' – in a state of rigid grief. Far from desiring or accepting change, he resists it. He is trapped, he tells us, in a determination to hold firmly to his first reactions to the news of his friend's death. 'Let Love clasp Grief lest both be drown'd', says the first lyric, and the second symbolizes this desperate and self-destructive state of mind in the single most memorable image of resistance to change which the early part of the poem provides:

> O, not for thee the glow, the bloom,
>   Who changes not in any gale,
>   Nor branding summer suns avail
> To touch thy thousand years of gloom . . .

Tennyson is addressing a yew tree in a graveyard: its darkness, persistence, and apparent exemption from the sexual cycle help make the tree a suitable fictive protagonist for a neurotic need to fix a single gloomy state of feeling. The yew is said to 'grasp' the gravestones and 'net' the bones beneath; the action is expressive of the emotional armlock Love has on Grief, and negatively exemplifies the affectionate embrace the protagonist has lost, and now longs for, an embrace he will finally re-experience in mystical form towards the close of the poem. At the end of this particular lyric we find him about to 'fail from out my blood' and 'grow incorporate into' the yew, like the skeletons interpenetrated by its roots. His distrust of his proper vitality has brought him to wish that he too, like his friend, should cease to participate in the changes of mortality.

Other images through this opening section of the poem re-express the same unwillingness to change, the same withdrawal of vital confidence. Thus we read of a girl whose affianced lover's death condemns her to 'perpetual maidenhood'. The speaker's heart seems a vase of tears shaken by grief to ice, a condition of chill and vacant stasis whose unnaturalness is retroactively emphasized by the many later images of warmth, fullness, rondeur, and flowing water. A second water image shows us a 'dead lake / That holds the shadow of a lark / Hung in the shadow of a heaven', a peculiarly hideous combination of immobility and unreality.

Lifeless immobility also appears in many images of repetitive motion. The low beat of the heart prevails everywhere through these first lyrics. Vitality on the verge of extinction is revealed equally by the clock that 'beats out the little lives of men', the funeral bell tolling 'Ave, Ave', the dove which 'circles moaning' endlessly, 'is this the end? Is this the end?' and such senselessly repeated rituals as the morning visit to the door of Hallam's house or the songs and games of the first Christmas celebration. Stars 'blindly run'; crowds 'eddy'; the poet 'wanders'. A persistent secondary metaphor for such multitudinous but meaningless cycles, too repetitive to involve the vital principle of change, can be seen in the references to 'dust' or 'ashes' or 'chaff'. The same kind of impression is presented through the metrical structure of the verse itself, with its unvarying stanza form and circular rhyme scheme, a monotonous formula which of itself invites the epithets Tennyson finds for some of his expressions of grief, 'dull narcotic', and 'mechanic exercise'. And such characteristically repetitive sound effects as 'On the bald street breaks the blank day' bring the mood up to the sensuous surface.

The first sign of recovery from this lifeless mood comes early. 'To Sleep,' he says, 'I give my powers away.' Sleep is everywhere in the poem Death's healthy analogue: to sleep is to resign the conscious self which has been tempted into identifying with fatal permanence to the ebb and flow of animal life, the cycle of night and day. Waking therefore brings an access of confidence that he 'shall not be the fool of loss'; by submitting to the course of time, the poet begins to recover a portion of his daunted vitality.

More striking evidence of a growing though still tentative willingness to trust to the motions of nature may be found in a sequence of waking perceptions which leads eventually to the close of the first section of the poem, the burial of Hallam. Lyric

XI in particular illustrates a possible strategy by which Tennyson can begin his recovery from the extremity of grief and the state of unnatural resistance which the shock of loss first induces. In it he looks down across a great plain to the sea over which he can fancy he sees the ship carrying Hallam's body home. He feels 'a calm despair' – the local name for the lifeless insensibility he wishes to conquer. His heart is still; but all around him nature is in gentle motion. Nature, too, is calm, but *her* calm is made up of a hundred small evidences of vital process. The chestnut 'patters' to the ground; the dews silently 'drench' the furze; the spider webs of autumn 'twinkle' in the light; the leaves actively 'redden'; and even the flat plain itself 'sweeps', with 'crowded farms and lessening towers', towards the distant sea. Nature is unceasingly alive in all its parts. The description is 'vivid', as our normal idiom of praise properly puts it, because its concrete details are each separately alive in its own way, each moving in the manner appropriate to it through its special verb.

Here then, by implication, is the solution to the rigid despair from which Tennyson suffers; a going out of the suffering soul into the reassuring particulars of natural life, whose principle of motion, of alteration in position or condition, so elaborately exemplified everywhere he looks, might become by sympathetic identification a source of new vitality for himself.

At this stage in the progress the poem charts, though, Tennyson is not quite able to enjoy the life he so clearly sees. He contemplates the active calm of nature, as he can later notice the contrasting 'wild unrest' of an equinoctial storm, without taking these slight and grand outward changes into the 'deep self' which still prefers to identify itself with a 'dead lake'. But the vividness of the natural descriptions is a good omen, like the sustained image of directed motion created by the voyage of the ship bearing Hallam, and the complementary image of the dove embodying his far-ranging eagerness to see the ship safely home. The sequence ends in a closing note of hope, the change prospectively to be undergone by Hallam's body from 'ashes' to 'violets'. This thought, indeed, represents the first deliberate focussing on a natural alteration with positive implications for Tennyson's own soul.

Home burial is 'well, 'tis something'; his immediate profit is a renewed expectation of moral development, of a slow but equally natural transmutation of sorrow into 'the firmer mind'.

The first Christmas is a good place to see a newer trust in the processes of natural change and the old despairing identification with permanence or repetition in conflict. The bells, 'four changes in the wind', themselves repeat, but the monotony of their action is somewhat transformed by their message: 'Peace and goodwill, goodwill and peace, / Peace and goodwill, to all mankind.' Their vital voices 'swell out' and 'dilate', 'answering' each other companionably, though hidden from the listener by mist and distance, 'as if a door / Were shut between me and the sound' – the same door which elsewhere stands between Tennyson and the embrace he desires. The lyrics which follow complain of the useless Christmas pastimes in the way we have mentioned, but even these repetitious motions end in a song of 'higher range', affirming that the dead 'do not die' but 'sleep'; they do not 'lose their mortal sympathy, / Nor change to us, although they change'.

Christmas, after all, is the birthday of Christ, who conquered death, as the sermon which follows indirectly affirms, not only in his own person through the resurrection, but representatively in the evocation of Lazarus from the tomb. Christ has sanctioned belief in immortality by his actions; a trust in these, of course, defines the Christian. Christianity converts death into the last of the changes to which the soul is subject, and simultaneously makes it possible to see the lower alterations of nature as types of this final spiritual metamorphosis. The cycles of nature in themselves are merely repetitive when the secular mind stands back far enough to see them as a whole and in quantity: 'I bring to life, I bring to death; / The spirit does but mean the breath; / I know no more,' says Nature, and the 'knowledge' of mortal men can go no farther. But if 'trust' in immortality is possible, then this same circular motion, whatever the natural context in which it appears, can be a metaphor of the transmutation from life below to life above, and redeem the changes of this world for souls still in the flesh. The Christian poet can allow himself to identify with the vitality nature's changes embody, in the expectation that this power of life will re-appear appropriately on the higher levels of the soul's action. Belief in upward metamorphosis after death reverberates in the believer's moral will, which thereby acquires confidence in its ability to rise above the urges of the beasts here and now, and also faith in the triumph of love, whose object becomes constantly present, however altered and hard to get in touch with. There is 'comfort clasp'd in truth reveal'd' because Christ's life and actions testify to the truth of a development from which Tennyson's emotional and ethical confidence derive.[7]

Christianity, then, conveys objective evidence for the immortality of the soul; subjective evidence that change for the better prevails past death is provided by the unsupernatual experiences of memory and dream. 'Nor can I dream of thee as dead.' To the senses and understanding Hallam is dead, but to the other faculties he is still alive, not now as a body but as an image or idea or influence upon the conscience of his living mourner. As long as his friend can still think of him, awake or asleep, Hallam is still *there*. Of such inward continuities and conversions the processes of actual nature are a mutely encouraging symbol.

The dramatic effect of the sequence of lyrics devoted to the problem of immortality, then, is to free Tennyson from the compunctions that kept him from yielding wholly to the visible motions of the natural scene. Criticism cannot begin to report justly the whole presence of natural images of movement, change, and organic metamorphosis which fill the middle portions of the poem. The relevant facts are too varied, too elaborate, too pervasive in their effect. The appeal to nature becomes as delicately complex as nature herself, and works in the same half-conscious fashion, by small oblique touches of language even more than by full dress appeals to the dawn or the spring; though these necessarily constitute the occasions through which a reader alerted to the omnipresent theme may focus his sense of the psychic progress towards which all elements work. Here are those passages of natural description which so attractively perfume the most casual reader's memory of *In Memoriam*. The non-believer in the poem's unity invariably appreciates them for their own sake. He need only add, to his approval of their beauty, a secondary recognition that the reasons why they are beautiful incorporate the meaning of the poem as a whole.

A connection between the conviction that Hallam has become immortal, and the faith that nature is God's image for such transitions, and therefore a trustworthy vehicle for the sympathies of the poet, is made clearly in a pair of lyrics near the center of the poem. In the first Tennyson protests his indifference to the changes Hallam's body is undergoing:

> Eternal process moving on,
>   From state to state the spirit walks;
>   And these are but the shatter'd stalks,
> Or ruin'd chrysalis

of his metamorphosed friend. 'I know transplanted human worth / Will bloom to profit, otherwhere.' His faith that this is so permits him, in the second lyric, to call vigorously on the Spring to 'dip' down upon the world and him: the meaning of the season cannot now be other than good. 'Trouble' *now* will not 'live with April days':

> Bring orchids, bring the foxglove spire,
>   The little speedwell's darling blue,
>   Deep tulips dash'd with fiery dew,
> Laburnums, dropping-wells of fire.

The separate aspects of the longed-for scene are not merely not neglected, but adored: the imagery of color, fullness, fluidity, and light contrasts sharply with the dark frozen emptiness we have seen associated with rigid changelessness when 'faith' was 'dry'. The invocation further on to the 'ambrosial air', with its long sentence winding through the verses, laden with opulent verbs of motion, is a still more entire opening of its speaker to the living power of nature: 'sigh,' he exclaims, 'the full new life that feeds thy breath / Throughout my frame,' so that his fancy may fly as far as the wind, free from 'Doubt and Death'. Even the yew, when Tennyson returns to it, proves no exception to nature's rule: 'to thee too comes the golden hour / When flower is feeling after flower'; it 'answers' a stroke of a walking stick with 'fruitful cloud and living smoke' of pollen. To be sure busybody

Sorrow reminds the observer that this 'kindling' is temporary, but her words are definitely called a 'lie'.

The seasonal cycle is the most prominent and traditional sequence of natural change in which Tennyson can see instances of affirmative motion. But he has at his disposal every type of natural pulsation from the alternation of day and night to the immensely slow but equally sure processes of geologic change.

> O earth, what changes hast thou seen!
> There where the long street roars hath been
> The stillness of the central sea.
>
> The hills are shadows, and they flow
> From form to form, and nothing stands;
> They melt like mist, the solid lands,
> Like clouds they shape themselves and go.

The tone of these verses trembles between awe and melancholy. The progressiveness of nature, whatever the scale, is evidence of life in the system of things and therefore by sympathy in the observer. To be sure geology can also induce a lapse back towards static despair, if in place of vital transmutation one sees merely a mechanical interchange of 'form' for 'form'. But Tennyson is saved from yielding permanently to the idea of a universe of motionless motion not only by his Christian faith in immortality but by a typically pre-Darwinian confidence that evolution has a direction. For him these larger cycles of inorganic and organic change are an upward spiral benignly incorporating the realms of civilization and individual culture.

The special form of motion most crucial to a poet is of course speech. Muffled speech is a mark of inhibited or falsified life; it is one of the marks of Sorrow's 'lying lip' that it 'whispers', and the dying sun cannot speak out, but only 'murmur'. The wretched child afraid of the dark 'has no language but a cry'. When Tennyson's gloom returns upon him his own sorrow seems to him inexpressible; his verses then express only his shallower griefs. The family mourners at the imagined funeral of a beloved parent find their 'vital spirits' so 'sunk' that 'open converse' is impossible. A more developed image links Tennyson's death-like inability to mourn his dead friend with the tidal movements in the Severn estuary beside which Hallam was buried. When the 'salt sea-water', always an image for the absolute negation of life in Tennyson's work, fills the river mouth, the speaker's grief is 'hushed'; when the tide runs out, and the flow of the river is re-established, his 'deeper anguish' falls with the level of the waters, and 'I can speak a little then'.

Living beings typically move towards each other for food, companionship, and love. Once Tennyson has persuaded himself that the spirit survives death, he is free to appreciate the motions of nature as evidence of progressive life for Hallam and for himself. But though Hallam continues to live, the change of death has 'put our lives so far apart / We cannot hear each other speak.' The ache of broken companionship therefore becomes the chief negative of lost life that still concerns him during and after lyrics in which the motions of the seasons are fully accepted. Contact is still missing.

The forming pressure of the poem's organic imagery shifts the motif of friendship into an intimately physical key. Sexuality, the chief act of mortal life among humans as among trees and flowers, appears in an enormous reliance on the idea of marriage, which gives Tennyson his happy ending and, in various forms, his principal image for the desired relation with Hallam in the past and present alike. Detached images of touching and embracing are diffused through the whole body of the poem, as most readers soon notice. Hands reach out; those of Science, 'feeling' for knowledge from world to world; those of faith, groping 'through darkness up to God'; those of domestic affection, seeking to comfort the fearful child. The 'dark hand' which 'struck down thro' time' killed Hallam; but touch is usually creative, as when the 'random stroke' drives pollen from the yew, or Hallam's hand, in a dream, touches 'into leaf' a crown of thorns worn by the dreamer.

A negative complement to these images of fruitful organic contact is the chorus of references to doors, which separate lovers and friends from the desired embrace. Thus Tennyson finds himself outside the door of Hallam's old room at Cambridge, listening to the racket of an undergraduate party within, and unwilling to knock; for his friend is no longer there to answer and take his hand. This memory will also illustrate another negative of intimacy. The gregariousness of an unloving crowd is a counter to the fruitful juncture of friends and lovers: people in large groups are 'flies of latter spring', mere units, like the grains of dust we have already identified as an emblem of meaningless non-existence. In positive contrast is the happy moment in a dream when the door opens: 'thro' a lattice on the soul / Looks thy fair face and makes' all 'still'.

All forms of human connection mentioned are metaphors for the desired contact with Hallam, and the changes the figure of Hallam undergoes in the course of the poem each involve different relations between his spirit and that of his friend. To start with, Hallam is simply a dead man, and sympathy with him prompts the survivor to seek a kind of death himself. But soon the emphasis shifts to Hallam the remembered friend. Still later Hallam becomes a puzzle; who, or what is he at the present moment? Images from mortal experience, babyhood, marriage, social mobility, are invoked in an attempt to define the indefinable state of being he now occupies. Is Hallam merged within the general soul? Or is he still a striving figure among the worthies of heaven? What kind of contact can the poet have with these immortal identities? His friend becomes someone to dream of, more than once; someone whose impossible future career may be fantasied; even someone to pray to, an interior power that merges with the speaker's conscience.

The climax to these changes provides an answer to the question of Hallam's final identity and a demonstration of the kind of relation it is now possible to have with him. This comes in the long lyric telling the story of a mystical vision. The circumstances are memorable; Tennyson stays up late out on the lawn. The 'wheels of Being' have reached their seasonal perfection in the warmth of full summer. Tennyson feels as calm as the air, which barely stirs the flame of a spirit lamp under the tea urn by his side. The cattle grazing in the distance gleam through a 'silvery haze', and the trees embrace the field with 'dark arms'. Harmony of nature

and soul have been attested by 'old songs' earlier in the evening,
but now his companions have left him alone to read some old
letters Hallam had written long ago. As he reads,

> Strangely on the silence broke
> The silent speaking words, and strange
> Was love's dumb cry defying change . . .

> So word by word, and line by line,
> The dead man touch'd me from the past,
> And all at once it seem'd at last
> The living soul was flashed on mine,

> And mine in this was wound, and whirl'd
> About empyreal heights of thought,
> And came on that which is, and caught
> The deep pulsations of the world . . .

'The dead man *touch'd* me from the past' – here is a consummation of the yearning for a new companionship to replace the old.
This mystical marriage dissolves the separate identities of the two
friends: 'the living soul was flashed on mine, / And mine in this
was wound.'

What has happened here? If I understand the poet correctly,
something quite simple but always extraordinary. The experience, recollect, is the reading of words, whose tones echo on
Tennyson's inward ear. The 'soul' of Hallam is 'living' because
Tennyson's reading brings it back to life as he hears in his mind
the words in which it is eternized. The climactic proof that Hallam is both immortal and available to him is appropriately a
literary proof; Hallam lives eternally in precisely the same way
that Tennyson's own experience lives for the reader of *In Memoriam* – in words.

This climactic moment confirms an essential lesson of the
poem as a whole. Hallam lives in Tennyson's own vital actions;
his power to feel, to remember, to dream, to aspire, to see the life
of outward nature, but especially in his power to read words. So
far as Hallam is the object of his surviving friend's contemplations,
or the tenor for which these objects are vehicles, he is still alive;
he cannot, in fact, ever die, for the act of contemplating, itself a

living action, becomes immortal by turning it into poetry. At this moment, Tennyson possesses not merely Hallam's point of view, but God's. He is 'whirl'd', he says, to 'heights of thought' from which he can overlook the whole of the natural process to whose motions he has been instinctively appealing. He comes on 'that which is', and hears 'Aeonian music measuring out' the whole temporal process. In God 'is no before', – and no after. Thus the consummation of friendship can 'master Time indeed, and is / Eternal'.

The effects of this trance contact, the last of the important identifications, are chiefly moral. The poet vows he will 'partake' in the changes of life; outwardly, for he leaves his old home for a new one, inwardly, by proposing a new identity as a poet of public issues. This inner alteration is signalled by a final dream, in which a voyage out to sea stands both for acceptance of the prospect of death and for commitment to the active life. The poet of private woe will be transformed into the prophet of the larger progress of humanity: 'I will not shut me from my kind . . .' In the preacher's voice appropriate to this new role Tennyson presides imaginatively over a penultimate course of bells announcing renovation for the world: 'Ring out the old, ring in the new . . . / Ring out, ring out my mournful rhymes, / But ring the fuller minstrel in,' who will sing the 'larger lay' he dared not risk before. From the assured point of view to which sympathy with Hallam's spirit has lifted him the cycles of nature and history are not 'seeming-random forms, / The seeming-prey of cyclic storms,' but parts of a slowly spiraling ameliorative progress of which such individuals as Hallam are an inspiring prophecy, heroes for the epic muse.

'What art thou then?' he asks once again in a lyric near the end of the poem, and the answer comes; Hallam is 'mix'd with God and Nature'. Hallam is mixed with nature because he is involved with the whole of the natural process and its metaphoric moral and spiritual analogues; he is mixed with God because he is identified, through love, with the point of view from which that whole process is visible as a vital and progressive motion. That point of view is available to Tennyson by faith, which is to say, by solitary but sympathetic imagination. Hallam, then, is revealed

finally as a name for the powers of life growing into consciousness, of the mind's ability to act in accordance with its own
nature, to believe, fancy, observe, dream, and participate in the
hopes of mankind. 'I cannot', as he says, '*think* the thing farewell';
he cannot unthink his own thought. The only way for Hallam
and what he comes to represent to cease to exist would be for
Tennyson himself to cease to exist; a possibility that is real enough
at the beginning of the poem, but impossible later not only because Tennyson was able to recover his power to live, but because
he succeeded in embodying the actions of that life in the poem
itself, which makes both it and Hallam immortal.

There is a degree of pathos, though, in this moment of
triumph, which is reflected in the rather forced rhetoric of the
optimistic social lyrics. They are less convincing poetically than
the 'swallow flights of song' in which seasonal rather than moral
change is the expression of the speaker's confidence. The life of
nature can be directly experienced; even the 'flow' of the hills is
visible to the exalted eye; but the forward movement of mankind
is rather demanded than seen or felt. The motion desiderated is
putative, and the strain of carrying out the metaphor of organic
change into the paler dimensions of history shows up in the tone.
The proper imaginative climax of the poem still remains the mystical contact; what follows is anticlimactic in the tedious as well as
the technical sense.

There is, perhaps, a deeper reason for the relative failure of the
last sequence of lyrics than their subject matter. The reality of
Tennyson's hopes for moral adjustment to the hopes of his
readers depends on the confidence he derives from his mystical
self-involvement with Hallam. But this crucial event fulfills the
poet's longing for communion with his kind only indirectly. He
does not, after all, meet Hallam and embrace him, as he once
could do; he raises Hallam from the dead in the shape of a voice
he reads from words. This voice is intimately present, but only
as a sound within the mind's ear. We can be reminded when we
notice this that the lesser versions of Hallam which anticipate this
climax are all equally ideas or images sustained by the interior
powers of the poet. Hallam, like the other persons and objects the

poem presents, is always a re-creation of the imaginer whose voice we hear and whose mind we never leave. And images, though proper objects of the imagination, are 'phantoms', which cannot finally satisfy the social longing for dramatic response. Had he not earlier called the idea that the dead merge 'in the general soul' unsatisfactory, and yet has not a version of this impersonal assimilation in fact been the way he and Hallam have been able to meet? The one change of all changes which the poem does not show is a change of address. The mind of its creator is caught in a lyric monotony, able to fancy a variety of fictional listeners for just so long as a single lyric takes to peruse, but always falling back on the quality of its own mode of acting. The resources of isolation are repeatedly re-experienced, but they are not escaped. Sometimes Tennyson feels himself *too* free to explore possibilities of doubt and belief, fancy and knowledge, which because they are untested by any social response blur into mutual obscurities of tremulous feeling. 'So', he says, 'hold I commerce with the dead: / Or so *methinks* the dead would say; / Or so shall grief with symbols play / And pining life by fancy-fed.' Self-doubt of this sort is the native curse of the Romantic imagination, as Tennyson's master Keats had found long before the young Tennyson had repeatedly faced this issue in his own early verse. There is no way for the artist to resolve these doubts, which are intrinsic to his creative activity, except by ceasing to write.

His resource is the reader, in whom the monologue is renewed as soon as the poem is taken up. 'In my thoughts,' says Tennyson on his second visit to Hallam's house, 'I take the pressure of thine hand.' In his own thoughts, the reader recollects, the whole action of the poem takes place. For the reader, after all, is the one lost soul whose immortality the poet can have confidence in: 'trust' is then and there made good by the present action of the person – you, me – who reads the words. And the point of contact is exactly that point of view from which the elaborate whole the language builds lives, in all its rich cycles, before the eye. It is the reader, then, who achieves the unity of the poem.

SOURCE: *The Victorian Newsletter*, no. 21 (Spring 1962).

NOTES

1. *Victorian Poetry and Poetics*, ed. Walter E. Houghton and G. Robert Stange (Boston, 1959) p. 6.

2. Paull F. Baum, *Tennyson Sixty Years After* (Chapel Hill, 1948) p. 105.

3. A. C. Bradley, *A Commentary on Tennyson's 'In Memoriam'* (1901).

4. T. S. Eliot, see supra, p. 132.

5. C. R. Sanders, 'Tennyson and the Human Hand', *Victorian Newsletter*, no. 11 (1957) 5–14; E. D. H. Johnson, see supra, pp. 188–99, and John Rosenberg, see supra, pp. 200–15; J. L. Kendall, 'A Neglected Theme in Tennyson's *In Memoriam*', *Modern Language Notes*, LXXVI (1961) 414–20.

6. Jerome Hamilton Buckley, *Tennyson, The Growth of a Poet* (Cambridge, Mass, 1960) p. 119.

7. It is the custom to speak slightingly of the Victorian devotees who read *In Memoriam* for religious comfort; to think Kingsley, say, foolish for calling it the great Christian poem of the nineteenth century. But is such a reading really wrongheaded or hopelessly sentimental? Granted that the poem is not all Christian, is not the part which deserves the name profoundly resonant with an important aspect of Christianity, the new relation Christ establishes between God and nature, the soul and the conditions of organic life? Let theologians judge, but to an amateur outsider Tennyson's poem seems rather an extension of orthodoxy into certain of its possible lyric and personal ramifications than a shallow misunderstanding. Hallam seems to be a sacrifice, and Tennyson a communicant. We have recently had in *Doctor Zhivago* an extension of the Russian Christian tradition in a similar direction, with comparable thematic consequences. In both works life is the key; life dramatically repeating the Christian discoveries in moments of individual perception and affection. One obvious difference is that Pasternak–Zhivago knows this kind of Christianized experience stands in opposition to the prevailing Philistia of abstract compulsion, while Tennyson more optimistically and perhaps muddle-headedly hoped to incorporate the yearnings of the age within the scope of his private and traditional metaphors.

Carlisle Moore

FAITH, DOUBT, AND MYSTICAL EXPERIENCE (1963)

WE are still wont to think that Tennyson must abide our question because he confused personal confession and public prophecy. *In Memoriam* especially, with its wavering progression from a deeply-felt religious doubt to the proclamation of a universal faith, has been dismissed as a typical instance of Victorian rationalization which no longer speaks to us. Yet with all the commentaries, analyses, and keys which have appeared since 1850 the poem still eludes consensus. In its own time readers generally accepted it as a poem of faith and rejoiced with Kingsley to find 'in the science and history of the nineteenth century new and living fulfilments of the words which we learnt at our mother's knee'.[1] But the praise was not unanimous. Some critics thought the doubt which they saw there made the faith less than 'honest', and objected to Tennyson's admitting it even into the concluding sections.[2] Nevertheless, for half a century *In Memoriam* brought solace to worried and struggling believers, many of whom did not perceive and were therefore not troubled by its ambiguities, while those readers who did perceive them were comforted by the commentaries which, like A. C. Bradley's, charted the triumphal journey from doubt to faith.[3]

The critical reaction came when religion began to lose its hold on the individual conscience. Carlyle's loss of the traditional faith in which he had been reared produced what William James called 'the sick shudder of the frustrated religious demand'.[4] Leslie Stephen, writing about his own similar loss a generation later, confessed, 'I did not feel that the solid ground was giving way beneath my feet, but rather that I was being relieved of a cumbrous burden. I was not discovering that my creed was false, but that I had never really believed it.'[5] As the need for spiritual

support diminished, or was satisfied by other supports, religion
as an institution began to lose its social value. Separated from
ethics it did not have to be regarded as the indispensable basis of
all moral conduct. One could be both happy and good, apparently, without benefit of faith. *In Memoriam*, therefore, with its
intense spiritual struggles seemed to an agnostic to be a somewhat foolish and misguided poem, the faith attained therein
meaningless or insincere. It is not without irony that Tennyson
was rescued from the neglect in which most Victorians languished
during the early decades of this century when it was discovered that
those struggles had produced some of his best poetry. It mattered
little that in the hands of Sir Harold Nicolson the rescue involved
splitting Tennyson in two and throwing away the worser half:
the 'prosperous Isle-of-Wight Victorian' wrote pontifical verse
lacking both inspiration and sincerity, but elsewhere, in the lines of
the 'lonely, frightened spirit crouched broodingly over thoughts
of death . . . the mystical genius of Tennyson comes upon one in
a flash, and there can be no question of the reality of his emotion
and his impulse'.[6] Later T. S. Eliot's critical authority made it
more than ever impossible to read *In Memoriam* as a poem of
faith, though he did defend it against the charge of insincerity.[7]
All that remained to be said in behalf of Tennyson's long struggle
for faith was that he had fought a good fight and remained a good
doubter.

The critical wheel had thus turned full circle. From being hailed
as a noble poem of faith despite its admixture of doubt, *In
Memoriam* came to be defended as a moving poem of doubt despite its unconvincing faith. In both cases large portions of the
whole were ignored or ruled out of consideration. Each judgment reflected special views of its age: post-Darwinian and post-
Freudian. But it may be asked whether such partial readings of
the poem can be said to do it justice. Having discovered the
genuineness of the doubt, perhaps we should re-examine the faith,
should ask whether in the light of that 'mystical genius' of Tennyson's which Nicolson recognized both are not admissible and,
indeed, wholly reconcilable, when the poem is seen in relation to
the phenomenon of religious conversion.

In its external, formal aspect *In Memoriam* is a public utterance, a conspicuous attempt to reconcile opposing tendencies which seemed to Tennyson and his contemporaries to be threatening the foundations of English society. Viewed thus it is fundamentally an effort to save religion from science by adducing a Coleridgean philosophy of religious experience against the demonstration of God from nature, or by reconciling the nineteenth-century belief in the progress of the species with the Christian concept of salvation.[8] Beneath this great argument lies Tennyson's intimate response to Hallam's death cast into language which expresses his shifting thoughts and moods over a period of seventeen years. Though he employed many of the familiar terms and concepts of his time he also, in a remarkable way, conveyed the mystical quality of his own vision and experience. T. S. Eliot remarks that Tennyson's 'surface' (by which he means technical skill) 'is intimate with his depths'. But for Eliot, Tennyson's depths are depths of sorrow; Tennyson is 'the saddest of all English poets'.[9] It is strange that the poet of 'the moment in the rose-garden' should have taken no notice of Tennyson's similar moment in the garden at Somersby. The trance-like experience of Section xcv marks the climax of the poet's efforts to commune with the spirit of Hallam; it provides a nexus between the disparate elements of doubt and faith; and it tends to draw the poem away from the tradition of the pastoral elegy, in which the turning point, 'He is not dead, he lives!', is so often merely a rhetorical device, and associates the poem with another kind of tradition altogether, that of religious conversion. Jerome H. Buckley pointed out in 1951 that 'Though loosely organised as an aesthetic whole, *In Memoriam* closely followed the general pattern of nineteenth-century conversion' in the way it 'traced the soul's growth from unshadowed hope through the denial of life itself towards the final conquest of doubt and despair'.[10] But he did not explore the work from this point of view except to demonstrate that in it and similar works the pattern of conversion often found expression in certain recurring images of fire and water, of which Teufelsdroeckh's 'Baphometic Fire-Baptism' in *Sartor Resartus* is probably the clearest example.

As the stock-in-trade of Methodism, conversion became immensely popular in the late eighteenth and early nineteenth centuries. Against a background of philosophic skepticism on the one hand and of the hard Calvinist creed of damnation on the other, there developed a widespread feeling that a saving faith was attainable by everyone, whatever his status, through a sudden electrifying emotional and spiritual crisis, and thousands were 'reborn' in a quick and easy way that sensitive minds distrusted. Herr Teufelsdroeckh observed sardonically that such conversions represented 'a new-attained progress in the Moral Development of man; hereby has the Highest come home to the bosoms of the most Limited; what to Plato was but a hallucination, and to Socrates a Chimera, is now clear and certain to your Zinzendorfs, your Wesleys, and the poorest of their Pietists and Methodists.'[11] Teufelsdroeckh's own conversion belongs to a different order, for it was not primarily an acceptance of Christ nor was it induced by a heavy burden of sin, but rather by a fear that God did not love the world. With some romantic dramatization, Teufelsdroeckh repeats in its main outlines Carlyle's own spiritual crisis experienced on Leith Walk, in 1821.[12] Not a doctrinal conversion, like Newman's adoption of a creed and submission to authority, this was rather, like Mill's reading of Marmontel, a spontaneous awakening, an intellectual and emotional discovery of new truths which though not self-induced answered a personal need and, in Carlyle's case, was strongly mystical. Moreover, it was attended by the two conditions which seem to characterize the intellectual species of conversion. The first of these conditions is a state of mind which for reasons known or unknown has become unbearable and is rationally irremediable. The occasion may be a fear for one's own security, or virtue, or a broader concern for the spiritual welfare of society or the cosmos. The second is the occurrence of a climactic experience during which a power greater than oneself is felt to be taking control and directing one towards a solution.[13] Often this does not complete the conversion but only begins it. Sometimes it is followed by a prolonged period of doubt which delays and modifies the faith ultimately attained. Sometimes there are repetitions of the original experience. Even

John Wesley's conversion, which he dated precisely at a quarter of nine, 24 May 1738, was followed by fears and agonizing doubts.

Both of these conditions are to be found in *In Memoriam*. The grief and 'wild despair' which are now so much admired cannot be endured indefinitely. Hallam's death, the 'soul-shaking event' in his otherwise undramatic life, had exacerbated Tennyson's already brooding and hypersensitive temperament to a state of depression which no mere passage of time can remedy. Domestic and personal troubles before 1833 had prepared the way: the death of his father in 1831, the mental breakdown of his younger brother Edward and the opium-addiction of Charles in 1832, and Croker's harsh treatment of his 1832 *Poems* in the *Quarterly Review*. After 1833 the burden of family business fell on his shoulders when Frederick left on a pleasure trip to Italy. He was concerned for his mother, for his sister Emily who had been engaged to Hallam, and for Septimus who was also, for a time, threatened with a mental breakdown. The unfriendly reception of his poems continued to worry him, and kept him from venturing to publish another volume. There was little money to support the large family, and when his grandfather died in 1835 the Somersby Tennysons were, as always, slighted.[14] Upon these depressing circumstances the loss of Hallam came like the jolt which turns already sub-freezing water to ice: 'Break, thou deep vase of chilling tears, / That grief hath shaken into frost!'[15] Preoccupied already with the bearing of science on religion, he could not fail to find in this personal loss a demonstration of the finality of death and the remoteness of God.

It is significant that there is no sense of sin, or sinfulness, in Tennyson's unhappiness. He fears divine neglect, not divine punishment (LII), and grieves because he has been left desolate, 'widowed', and alone, with no sure prospect of reunion with the one in whom he had found not only affection but support in a world growing increasingly harsh and alien. With Hallam gone even Christ seemed distant. During that first Christmas of 1833 he thought of Christ only in connection with the miracle of Lazarus which occurred long ago (XXXI), and the second Christmas did not banish his sense of loss.[16] There is some tendency to identify Hallam and Christ in spirit, to think longingly of Christ as a human savior (XXXII, XXXVI) who, as he saved Lazarus and inspired Mary's perfect faith, may with 'mortal sympathy' and love save Hallam in the other world; but this develops slowly. Meanwhile, God is remoter still. Although His existence seems sure, His goodness and love cannot be seen in His creation of nature 'red in tooth and claw' (XXXIV, LV, LVI). However self-centered his despair, Tennyson's concern for the immortality of all souls is real: 'Else earth is darkness at the core, / And dust and ashes all that is' (XXXIV). The threat of current evolutionary ideas to the doctrine of immortality was equally real, and the more disturbing because it did not help, as Lionel Stevenson remarks, to read into these ideas a spiritual principle of successively higher incarnations of the soul. For he had still to persuade himself (and others) in a more than purely rational and logical way that man's 'inward sense of immortality is stronger and truer than the inconsistent physical forms of the universe'.[17] Even after the intellect was satisfied the heart still felt the loneliness and grief of personal loss: 'We cannot hear each other speak' (LXXXII). It remained for an intuitive conviction of immortality to be achieved through an actual, possibly a mystical, contact with the spirit of the lost one.

This brings us to the second necessary condition of conversion. 'Tennyson was at heart a mystic,' wrote Sir Charles Tennyson, 'with a capacity for true mystical experience.'[18] Many evidences of this may be found in his poems, from among the earliest ('Armageddon', 1823–4) to the latest ('The Ring', 1889). *In Memoriam* contains many signs of it, and in an important group of sections, from XC through XCIV, there is a plea for a vision of Hallam which is answered with the trance-like experience which ultimately gives him the assurance he has sought.

Everything had led up to this episode. The opening sections, with their mood of enforced calm expressing the poet's loss and initial shock, the subsequent despair and confusion, nevertheless constitute a developing (if not orderly) series of lucid pictures of the past (the yew tree, the house on Wimpole Street) and the imagined present (the ship returning, anticipations of its arrival, the burial) which are threaded with his increasing anguish. As efforts to control it, or divert it, or reason it away, fail, the larger significance of Hallam's death becomes clearer, creating fresh fears, and Tennyson comes to feel the need of some sort of contact with Hallam's spirit to revive his belief in man's immortal spirit and in love as the universal law (XLII).

In response to this need, but also as a direct expression of Tennyson's sensibility, there are mystical intimations throughout the poem, from the earliest sections, in which he hopes that he may 'reach a hand thro' time to catch / The far-off interest of tears'; and in the presence of the old yew tree he feels himself disembodied: 'I seem to fail from out my blood / And grow incorporate into thee.' In Section XII he again describes himself as leaving his own body, 'I leave this mortal ark behind, / A weight of nerves without a mind,' and hasting over seas to the ship which brings the dead Hallam home he can only 'circle moaning in the air' and return 'to where the body sits, and learn / That I have been an hour away.' This half-dream, half-trance leads to the fear, in Section XVI, that his grief has unbalanced his mind, 'made me that delirious man / Whose fancy fuses old and new, / And flashes into false and true.' When with the oscillating movement of the poem calm returns, and the first Christmas brings a degree of resignation (' 'Tis better to have loved and lost . . . '), he begins to search for convincing evidence of immortality in man's life ('My own dim life should teach me this, / That life shall live for evermore' (XXXIV)), or in the 'tale' of the life and resurrection of Christ (XXXVI), or, hopefully, within his own consciousness. Truths lie 'Deep-seated in our mystic frame', but 'darkly-joined'. Perhaps in the same way that there existed the Wordsworthian possibility of receiving intimations of our life before our birth, in 'A little flash, a mystic hint', so there is the possibility of communication between souls in the afterlife and here.

> If such a dreamy touch should fall,
> 　O turn thee round, resolve the doubt;
> 　My guardian angel will speak out,
> In that high place and tell thee all.　　　(XLIV)

This seems to anticipate, though as yet without much hope, a communion with the spirit of Hallam in some sort of trance or vision, and it is clear that Tennyson attaches immense importance to such experiential evidence in the resolution of his doubts. Soon he gives more direct expression to his desire to be made aware of Hallam's actual presence: 'Be near me when my light is low . . . Be near me when the sensuous frame / Is rack'd with pangs that conquer trust . . . when my faith is dry . . . when I fade away' (L); then more generally:

> Be near us when we climb or fall:
>   Ye watch, like God, the rolling hours
>   With larger other eyes than ours,
> To make allowance for us all. (LI)

If Hallam remains distant it is not, Tennyson believes, because of his own human shortcomings, the despair, the sensuous nature, the spiritual dryness, of which he is humbly aware, for he is confident his love for Hallam will redeem him (LII).

Meanwhile rational consolation ('Oh yet we trust that somehow good / Will be the final goal of ill' (LIV)) yields inevitably to rational depression: 'O for thy voice to soothe and bless! / What hope of answer, or redress? / Behind the veil, behind the veil' (LVI). The next large group of sections (LVII-LXXXIX) dwells on wavering moods of resignation and despair, while the anniversary of Hallam's death (LXXII), the second Christmas (LXXVIII), and the New Year (LXXXIII), pass him by without much helping or hurting. He did dream of a 'mystic glory' shining on Hallam's grave (LXVII), but in this dream ('kinsman thou to death and trance') his efforts to see Hallam's features are frustrated and confused,

> Till all at once beyond the will
>   I hear a wizard music roll,
>   And thro' a lattice on the soul
> Looks thy fair face and makes it still. (LXX)

Still, there is no communion or sign of recognition in such dreams or fancies, and the poet reaches a state of emotional equilibrium (LXXXII, LXXXIII) in which, blaming no person or thing ('I wage not any feud with Death'), he seems resigned to his 'low beginnings of content' (LXXXIV), and grateful at least for the memory and friendship of Hallam. It is in such a state of resignation that, according to James,[19] religious conversions are likely to occur. It is the turning point both of the poem and of the poet's hopes. At the very bottom of his fortunes he realizes that there is 'in my grief a strength reserved'. There are 'mighty hopes that make us men'. And though 'in dear words of human speech / We two communicate no more', he has a premonition that 'I shall prove / A meeting somewhere, love with love' (LXXXV). Still sad, he now thinks less about himself, more about Hallam's days at Cambridge (LXXXVII) and at Somersby (LXXXIX), and this leads directly into a group of sections (XC–CVI) in which Tennyson invokes the spirit of Hallam: 'Come, beauteous in thine after form, / And like a finer light in light' (XCI), culminating in the unmistakable awareness of his spirit in Section XCV.

The trance occurs in a large group of sections in which Tennyson describes the circumstances leading up to his mystical experience and records its immediate consequences. In Section XC he begins to think about what he desires so much, namely the return of Hallam. But the subject is, at this stage, general and hypothetical. If men could return from death they might not be welcomed back either by their wives, now 'in other hands', or by their sons, jealous of their inheritance; but these wives and sons have not felt love. Tennyson, who has, can only cry to Hallam, 'Come thou back to me!', and in the next section (XCI) he asks Hallam to appear either in body or in visible spirit. Ever prone to doubt, Tennyson now fears that he might distrust such a vision (XCII) as a 'canker of the brain', and might discredit the phantom's spoken prophecies as mere presentiments. 'I shall not see thee,' he writes in the next section (XCIII). Therefore, he begs Hallam to 'Descend, and touch, and enter' so that he may feel his presence. Yet, this may be impossible, since (XCIV) one needs a peaceful and serene spirit to hold communion with the dead.

It is clear that up to this point Tennyson has been preparing both himself and us for the climactic experience which is told in

Section xcv. Providing an effective change of pace and tone, this section is the richly descriptive narrative of one summer evening at Somersby (1835), spent singing old songs with the members of his family and watching the approach of night, when, after the others had gone to bed and he was alone, he reread Hallam's letters, and suddenly felt a presence.

> So word by word, and line by line,
>   The dead man touched me from the past,
>   And all at once it seem'd at last
> The living soul was flashed on mine.
>
> And mine in this was wound, and whirl'd
>   About empyreal heights of thought,
>   And came on that which is, and caught
> The deep pulsations of the world.   (xcv)

It is well known that until 1878 the phrases 'The living soul' and 'mine in this' read 'His living soul' and 'mine in his'. For twenty-eight years this section of the poem described a personal contact with Hallam's spirit, a contact which by itself could indeed resolve all doubts and restore one's faith in immortality. It was a record of genuine mystical experience, a clear sign from a beloved spirit in the next world which, because it effected, or seemed to effect, the dispelling of all religious doubts, had all the earmarks of a conversion comparable in its way with St Paul's.

Among critics Section xcv has occasioned both perplexity and indignation. Why, if he wanted to record a conversion, did Tennyson make emendations which removed the personal element, and throw the whole thing into doubt? And why did he wait so long to make them? John D. Rosenberg writes, 'If "The living soul" is not Hallam's, the lines are without meaning'; for Paull F. Baum they cause the whole section and with it the whole poem to fail as a clear and honest work of art.[20] It is certainly true that the earlier version is the clearer. We may well ask why it did not satisfy Tennyson. Certainly the bereaved poet desired an intimate, even a physical contact. But we have seen that he has already rejected this possibility (xcii, xciii) in favor of a vaguer if no less real spiritual one. We have no way of knowing whether the contact described in the earlier version is what he thought he had felt, or what he wanted to think he had felt. In time he was convinced that it suggested a more personal contact than the trance justified. There is, indeed, ample meaning in the amended version if it is understood that Hallam's spirit is not in a state of isolation but exists as an all but indistinguishable part of the universal spirit of the Deity. The poet, reading Hallam's letters, feels in his trance the touch of this spirit, which conveys a comforting sense of the closeness of his friend and convinces him for the moment that they have touched. It is this necessary ambiguity that the final version seems meant to convey: the contact suggested both Hallam and the Deity. The poem cannot be called dishonest unless its maker is here compromising his belief or distorting his actual experience. Tennyson seems to have tried, rather, to correct the record. To James Knowles he said later that what he felt was 'perchance the Deity . . . my conscience was troubled by "his". I've often had a strange feeling of being bound and wrapped in the Great Soul.'[21] Nor does it seem just to commit the poem to clarity, if it deals with an experience that by its very nature is beyond clarity, and if its parts are consistent with the whole. The idea of Hallam merged in the Deity is no afterthought but finds grateful expression in many of the later sections (e.g. XCVII, CXXII, CXXIV, CXXX):

> To feel thee some diffusive power,
> I do not therefore love thee less . . .
> Tho' mix'd with God and Nature thou,
> I seem to love thee more and more. (CXXX)

Though at the expense of clarity, the emendations enlarge and universalize the whole experience of the trance. They also introduce an admixture of doubt into the very middle of the newly-awakened faith which, religiously and psychologically, is not unprecedented. The faith of the saints was made arduous by doubt. Quite apart from the emendations, however, Tennyson's trance was followed immediately by doubt: 'At length my trance / Was cancell'd, stricken through with doubt.'[22] It is not surprising that its end should have been sudden, the return to reality a shock.

'Sometimes,' he told Knowles, 'I get carried away out of sense and body, and rapt into mere existence, till the accidental touch or movement of one of my own fingers is like a great shock and blow and brings the body back with a terrible start.'[23] It is the nature, not the actual occurrence of the experience that the poet doubts. Tennyson is not, in fact, so worried as his critics are by the uncertainty of his trance-contact, but seems content not to know whether it was Hallam or 'some higher name' he has touched, or both. The last four stanzas of this section, which Bradley calls 'one of the most wonderful descriptive passages in all poetry',[24] express a mood of exalted calm.

That the experience belonged to the phenomenon of conversion is clear from what follows. Through it his doubts have been scotched, his faith has become stronger. He thinks now of another, perhaps Hallam, who fought against doubt to a stronger faith (XCVI); he reflects that honest faith in these times does not exclude doubt, that even the strongest faith 'Dwells not in the light alone / But in the darkness and the cloud, / As over Sinai's peaks.' His own faith was intuitive, based not only on 'the unreality of the material and the reality of the spiritual world but on the mystic's power of spiritual communion and the capacity of the human mind to transcend the material and in some sense apprehend infinity'.[25] Rational argument had failed as the basis for religious evidence, but there was the appeal to experience, the same appeal which is found in Coleridge, Carlyle, and Maurice, and earlier in Kant and Schleiermacher: 'the heart / Stood up and answer'd "I have felt" ' (CXXIV). The 'Ring out wild bells' passage (CVI) celebrates his victory, and he resolves to cease his introspective grief and, after Goethe and Carlyle, accept sorrow as a strengthener of the soul. In Section CXX he compares his struggles with St Paul's; he recalls the climactic trance of Section XCV, repeating his uncertainty about its precise nature ('Oh, wast thou with me, dearest, then, / Whilst I rose up against my doom'), and asks Hallam to return ('be with me now, / And enter in at breast and brow') in another mystical experience

As in the former flash of joy,
I slip the thoughts of life and death;

> And all the breeze of fancy blows,
>   And every dewdrop paints a bow,
>   The wizard lightnings deeply glow,
> And every thought breaks out a rose.   (CXXII)

No second trance occurs, but Tennyson is not despondent on this occasion either, for his memory of the first has enabled him to accept the ordinary state of human ignorance. Having transcended this state once, in a 'flash of joy', he is strong enough to withstand all rational doubts and natural terrors:

> And all is well, tho' faith and form
>   Be sunder'd in the night of fear;
>   Well roars the storm to those that hear
> A deeper voice across the storm.   (CXXVII)

Natural terrors will remain, though deprived of their old effect because of the 'deeper voice' which came to him from a divine source 'across' (not in, or through) the storm.

Yet the repeated 'all is well' of Sections CXXVI and CXXVII, mentioned along with war, social injustices, and dying aeons, conveys a profound sense of sadness that so much evil should be prerequisite to eventual good. The triumph is muted. Such faith as he has won leaves great questions unanswered: Why so much evil? Why is our vision so limited? Like religious skeptics of all ages, he 'would see a sign'. He had felt one, and he was grateful for the evidence which despite 'The freezing reason's colder part' enabled him to believe that 'all is well'. The attitude is not very different from T. S. Eliot's in 'Little Gidding': 'Sin is Behovely, but / All shall be well, and / All manner of thing shall be well.' Beginning with doubt and fear, Tennyson ends with doubt and hope. It should not be giving him too much the benefit of his doubts to say that this attitude is not dated, but will have relevance for as long as man separates faith and reason.

It is at this point that we can see why *In Memoriam* is neither a poem wholly of faith nor one wholly of doubt. Its faith admits an ignorance of the whole truth and leaves room for doubt; its

doubt, having made room for itself after Hallam's death, had to
make room for faith after the trance of Section xcv. Love and
hope are the bonds. For if religious faith is necessarily incomplete, so is science. A faith which is at once intuitive and intellectual will not be attainable until faith and knowledge meet.
Tennyson hoped that with evolutionary progress man would
ultimately find that religion and science reveal one and the same
truth.[26] Meanwhile, one of the strengths of the Christian religion,
as Sir Thomas Browne had observed, is its absence of logical
proof. If miraculous visions occurred daily we should depreciate
or ignore them, like the Israelites who 'made their gods of gold, /
Altho' the trumpet blew so loud' (xcvi). Not that doubt is to be
nurtured; it is to be endured, like a hairshirt, as a chastener of
one's faith. Far from falling back on the standard affirmations of
his day,[27] Tennyson chose a limited faith which required courage
to sustain. The position taken in the concluding sections and the
Prologue was his final position. That he never went beyond it has
been lamented and deplored, but considering its dependence on
the progress of the species, it is a position which hardly admits of
much advancement in a lifetime.

When all is said, *In Memoriam* remains one of the most egoistic
of elegies. The selfless sorrow felt for Hallam's premature death is
soon obscured by Tennyson's tragic bereavement, by his an-
guished desire for sensible contact with Hallam, and by his prolonged efforts to establish the idea of a loving deity. The poem
would be more autobiography than elegy if Tennyson had not
contrived so well to work his experience into the traditional
elegiac form. It was, I think, the trance that enabled him to use
the elegiac turning-point, 'He is not dead, he lives!', with conviction, to combine the pattern of elegy with the pattern of conversion. Yet he departs more from that of elegy. As Bradley
observed, the turning-point is not so clearly marked as in *Lycidas*
and *Adonais*. Indeed it is hard to locate at all.[28] But this is because
Tennyson is following his own experience rather than poetic
tradition. The announcement that 'he lives!', accordingly, had
to be delayed until after the period of uncertainty and doubt that
succeeded the trance, and as with Carlyle, whose 'Everlasting

Yea' had to follow the long 'Centre of Indifference', his faith evolved slowly.

But if *In Memoriam* is not pure elegy, neither is it a straight record of experience. Tennyson arranged the elegies to lead from the moment of mystical contact through a slow recovery to a faith that stopped short of completion, at least in the Wesleyan sense. Brought up in the evangelical tradition, he came naturally by his knowledge of conversion and its various stages. For his final construction of the whole it was his own much less dramatic conversion that supplied the pattern, but even this was modified to admit discourses and arguments that had little to do with that experience. The result is a form which, like the envelope-quatrain, he made uniquely his own. His success, considering the difficulties he encountered, is almost without precedent. Few long poems achieve such a synthesis of disparate parts. During the long period of its composition Tennyson gained not only artistic development[29] but religious and emotional maturity. We have seen that along with the many strands of thought and feeling that run through it – reflections on science, on nature, on society, on the relationships between this life and the next, on the Christmases and the anniversaries, and on his concern for his relatives and friends – there is the clear strand of mystical experience leading up to and beyond the gentle but significant trance in the garden at Somersby which enabled him to recover his faith, determined the peculiar leaven of doubt in that faith, and, finally, enriched the inner character of the poem itself.

Source: *Victorian Studies*, VII (1963).

NOTES

1. Edgar F. Shannon, *Tennyson and the Reviewers* (Cambridge, Mass., 1952) p. 149.

2. See the reviews in *The English Review* and *The Times*, supra.

3. *A Commentary on Tennyson's 'In Memoriam'*, 3rd ed. (1936) pp. 36–43. Among the many which preceded Bradley's (originally published in 1901) were F. W. Robertson, *Analysis of Mr Tennyson's*

'*In Memoriam*' (1862); Alfred Gatty, *A Key to Tennyson's 'In Memoriam*' (1881); John F. Genung, *Tennyson's 'In Memoriam': Its Purpose and Structure* (1881); and Elizabeth R. Chapman, *A Companion to 'In Memoriam*' (1888).

4. *Will to Believe and Other Essays* (New York, 1927) p. 42.

5. *Some Early Impressions* (1924) p. 70.

6. *Tennyson* (1923) pp. 14, 27.

7. Supra, pp. 129 ff. Following Eliot, Samuel C. Burchell, in 'Tennyson's Dark Night', *South Atlantic Quarterly*, LIV (1955), thinks the twentieth century first to appreciate *In Memoriam* as an expression of anguish and doubt: 'There is a concreteness in the pessimism and despair of Tennyson and *In Memoriam*, and it is something for which we can have great sympathy ... after a period of being a schoolboy's medicine and a clergyman's platitude, *In Memoriam* now finally merits the serious attention of modern critics' (p. 81).

8. See Graham Hough, supra, pp. 138–54, and John D. Rosenberg, supra, pp. 200–15.

9. See supra, p. 136.

10. *The Victorian Temper* (Cambridge, Mass., 1951) p. 87.

11. *Sartor Resartus*, ed. C. F. Harrold (New York, 1937) p. 198.

12. See my '*Sartor Resartus* and the Problem of Carlyle's Conversion', *PMLA* LXX (1955) 662–81.

13. For more detailed analysis of conversion see William James, *Varieties of Religious Experience* (1902) pp. 189–258; A. D. Nock, *Conversion* (Oxford), 1933 pp. 1–16, 254–71; and Robert H. Thouless, *The Psychology of Religion* (Cambridge, 1923) pp. 187–224. Among the class of spontaneous, or involuntary, conversions, James distinguishes the moral conversion, involving little or no intellectual readjustment, from the fuller, spiritual one which involves far-reaching intellectual and emotional changes. These vary in three main respects: the state of consciousness out of which they arise, the nature of the crisis itself, and the effects of the crisis. The inductors may be a feeling of personal sinfulness, weariness of self (accidie), or the fear of a godless world. (For Carlyle, Mill, and Tennyson, the crux was not a burden of sin, or even the loss of belief in God, but the lack of moral, rational meaning in the universe and human life.) Though sometimes gradual the crisis is more often instantaneous, attended by trance or vision: and the effects are a feeling of peace and harmony, a perception of truths not known before, and an enhanced view of the objective world (pp. 248 ff). There is an interesting discussion of 'The Metaphysics of Conversion' by R. H. Hutton in his *Contemporary Thought and Thinking* (1894) I 369–76.

14. Charles Tennyson, *Alfred Tennyson* (New York, 1949) pp. 105–54.

15. Sec. IV; see Thomas Bayne, 'Carlyle and Tennyson', *Notes and Queries*, 7th ser., XI (1891) 204.

16. Sec. LXXVIII. Though few readers doubt the depth of his grief, some have wondered whether it was quite healthy for a man to grieve so long for another man, as if there were a decent maximum as well as a decent minimum for mourning. Paull F. Baum's view, in *Tennyson Sixty Years After* (Chapel Hill, 1948) is that 'the composition of these elegies [became] a kind of habit and the death of Hallam a kind of convenience to the muse' (p. 116), but this deliberately ignores the early and lasting association in Tennyson's mind of Hallam's death with the distressing problem of man's ultimate destiny.

17. Lionel Stevenson, *Darwin Among the Poets* (Chicago, 1932) p. 89.

18. *Six Tennyson Essays* (1954) p. 96. See also James Knowles, 'Aspects of Tennyson', *Nineteenth Century*, XXXIII (1893) 169, 186. According to Sir Charles, Tennyson was not a complete mystic but 'possessed in some degree the power mystics have claimed through the centuries, to establish immediate communication ... between the spirit of man, entangled among material things, and ... God' (p. 71). Tennyson believed that he possessed this power and told both Tyndall and Knowles how he could induce trance-states by concentrating on his own name (*Alfred Lord Tennyson, A Memoir, by His Son* (1897) II 473–4). He described it also in 'The Ancient Sage'. This has led some critics, e.g., Robert Preyer, 'Tennyson as an Oracular Poet', *Modern Philology*, LV (1958) 250, to dismiss his mystical experience as self-hypnosis. That it is larger than this, and unforced, seems evident from its presence throughout his poetry. The experience described in *In Memoriam*, as we shall see, is spontaneous. He distrusted the current cult of spiritualism, and was self-conscious about his own modest capacity, protesting to Tyndall: 'By God Almighty, there is no delusion in the matter! It is no nebulous ecstasy, but a state of transcendent wonder, associated with absolute clearness of mind' (*A Memoir*, II 473–4).

19. James cites the apathy and exhaustion of Teufelsdroeckh on the Rue de l'Enfer. Tennyson's mood of resignation and acceptance, bringing a certain relief, invites the mystical contact: 'So long as the egoistic worry of the sick soul guards the door, the expansive confidence of the soul of faith gains no presence. But let the former faint away, even but for a moment, and the latter can profit by the opportunity' (*Varieties of Religious Experience*, p. 212).

20. Rosenberg, supra, p. 215 n; Baum, *Tennyson Sixty Years After*, pp. 307–8. While granting beauty in many of the lyrics Baum accuses Tennyson of 'perverting' his poem; he should not have attempted to 'arrange' them at all. Further, his glossing of 'The living soul' as 'The

Deity, maybe' betrays a 'weakness inherent in Tennyson's character
. . . we have a right to expect some sort of clear statement: either it *was*
the Deity – for the purposes of the poem, of course – or it was not'
(p. 307).

21. Knowles, in *Nineteenth Century*, XXXIII 186.

22. Sec. XCV. I take it that 'cancell'd' does not mean repudiated but,
rather, brought so suddenly to an end that Tennyson could not be sure
of either the nature or the identity of the spirit whose presence he had
felt. Bradley concludes: 'Probably at the moment of the experience
he did think his friend's soul was present, but thereafter never felt any
certainty on the subject' (p. 191 n). But this uncertainty did not 'cancel'
the growing certainty, stemming from this experience, that his plea
for contact with Hallam had somehow been granted.

23. Knowles, in *Nineteenth Century*, XXXIII 169.

24. *Commentary*, p. 192.

25. *Six Tennyson Essays*, pp. 110–11.

26. Sec. CXXVIII, and the Prologue; also *A Memoir*, I 323.

27. This indictment still persists. See Jacob Korg, 'The Pattern of
Fatality in Tennyson's Poetry', *Victorian Newsletter*, no. 14 (Fall
1958) pp. 8–11.

28. *Commentary*, p. 30.

29. See E. D. H. Johnson, supra, pp. 188 ff.

J. C. C. Mays

AN ASPECT OF FORM (1965)

THE form of *In Memoriam* is not an academic question only. Here, as in other cases, to speak of the form of the poem is to describe its total effect. It is to describe our conclusions on the experience of reading the entire thing.

There are two important discussions of the poem's form to which a reader might turn in the expectation of adding to or sharpening his own conclusions. A. C. Bradley's discussion is probably the best known. He bases his reading on Tennyson's remarks included in the *Memoir* and in the Eversley edition; and they lead him to conceive of the three Christmas lyrics as a kind of structural framework, around which the rest of the poem is arranged. The other account has received its most persuasive statement from Miss Pitt, in one of the most sympathetic and balanced among recent studies of Tennyson.[1] She bases her account of the form of *In Memoriam* on Tennyson's remarks to James Knowles. These remarks lead her to consider the two Anniversary lyrics, not the Christmas lyrics, to be the principle of the poem's form; and she goes on to discern a Dantesque pattern of Inferno, Purgatorio, Paradiso.

Each of these interpretations is in its way consistent, and each is able to point to aspects of the poem for support. At the same time, each interpretation is valid only if the other is denied, even if the other may appear equally justifiable and on similar terms. It seems then as if, when we turn for help in understanding the poem's form, we have to assume that Tennyson planned his poem in one of two ways. And the poem itself does not much help us to decide which of these two ways he intended, because we have also to assume that the plan was partially obscured in its working-out during the process of composition. The fact that

each interpretation is simultaneously consistent and contradictory suggests in itself that each of them might approach the poem
in a similarly inappropriate way. It suggests each might be based
on characteristics of the poem which are superficial, or at least
secondary, on proximate effects and not upon their cause. Also –
and more important, since we are concerned here with the poem
more than with its critics – neither of these alternative interpretations is reinforced by our reading. We have continually to import
them: we cannot carry them away. They are most inadequate because, while they work well enough between their own two covers,
when we turn back and read *In Memoriam* again, they are either
forgotten or, if they are remembered, they raise a good many more
problems and doubts than they settle.

One other way of understanding the poem's form may be mentioned. This is to assume that it has no form, that it is essentially
a number of individual lyrics which are related to each other by
shared themes and images but by little else. This way is perhaps
nearer to the truth, because it is at least more honest. At least it
shows a willingness to draw conclusions about the form of the
poem from reading the poem itself, even if the reading has not
proved altogether very conclusive or rewarding. A little more
help than this may, I feel, be offered.

Tennyson's later comments to Knowles and to his son are not
immediately relevant as a means of approaching the poem as it is.
To understand its form, in a way that corroborates our experience while and after reading it, we must turn in the first place to
the attitudes towards form expressed in the poem itself. When
these attitudes are properly recognized, it is appreciated more
readily why Tennyson was encouraged to give *In Memoriam* a
form of a somewhat peculiar kind. They also help to describe the
relation between the important themes of the poem and its more
striking characteristics of technique. Finally, they are not irrelevant to the grounds of the shortcomings of the poem, as they appeared to Tennyson himself and as they remain for us, as well as to
what constitutes its achievement.

I

The word 'form' is repeated more frequently in *In Memoriam* than in any other of Tennyson's poems. Some of its occurrences are of course without much significance, but a larger proportion bear the weight of more important meaning. Tennyson discusses form in general at most length in the lyrics following the Lazarus lyric, especially in XXXIII. The essential point here lies in the contrast between form and faith. The sister's simple reliance on outward conventions, her 'faith through form', is contrasted with the poet's own restless and more uncertain longing to derive authority solely from inward feeling, from 'the law within',

> Whose faith has centre everywhere,
> Nor cares to fix itself to form.

The same distinction between form and faith emerges explicitly elsewhere in the poem, as for example in the first stanza of CXXVII; and it crops up again in many other poems, such as 'The Ancient Sage'. The most important revelation of Tennyson's attitude towards the distinction, outside *In Memoriam*, is expressed in the posthumously published 'Akbar's Dream'. The instances and discussion within and outside *In Memoriam* show surprisingly consistent underlying assumptions, which may be stated fairly simply.

Tennyson's attitude is essentially a divided one, deriving from the apparent opposition of form to faith. Form is seen as a necessary evil: faith can express itself only through form, and yet form circumscribes and distorts the expression of faith. On the one hand, 'He urged men "to cling to faith beyond the forms of faith".' On the other, the *Memoir* also records him saying, 'I dread the losing hold of forms. I have expressed this in my "Akbar".' His divided attitude is summed up in the complaint, 'There must be forms, but I hate the need for so many sects and separate shrines.'

Tennyson's attitude towards form as a regrettable necessity, the notion that only through form can faith express itself for men and yet imperfectly, is one whose working-out is a central theme of *In Memoriam*. It is important to recognize also that this attitude is expressed in a similar way in the many other oppositions that run through the poem. It is echoed, for instance, in the notion that love knows itself only through mortality (XXXV), or that the soul, issuing from 'the general Soul', 'the deep', 'the vast', 'strikes its being into bounds', and only in this way becomes individually itself (e.g., XLV). This is echoed in LIII, which, taking up the suggestion perhaps of 'No shell, no pearl' from the close of the previous lyric, hints that good might know itself only through evil:

> That had the wild oat not been sown,
>   The soil, left barren, scarce had grown
> The grain by which a man may live?

The fact that the opposition between form and faith is but one aspect of a larger theme of opposition running through the poem will be considered later. What is more important at the present stage is that Tennyson's attitude towards form in general applies to poetic form in particular. On the one hand is faith, or what Tennyson believes or wants to believe, in other words, what he wants to say. On the other hand is form, or the means at his disposal by which he can communicate what it is he believes, what he wants to say. His attitude is born from the assumption that communication, or putting into form, necessarily demands some restriction of expression, or faith. The fifth lyric states the assumption clearly:

> I sometimes hold it half a sin
>   To put in words the grief I feel;
>   For words, like Nature, half reveal
> And half conceal the Soul within. . . .

> In words, like weeds, I'll wrap me o'er,
>   Like coarsest clothes against the cold:
>   But that large grief which these enfold
> Is given in outline and no more.

Tennyson's divided attitude is not without parallel. It may be found for instance in the *Four Quartets*, where it is resolved in a not altogether dissimilar way. Nevertheless, it is sufficiently distinctive to have been too frequently misunderstood. It is particularly important to recognize how closely it bore on the difficulties facing him when he came to combine his many lyrics into a single poem.

Tennyson was first occupied, in the majority of the *In Memoriam* lyrics, with the expression of single and private moods. All that the lyrics themselves, or small groups of lyrics, have in common is their foundation in emotional tension or intellectual contradiction. It is natural, in other words, that they should all approach a central concern; but it is incidental to the way in which the majority appear to have been written that they should reflect a consistently developing interpretation of it. Though Tennyson probably had some hope that the lyrics could be fitted together at an earlier stage than is often thought,[2] it is essential to bear in mind that they were for the most part composed almost haphazardly, at many different times, in many different situations, in many different moods. Whatever his vague hopes for them, they were first of all his 'Elegies', held together only by the Butcher's Book.

Tennyson's purpose, when he later came to arrange his lyrics in some order, was most of all to provide some excuse and real occasion for presenting them together. The obvious way to maintain interest in a number of single lyrics following one after the other is to arrange them in such a way that they progress as a narrative or as an argument. It is to attempt to give them some connection, so that reading them in succession offers some attraction in itself, to give a number of 'seeming-random forms' some pattern in which they do not cancel out each other's effects, but enhance them.

It may be appreciated that Tennyson's purpose at once conflicted with the means at his disposal. If his lyrics were going to be read together, fruitfully, he would have to impose on them some form. He would have to relate them to each other by providing a developing thread of interest, and so, by making some matters more distinct, play down others. To make his particular lyrics into one whole poem, he would have to relate them to each other in a way that would not do justice to his experience as he wrote them. He would be obliged to isolate and suppress, to channel, mute, and categorize, and even to some extent adopt methods which appalled him in contemporary science. Any narrative or argument would distort and violate his meaning, just as form petrifies, stratifies, and is a reduction of faith. Tennyson describes the predicament facing his muse in XLVIII:

> Her care is not to part and prove;
>   She takes, when harsher moods remit,
>   What slender shade of doubt may flit,
> And makes it vassal unto love . . .
>
> Nor dare she trust a larger lay,
>   But rather loosens from the lip
>   Short swallow-flights of song, that dip
> Their wings in tears, and skim away.

The issue, of course, is that all 'these brief lays' nevertheless had to be in one sense or another 'a larger lay', if they were to be published together under a single title. Tennyson's attitude led him to want to give his lyrics a sense of movement which did not move anywhere, to want his whole poem, in R. L. S.'s terms, to travel rather than to arrive.

The way in which Tennyson solved the problem of form was the way closest to his own experience: he presents the drama of himself in the very process of discovering it, so that the continuity which underlies the whole poem's form is in the first place provided by himself in the role of hero. Tennyson attracts continuing interest, and establishes the relation of this interest to his reader's concerns by displaying his own struggles as ones his reader cannot ignore. The sheer intensity of his own apparent involvement is such that it demands participation. The solution works itself out in the individual lyrics in many different ways, but the effect is similar. One of the most characteristic of Tennyson's techniques is to speak in a way that leads us to assume not that we have heard, but have overheard. He frequently speaks as would only a person in the isolation of the confessional, and the effect of this manner is to compel sympathy which extends almost to the point of identification. Not to take notice would seem almost like betrayal, like remaining unmoved by a soul bound upon a wheel of fire or by a soul in bliss.

The effect is achieved in different lyrics by different means. Frequent apostrophizing either of objects or of concepts, like the Yew or Sorrow herself, at once places us as readers in the position of eavesdroppers. Also, we tend instinctively to assume to some degree the role of what is apostrophized, and to be all the time semi-conscious of the poet's dependence upon our powers. The frequent addressing of Hallam or some scene again encourages the substitution of our own selves for the person or the landscape addressed; we are led to apply Tennyson's caressing, or longing, or laudatory words to some degree to ourselves, and thereby more strongly encouraged to accept Tennyson's evaluation of his needs and progress. Questions, especially in the central and more abstract part of the poem, sustain our sense of participation. Tennyson's commands to such assumed companions as his fellow mourners, or his dialogues, as with the almost animate 'Dark House' or Urania, likewise draw us more closely into the experience taking place. The direct and uninhibited way in which Tennyson appears to utter his inmost feelings is not without its magnetism. There is something awesome and yet deeply attractive in his constant tone of open, explicit honesty; and its whole effect is constantly to pull us into a more intimate relationship. We would not expect anyone to speak in this way, except to the most intimate of associates, so that to escape embarrassment we are almost compelled into concern, to participate directly in Tennyson's own feelings.

The fact that most of the memorable lines and phrases in the poem are so general, and so true as to be in themselves nearly trite, reminds us how far Tennyson's method depends upon the shared sense of tremendous personal involvement. The whole power of ' 'Tis better to have loved and lost / Than never to have loved at all' depends on Tennyson's control over the way in which we read it, as we particularly appreciate when Bradley reminds us of the very similarly phrased sentiments in Congreve and Campbell. It seems that a poet who can wring so much out of statements as flat as this must have a giant's grip upon our attention. It might finally be mentioned that the fact that the *In Memoriam* lyrics are so easy and so tempting to parody is yet another indication of how much their power rests on our identification with their speaker, rather than on his argument. The way in which they are spoken or read is all-important. If they are read without sympathy, the same lines that are so admired become laughable. One might contrast a representative poem by, say, Donne, where the sense leads to the sound and not vice versa; and where, consequently, parody requires as much a reversal of argument as of feeling, so that it is often more exactly described as answer- or debate-poetry. That it takes only a slight shift or disengagement of sympathy to disintegrate the effects of Tennyson's lyrics perhaps explains why the best parodies read more like imitations, with only a nudge to alter the tone in which one reads them.[3] It reminds one that the most important means to unity in *In Memoriam* is the feeling that all the time Tennyson is there beside us, talking.

Such an answer to the problem of form demands that the progress of the poem should be felt to lie in the poet himself, as a moral and spiritual example. It is an answer that recommended itself strongly to Tennyson's cast of mind. While his concern in *In Memoriam* is to present the search for faith together with its justification, he had less aptitude for tidy systematic thinking than for depth and constancy of reflection – in his own terms, less aptitude for knowledge than for wisdom. His method is entirely at one with his premise that argument should convince no one. Just as he overwhelms the uncertainties of his own mind by repeated assertions rather than by intellectually resolving them; so he chooses to assume an audience of sympathizers, even of initiates, to evade the discipline of logic and the distortions brought about in categorizing.

Tennyson's method is thus also at one with his attitude towards form. His premise that belief is prior to experience, and that faith cannot be derived from form, encouraged him to avoid an intellectually progressing argument, where defined terms move economically from stage to reasoned stage by cause and effect.

One of the themes of the poem is a winning through to confidence in form, and to an ability to sustain it by faith. The growth through the poem of Tennyson's confidence in poetry itself has been remarked on by E. D. H. Johnson.[4] The way in which Tennyson in the end arranged his lyrics similarly reflects his recovery and growth of confidence in his art. The form of the narrative gains shape and discovers its direction, its destination, as its speaker wins through to equilibrium and stability of mind. And as he comes gradually to recognize faith in himself and in all else, so his argument, too, discovers its own coherence and significance.

II

The workings-out of the principle of form in the poem can be described in more detail. The theme of all the separate lyrics or groups of lyrics is founded upon tension and opposition, even if towards the close of the poem it is opposition largely reconciled. The recurring pattern of opposition is stated in many ways, and is applied analogically to every subject. Death, for instance, is set against Life, Time against the Timeless, Nature against Art and Mind, Body against Soul, Flux against Permanence, Science against Belief, Form against Faith, and so on. The pattern takes multiple forms, and is metaphorically related at all levels. It is repeated in the poem's imagery: in the contrast between, for instance, Tennyson and Hallam, Orpheus and Eurydice (e.g., XLVI), Masculine and Feminine, Darkness and Light, North and South, Vesper and Phosphor, and also in the imagery of widows and widowers, ladies and their suitors, and of the two hands. There is opposition, too, in the juxtaposition of succeeding moods. Positive moods contrast with negative ones, hope alternates with despair. And just as each knows itself only through the other, Life through Death, Good through Evil, Faith through Form, so the whole progression of the poem is through opposition playing against itself. Moods oscillate so that the themes they centre on advance by surges and lesser retractions, in a kind of decreasing undulating movement.

Tennyson describes the pattern of opposition fairly clearly in the first two stanzas of XLV:

> The baby new to earth and sky,
>   What time his tender palm is prest
>   Against the circle of the breast,
> Has never thought that 'this is I':
>
> But as he grows he gathers much,
>   And learns the use of 'I', and 'me',
>   And finds 'I am not what I see,
> And other than the things I touch.'

The form of the poem is founded on the progress of resolving this objective-subjective, centrifugal-centripetal opposition. It advances as it were by the dilation and contraction of the poet's spirit in its hopes and fears, in a diastolic-systolic rhythm.

For such a reason, Tennyson's rhetorically invited alternatives in the sixteenth lyric are not exclusive, but complementary. On the one hand, his insecurity and sorrow is known only in its bewilderingly confused occasions,

> But knows no more of transient form
> In her deep self, than some dead lake
>
> That holds the shadow of a lark
> Hung in the shadow of a heaven.

On the other hand, 'wild unrest' is more characteristic of this earlier part of the poem than 'calm despair'. The speaker is, if judged by his own words,

> ... that delirious man
> Whose fancy fuses old and new,
> And flashes into false and true,
> And mingles all without a plan.

The largest oscillations in mood are at the beginning of the poem because this is its theme. As the poem progresses, and Tennyson attains to some belief in form, the oscillations become less extreme; until, with the last of the dream lyrics (CIII), the basis of a final resolution is reached, and thereafter the remainder of the poem is a sort of exemplum, which broadens, strengthens, and confirms.

The concerns of Tennyson's poem are presented as the speaker's efforts to unify his shattered consciousness, to integrate his sensibility. What links and merges the dialectic of contrasting moods, so that they make up a progression, is Time. How Time, or Memory, is the means by which self-consciousness is attained is described in the two remaining stanzas of XLV:

> So rounds he to a separate mind
>> From whence clear memory may begin,
>> As thro' the frame that binds him in
> His isolation grows defined.

> This use may lie in blood and breath,
>> Which else were fruitless of their due,
>> Had man to learn himself anew
> Beyond the second birth of Death.

It is essential to grasp the relation of these stanzas to the two that precede them if the poem's form is to be properly understood.

The resolution of opposite themes, moods, and images is won not through argument, but through Time. Though Time is in one sense the villain of the poem, it is increasingly apprehended as the means to salvation. Tennyson's quest is to regain the emotional, intellectual, and spiritual harmony that existed in a paradisal past, a harmony in which all tensions and conflicts seemed resolved or not to exist. It is to regain the sense and the power of love, to be at one with the best in himself, and thereby with mankind. The notion that the means to his end is Time – that though love is immortal it can know itself only through mortality – is made explicit in the last two stanzas of XXXV:

> . . . If Death were seen
>> At first as Death, Love had not been,
> Or been in narrowest working shut,

> Mere fellowship of sluggish moods,
>> Or in his coarsest Satyr-shape
>> Had bruised the herb and crush'd the grape,
> And bask'd and batten'd in the woods.

Tennyson's purpose throughout the poem could be stated as to 'Redeem the time'. What the form of the poem shows is the slow and gradual recognition of the full meaning of the corollary, 'Only through time time is conquered'.

Time the destroyer, time the preserver, thus provides the other key to the form of *In Memoriam*. Tennyson's gradual winning of confidence in form and in all else is presented dramatically, as it happens, and not as an imposed conclusion. Though faith and form are 'sunder'd in the night of fear', they approach each other as the poem advances, until they are finally united by love working through time. The speaker comes at last to see and feel 'That all, as in some piece of art, / Is toil coöperant to an end,' and the realization gives his poem an emergent unity. Because this is the way that the whole poem is constructed, it not only gains shape but also speed as it goes along. The dual nature of the 'Victor Hours' reverses, and the pace picks up especially with the three succeeding groups of dream-vision lyrics. The time intervals become progressively shorter, just as the oscillations between hope and despair simultaneously become less extreme and are finally resolved. Doubt and suffering are finally recognized as having been creative, and

> . . . less of sorrow lives in me
> For days of happy commune dead;
> Less yearning for the friendship fled,
> Than some strong bond which is to be. (CXVI)

III

These suggestions about the form of Tennyson's poem may be made clearer by comparison. In an attempt to feel more precisely what is peculiar to *In Memoriam*, its readers have often compared it with other English elegies. Obvious comparisons no doubt have their uses: Professor Foakes' comments on Tennyson's and Shelley's very different attitudes towards the forms of nature are a case in point, which is relevant here.[5] Such comparisons have nevertheless frequently encouraged a confused or even misguided interpretation of the form of the whole poem.

It is, for example, as revealing to think of *The Prelude*, first published in the same year as *In Memoriam*, as it is of *Adonais* and *Thyrsis*. Even to remember the *Intimations Ode* might remind one of important aspects of Tennyson's poem which Shelley's and Arnold's do not; not only of 'Whither is fled the visionary gleam', but of the answer. It is significant that Mr Perkins' book on Wordsworth[6] suggested most of the remarks made above on the poet as hero, seeking to regain a sense of assured identity through a recovery of past experience, and on the relationship that this role encourages between poet and audience and in technique. If the remarks are accepted as pertinent, the point being made here is confirmed.

Further suggestions for comparison might be made. Though they might appear at first to be a little cranky, they may nevertheless serve some useful purpose; it seems we must be prepared to risk appearing cranky when our reward might be a better understanding of *In Memoriam*. It may be suggested, for example, that Tennyson's poem is probably as fruitfully compared with Donne's *Anniversaries* as, say, with *Lycidas*. Both poems are probably better described as 'meditations' than 'elegies'. Both poems hold a similar position in the work as a whole of each poet. The similar grounds of antipathy towards science, whether it be in particular astronomy or geology, are instructive and revealing; and so on. One might note also that Tennyson's Hallam has been criticized from an early date as being too extravagantly presented, for being presented almost as if he were the Saviour, just as Donne's presentation of Elizabeth Drury was held by Ben Jonson at least to have been more in keeping with the Virgin Mary. Yet, in the end, Hallam's role for Tennyson in the poem is close to Elizabeth Drury's for Donne, as 'the Idea of a Woman and not as she was'.

The shared influences of Dante and Petrarch on both poems is no doubt the basis of a large number of the similarities. Other shared reminiscences or obligations might explain other points of coincidence – as Aquinas might explain Donne's and Tennyson's shared distinction between *scientia* and *sapientia*, knowledge and wisdom – if such points of coincidence are to be dwelt upon.

Donne's sources nevertheless serve as a reminder of the one point of difference which is more essential than any other. The whole form of his poem is apparently founded upon a fairly coherent and balanced pattern of meditation, derived from strict principles established by Ignatius Loyola. In other words, the *Anniversaries* have an architectonic, however obscured it may be in its working out in the poem, and in a sense which *In Memoriam* emphatically has not.

This difference serves to introduce another comparison which might be useful. The poem which reminds one most fully of the essential principle of form in *In Memoriam* is not *Thyrsis*, *Adonais*, or *Lycidas*, nor even *The Prelude*, *The Anniversaries*, or an Elizabethan sonnet sequence, but *Piers Plowman*. A number of points of coincidence are relevant to the subject in hand. For example, both poets express a similar hesitancy to trust in poetry itself as a means of expressing their full intentions. Both assume that it is only through failure that success is possible, that only by knowing black do we recognize what is white. Again, the doubt and confusion raised in each poem by contemporary answers to perennial questions, whether the emphasis be laid on social abuses or on the claims made for theological or scientific certitude, occupy a similar relation to the shared central theme of the way of a soul to love.

Such coincidences, and many others of a like kind, lead one to become aware of an essential similarity between the form of the two poems, which throws light on Tennyson's achievement. Each poet expresses the course of pursuing an embodied ideal, Piers or Hallam, and presents that course with a like fidelity. This is what is most important of all, and what has led to similar misunderstandings of the form of each poem. In each case, form is supplied by simulating the experience of achieving formal understanding, not by imposing a comprehension attained after the experience itself. In each case, the pattern is emergent; one is given a direction rather than a destination, and in reading one follows the poet in his efforts to perceive and to attain to it. It is worth remark that the last of Tennyson's lyrics celebrates the living will to faith, which works through and conquers time, 'Until we close with all we loved, / And all we flow from, soul in soul': what sustains Tennyson is identical with what sustains the hero of Langland's poem, Long Will.[7]

In one sense, Tennyson's *Visio*, in which he states the inadequacy and torment of his own soul and in which he comes intellectually or externally to perceive the ideal he must attain, is given in the lyrics up to and following the first Christmas. Thereafter he moves through three successive stages in which this ideal is gradually attained; he progressively embraces by experience, or lives in this life, as does Langland in the three *Vitae*, a previously abstractly stated hope. On the other hand, Tennyson's *Visio* is of course assumed to have taken place before his poem opens. His whole journey in the poem is to meet again what has been lost, and to give it life again within himself. What is most interesting is the correspondence between the proportions of Langland's three *Vitae* and the proportions of *In Memoriam*.

Langland is at his apparently most digressive in the Life of Dowel; and his hero wanders uncertainly through many doubts, and many hopes show themselves false, before Dowel is vouchsafed him. Similarly, the earlier part of Tennyson's poem is that characterized by the most unrest, in which his oscillation between hope and despair is greatest, and in which the largest proportion of more abstract speculation is met with. He advances gradually to find some resting-place in merely mechanical actions, mere conventions, until he is able to think of his loss in social terms, and thence of his art as at least a kind of ritual. Dependence on such forms as ritual, as he says in 'Akbar', varies 'with the tribes of men'; and the consolation it can provide must prove only temporary to the inquiring spirit. Having come to terms with his exclusively personal concern and sense of loss, he is thereby able, after the first Christmas, to consider the notion of the continued life of what appears to be dead; he slowly wins his way forward against many setbacks by reflecting on this notion and the problems it raises, so that he achieves at least a semi-philosophical confidence in future reunion. Turning then to the hope that Hallam might be near him in this life, in the present, the tone becomes less reflective as Tennyson describes his more immediate personal fears, thoughts, and hopes. As lyrics and groups of lyrics succeed each other, the forward surging of emotion becomes stronger and the reactions to it less extreme. Sorrow slowly softens, and the sense of beauty and reconciliation grows, until, in the first group of dream lyrics (LXVII–LXXI), the speaker reaches for the first time a sense of all opposition gone –

> And thro' a lattice on the soul
> Looks thy fair face and makes it still.

However, just as Langland, having attained the Life of Dowel, at the very same moment perceives its inadequacy and enters upon the Life of Dobet, so Tennyson's course is not yet run. His feeling of defeat returns abruptly with the dawn of the anniversary of Hallam's death. The brevity, containedness, and almost fitful uncertainty of the first dream lyrics is at once shown to be insufficient to sustain the poet in his daily life; and the lyrics that follow are to enlarge on the experience of reconciliation, in terms both of relevance and permanence. As in Langland's poem, the pace quickens after the first stage has been reached, and doubts are fewer and more speedily overcome. Hallam is remembered not alone, by a solitary mind, but in situations of society and friendship, which are increasingly valued for their own sake. Tennyson thus comes to long not merely to recreate the experience of a circumscribed past, but for its more complete and permanent realization. And, once the desire is fully recognized and prepared for, he is vouchsafed a second dream in which it appears to be fulfilled.

The three occasional lyrics that follow immediately on the second dream are apparently designed to show the change that has taken place in the speaker's mind. Following a common pattern in the poem, the second anniversary lyric recalls and demands comparison with the first. The break with the past and the release from the hold of the dead is not, however, quite complete. One more stage is necessary before all opposition is resolved, before all experience is absorbed, and before Tennyson is completely free and strong to face what the future offers. In the last of the dream lyrics, he re-examines the states of mind he has passed through, travels in his sleep beyond Time's 'forward-creeping tides', and dedicates his poetry to its final end. It is the happiest of all three series of dream lyrics; there are no succeeding doubts, no immediate retractions or hesitancies, and from here on the poem moves more evenly. The growth of love for Hallam, who is dead and reborn, into a love for all that Hallam represents in all mankind and human activity is enlarged upon as a sort of coda throughout the remainder of the poem. If the lyrics up to the first Christmas or even to the close of the long semi-philosophical discussion form a sort of prologue – a more fitting one than the poem was finally given – the lyrics following the last great dream are its more fitting epilogue. Tennyson's progress in his poem is more ordered than Langland's, and it follows naturally that he should find his Piers. It is 'A statue veil'd' that he sees in this life, even so; and though hope of reunion or of final resolution and bliss is assured, it is to be fully realized only through death. The form of his poem is thus as open-ended as Langland's: the point at which it aims and from which it derives coherence, the 'one far-off divine event, / To which the whole creation moves', is ever and necessarily outside and beyond it. And even 'behind the veil', 'Eternal form shall still divide / The eternal soul from all beside'.

IV

This reading of *In Memoriam* differs from many others, and it may be of interest to comment on some points of difference. It was said above that the logic of the poem is polar and temporal, as distinguished from what can be called architectonic and spatial; and that its form is not one imposed by the poet in conclusion, but that it embodies the poet's dialogue with himself and his winning through to conclusions. If there are stages in Tennyson's meditation, they are, like Langland's, emotional and spiritual. The poem is not reducible to a diagram (as is to some extent an Ignatian meditation); it evolves in a way that gives higher value to honesty than tidiness, to faith than form. Each stage does not, therefore, cancel out its predecessors. It is not a ladder of perfection that Tennyson or Langland is climbing, whose rungs are kicked away in ascent; the pattern, while new in every moment, is also familiar. It is of movement forward, yet also retraction, and a going on again from there. Successive stages, moods, images, and triumphs thus gain their significance from the relation they bear to what has gone and still remains before, as well as, always, to what is to follow.

On account of this, it is not surprising that little of what is symbolic in the poem has a constant value. 'The late-lost form that sleep reveals' at the beginning of the poem (XIII) is recovered only to the varying extent that Tennyson is able to sustain form by the strength of his faith. The strength is drawn upon from his own resources; so that even Hallam appears to change and develop in accordance with Tennyson's demands upon him, in the way that Piers changes constantly for Langland. The poem's symbols must be read dramatically, in the light both of the needs that generate them and what they are later able to sustain. Just as the principle of Nature behind the dioecious Yew is 'a hollow form', which is only gradually invested with meaning by faith as the speaker himself acquires it (his increasing confidence is particularly striking in the spring lyrics preceding the second dream); so all occasions mean much less in themselves than what they are made to mean. Even towards the close of the poem, Tennyson recognizes that 'The hills are shadows, and they flow / From form to form, and nothing stands' (CXXIII): as he says in 'Akbar', such forms of nature are merely 'the spiritual in nature's market place'.

One might also point to Tennyson's similar use of language, of 'matter-moulded forms of speech'; and to the fact that words and phrases as frequently refer to other words and phrases elsewhere in the poem for their value and full meaning, as to any experience of our own that we can draw upon. Sometimes they are indeed explicable only with reference to other passages – as for instance the apparently very inappropriate 'landing-place' of the forty-seventh lyric, which Bradley nonsensically explains by referring to Coleridge's *Friend*, and yet which can be fully understood only by reading 'Timbuctoo'.[8] Understanding is thus gained not by searching one's own experience or by speculating on the etymologies of words, but by reading on and elsewhere. The relation between words, as between moods and occasions, is their larger meaning. Sometimes even their lesser meaning can be supplied only by Tennyson himself.

It may be remarked that this use of language not only coincides with Tennyson's general attitudes towards form and faith, but also with the technique demanded by his own role as hero. A range of fairly simple words, with familiar associations and obvious symbolic overtones, becomes in this way more capable of expressing a deeply personal meaning; he is able to be simple and concrete in descriptive detail, and at the same time to express the most private concerns. To take only one illustration, the symbolic overtones of the 'Dark house' lyric are obvious and clear enough; but when we later come to read 'How fares it with the happy dead?' (XLVII),[9] the previous lyric leaps onto a different level of significance. We recall it not only as one of the most beautiful single lyrics of the poem, but also as an image-reflection of an important underlying concern, and thereby related to all other houses, castles, palaces, and even cities and 'great Elysian solitudes', to which Tennyson repeatedly returns. Tennyson is in this way able to shape our experience in a manner that often depends on our not being fully aware at the time of what is really being talked about; and in this way he overrides, by the language of assertion, the possibility of our intellectual objection and the breaking of the spell. Guided by the pressure of the speaker's emotion, we are led to make the connection between words and phrases; and the meaning we arrive at is all the more persuasive because created apparently by ourselves.

It should now be clear why any initial assumption that the Christmas or the Anniversary lyrics are the structural cornerstones underpinning the form of the whole poem is intrinsically dubious. Tennyson exploits to some degree the symbolic significance of calendar events, just as Langland does, but consequently to assume that any detail or event possesses an inherently more or less permanent value in the poem is to run a serious risk of misunderstanding it. If the poem is read in the way that has been suggested – as it is, and not as Tennyson later thought it might be – the successive Christmas and Anniversary lyrics appear primarily as time notes. That is, they stand out as lyrics in which we are made as strongly aware of other similar occasions as of the particular occasion in itself. Each of the particular occasions encourages Tennyson not to explore and exploit all the *a priori* symbolic significances that we might perhaps expect, but rather offers itself because of its particular appropriateness as a vantage-point, looking both back and forward over time passing. Occasions are utilized to reflect rather than to lead to any new discovery. For such a reason, it is of the greatest importance that the first Anniversary lyric follows immediately on the first group of dream lyrics, jerking Tennyson into a realization of the impermanence of his apparent success; that the second follows the second dream at an interval, and provides such a contrast in mood; and finally that no anniversary, no reminder of Hallam's death, is described following upon the third. The inadequacy of the usual accounts of the poem's form may be described as the misreading of lyrics of form, like the first Christmas lyric, as if they were invested with faith; whereas Tennyson's whole meaning is that faith is not a constant. The usual accounts appear also to overlook the striking significance of the poem's proportions and accelerating time-scheme, as well as the 'spots of time', the telescoping moments of lived contact with Hallam in dream.

The successive dream or vision lyrics could probably be more meaningfully read than either the Christmas or the Anniversary lyrics as the most significant stages, 'landing-places', in the development of Tennyson's theme; with the forty-seventh lyric as their intellectual progenitor, the hope they try to embrace by experience. They are situations which are deliberately, even elaborately, prepared for and created, and their symbolic meaning is in each case sustained. They are the only situations in the poem, even after the departure from Somersby, during and through which the prevailing theme of opposition is explicitly resolved. Everything leads up to them and on from them; but this again, in the end, is the whole point. It is only proper to recognize the importance of the dream lyrics in our reading if we fully recognize their place in a complete experience: why, for example, the first dream-vision comes so relatively late in the poem; why succeeding dream-visions follow at increasingly shorter intervals, and why the pace of the poem quickens with them; why the third comes on the eve of departure from Somersby, and yet why nearly thirty lyrics follow, and more evenly. We have, in other words, to recognize in our reading what differentiates, what precedes, intervenes between, and follows the dream lyrics, because only by recognizing their dramatic value, or the degree to which form and faith interpenetrate at particular moments in the course of the poem, does their meaning emerge.

v

The significance to be attributed to the dream lyrics in the present reading would seem to be confirmed by attitudes expressed by Tennyson, in his poetry and elsewhere. It is instructive to look at his later attitudes towards the poem, not only to offer some explanation for them but because they are an interesting reminder of the inseparable relation between the form of *In Memoriam* and the quality of its faith.

The importance of the theme of dreams and visions in Tennyson's earlier published and unpublished poems hardly needs to be stressed. It has been described at some length in a recent book,[10] where its relevance to the dreams of *In Memoriam* is made clear. Although one would wish to add or to modify Mr Ryals' account in almost all its details, only two deserve particular mention here. It is important to realize that the visionary experience in which Tennyson is 'laid asleep / In body, and becomes a living soul' is, at least in its formulations, very much a conventionally literary experience: it must be read not only with Plotinus or even St Paul in mind, but also the great Romantics, especially Wordsworth and Keats. Comparison with Wordsworth and Keats at the same time brings out what is peculiar to Tennyson's experience; and this is something not unrelated to his different attitude towards nature discussed by Professor Foakes, or to his reluctance to impose form upon his search for faith.

The prelude to the first two dreams is described in some detail. In each case, the vision is precipitated not by surroundings of extraordinary natural beauty but by the reading of letters. In the first case, it is the letters on Hallam's tomb that Tennyson reads, though at the time of the lyric's composition he had not seen it. It would seem in fact, from poems in the *Two Brothers* volume like 'On the Moonlight shining upon a Friend's Grave' and (one of his most successful early efforts) the ode 'On Sublimity', that Tennyson was describing an experience more long-standing than his friendship with the historical Hallam. The original first edition reading of 'chancel' for 'dark church' again reminds one, in its material inaccuracy, that the *In Memoriam* lyric has a great deal to do with the sort of experience described in such early poems as 'The Walk at Midnight'. Again, the fact that the second dream lyric (xcv) draws upon the earlier unpublished 'Deep and Solemn Dreams' is not coincidental; and there are many further echoings and self-borrowings that could be cited. What all the evidence in the end suggests is that the central experiences in *In Memoriam* refer to the regaining of something besides what was lost with the person Hallam. They refer in part to the experience of repeating his own name, and the subsequent trance, which is also described for instance in 'The Ancient Sage' and the *Memoir*. (It is a process familiar to students of Yeats' MSS.) The very same 'Spectres' that long haunt his mind become in time a 'mystic Glory', a Shekinah, and both are essentially derived from self. This is what is important, and what distinguishes Tennyson's from many other similar experiences. Even at the moments of seeming reconciliation, form is not taken on its own terms:

> My love has talk'd with rocks and trees;
> He finds on misty mountain-ground
> His own vast shadow glory-crown'd
> He sees himself in all he sees. (xcvii)

Tennyson's later attitude towards these moments in which he appeared to 'see into the life of things', or rather into himself, is fairly clear. Reversing the direction of his earlier sympathy, it may be compared with that of the later Coleridge in *Constancy to an Ideal Object*. The glory once again became a spectre:[11]

> The enamoured rustic worships its fair hues,
> Nor knows he makes the shadow, he pursues!

Tennyson's later deprecatory attitude towards such moments is an important theme in *The Princess, Maud,* and the *Idylls* (especially 'The Holy Grail'); and it crops up time and time again elsewhere. 'Enoch Arden', for instance, is a poem written almost as if expressly to contradict any suggestion that paradisal happiness and unity of being, which have been lost, are and can be relevant to life as it must be lived here from day to day. The poem is in direct opposition to anything said in *In Memoriam,* in theme or in feeling; and the immediate appeal the story possessed for Tennyson, and the speed with which he interpreted it in verse, suggests it embodies more than superficial or transient attitudes.[12] It appears that Tennyson's reaction softened a little during his last years, but in no sense did he ever return wholly to his earlier attitude. He came again to acknowledge publicly his 'passion for the past'; but it would seem that as Laureate he never wholly forgot that he preached to 'rustics', 'To those that eddy round and round'.

Tennyson's changed attitude towards dreams and visions throws light on his later remarks on *In Memoriam,* particularly in its form. It explains why the remarks used by Bradley and Miss Pitt to describe the poem's structure are misleading: consciously or unconsciously, it does not matter which, they were intended to confuse and to lead his readers and himself away from attitudes which later embarrassed him. The remarks in the *Memoir* and in the Eversley edition, drawn on by Bradley, appear to express a later interpretation to which he gave most weight; and it may be noted that all the later additions to the poem attempt to shift its form in this direction. Tennyson's remarks to Knowles, who one suspects he might have found on occasions a more congenial spirit than his son Hallam, are less committed to suggesting a form that points towards meaning. Nonetheless, the way in which they are open to be interpreted in the light of later 'Laureate' attitudes is quite adequately demonstrated by Miss Pitt.

Tennyson realized in these after-years that his public would not allow any material alterations to the poem, which explains why his later additions to it obscure its form and meaning rather than succeed in giving it another one. It should also be noted that, even at the time of publication, his attitudes towards the poem's theme were not as assured as they had once been. Both Jacobs and Beeching[13] suggest that the poem originally ended immediately before the present lyric LVII, 'Peace; come away'; and certainly the break in the poem at this point is only explicable in terms of the hesitancy already suggested. It seems as if Tennyson was tempted to choke off his poem before the living of the progressively intense reunions experienced in the succeeding lyrics; to reverse Langland's progress and, as it were, retract his C and B texts to the *Visio* of A. The uncertainty also accounts for the obtrusively orthodox tone occasionally met; the Prologue and Epilogue, in particular, read almost as if they were deliberately intended to dull our repsonse to what comes between them. Or again, Miss Pitt's comments on the probably relatively early date of the composition of the lyric 'Tho' truths in manhood darkly join'[14] are pertinent to what we must conclude from Jacob's and Beeching's criticisms. Tennyson's 'return to orthodoxy', it seems, began earlier than is often supposed.

Tennyson's revisionary readings add a fifth dimension to the study of his poem; but questions such as why Goethe was introduced to obscure the reference to St Augustine in the opening lyric, or why Tennyson afterwards thought the 'You' of XCVIII imaginary, may be answered in many ways. What is important is that Tennyson never afterwards felt quite at ease with the poem, in a way that surprised many of its deep admirers. It represents an aspect of his attaining to maturity, in every sense – one that he had advanced beyond and which was nevertheless still with him. One can perceive his unease in the comments and changes discussed above, and even in such later gruff explanations that he never called Hallam 'dear' and 'dearest' and that 'this is a poem, *not* an actual biography'. His continuing embarrassment perhaps led him to do something that has confused his readers ever since; that is, to retain the poem, in all editions of his collected works, in the order of its publication, after *The Princess* in which the dreams are denied. He thus obscures what would otherwise be noticed, and influences the approach to our reading of the poem as effectively as through his later revisions and talk of the Christmas lyrics.

VI

Tennyson's uncertainty about the form of *In Memoriam* provides the basis for some concluding observations. An explanation might be offered for how it was possible that he could change his mind, how his faith could weaken, after the amazing demonstration of its recovery and power during the course of the poem.

Though at the end, Tennyson's heart 'Stood up and answer'd, "I have felt"', it is important to recognize in what sense this is true. While for Wordsworth poetry is 'the spontaneous overflow of powerful feelings', Tennyson finds that passion clogs the channels of speech (e.g., IV, XIII, XIX, XLIX, etc.). The fact is significant, and may be emphasized by recognizing some of the motives underlying his choice of stanza. Mr Robson,[15] in enlarging upon Arnold's remark on *Ulysses*, points to 'the radical discrepancy between the strenuousness aspired to, and the medium in which the strenuousness is expressed'; and, again, Miss Pitt discusses the relationship of the astonishing slowing-down of the speed of Tennyson's verse, its incantatory rhythms, to the natural tendency of his sensibility to reflect and passively absorb, to melt away definition and all exactness of objective reference.[16] These remarks are relevant to what has been said − to the fact that the poem's whole theme is one in which time provides the purpose and the means, and that its whole form embodies Tennyson's tendency to linger over the significance of previous moments, to look back and dwell on them, and finally to incorporate them into his experience. It is apparent also in his language: one may note his brooding over words (it is through this that the first two visions come), and even that the horror of 'On the bald street breaks the blank day' depends for its effect on the breaking-up of previously lengthening rhythms with emphatic sharp alliteration and the repetition of clipped final consonants. So, then, the form of the verse. It is particularly appropriate as a means to prevent the mind eddying round on itself. Edward FitzGerald felt the poem had the air of having been evolved from a poetical machine;[17] and his reaction is honest and to the point. Movement, mood, and grammar all play against the stanza continually; and yet they are held together and carried forward by the stanza's at times almost jingling mechanical movement. It is dubious to press any claim for the intrinsic properties of a particular verse form; but it seems fair to say that, in this case at least, the whole principle of coherence and progression actually depends upon the dichotomy between technique and feeling, form and faith.

The dichotomy which is in this respect generally so fruitful may nevertheless be noted as a contradiction of that honesty to experience suggested as the clue to the poem's form. And, indeed, it must be realized that Tennyson's honesty often extends only to the point of explicitly refusing to be honest. It extends ultimately to the point of conceiving a double standard of truth, as is made clear in the fifty-third lyric. This has a direct bearing on what has been said of Tennyson's attitude towards and use of language; he recognizes himself that his muse only

> ... sports with words,
> But better serves a wholesome law,
> And holds it sin and shame to draw
> The deepest measure from the chords. (XLVIII)

The attitude accounts for several obscurities and ambiguities which still, after the many commentaries, remain unresolved. It also suggests why Coleridge's penetrating analysis of what he calls the 'language of fanaticism'[18] should at times seem more appropriate than our milder modern discussions of 'the language of assertion' or of 'subtext'.

What is, if anything, of equal importance here is that Tennyson's double-standard is founded not only upon a notion of esoteric and exoteric meaning, but upon an attitude towards himself. If Yeats came to realize that all symbols start 'In the foul rag-and-bone shop of the heart', Tennyson refused to look there. He believed that the mind is not up to the task of confronting itself, that the unfathomable cannot be fathomed. If we attempt to interrogate what Lear calls 'unaccommodated man', we perform an injustice; and Tennyson would exclaim rather with Viola, 'O time! thou must untangle this, not I; / It is too hard a knot for me to untie!' It seems, therefore, as if Tennyson's symbols may often fail to have meaning for us, because the whole of their possible justification was never known. If the form of faith in his poem, in other words, was uncertain for him as well as being uncertain in many respects for us, it is perhaps because, in T. S. Eliot's words, 'Tennyson's emotion was so deeply suppressed, that it was hidden even from himself.'

This leads to some last comments. If, on the one hand, the comparison with Langland helps us to understand the form of *In Memoriam*, it is as well to remember at the same time what we have been taught by Eliot. The relation is again not one to be approached in terms of specific 'influences', 'echoes', and 'borrowings', but to achieve a clearer understanding. The very many particular coincidences need not be mentioned, but it may be suggested that Eliot might have had a greater degree of sympathy with Tennyson's mind than many critics who have written at greater length on him; indeed, and because of this, that his poetry itself is an illuminating comment on Tennyson's achievement. There is a great deal in common between the *Four Quartets* and *In Memoriam*, in purpose, theme, form, and images, but these aspects of Tennyson's poem have received sufficient attention for the present. It is instead more instructive to recall Eliot's earlier verse; and the limits of Tennyson's honesty, together with its relation to the failure and success of his poem's form, may all the more clearly emerge.

In Eliot's terms, 'Between the idea / And the reality' falls the Shadow. Though Tennyson is honestly aware of a like fact, he admits it to the extent where it appears justified. He in the end turned aside from the Heart of Darkness, and considered his action a necessary condition of his humanity:

> Beneath all fancied hopes and fears
> Ay me, the sorrow deepens down,
> Whose muffled motions blindly drown
> The bases of my life in tears. (XLIX)

The whole attraction and theme of Tennyson's poem is nevertheless conveyed by the overriding seriousness of the speaker's striving for personal and spiritual integrity. The relation between these two attitudes and the question of form is illuminating. The way in which nature remains throughout the poem a 'phantom', with little objective significance of its own, has already been remarked on. In a similar fashion, people and persons, 'blood and breath', continue to have little value in themselves, but only potential 'use'. Even Hallam continues to be seen, heard, and valued as a means to an end, which is the restoration and enlargement of Tennyson's own mind and sensibility. What all this amounts to is that the way of a soul is intrinsically the way of egotism, exalted into a distinctive technique. As in Eliot's earlier poetry, it involves a degree of blindness to all outside itself.

Nevertheless, Tennyson's failure to know the outside world on its own terms paradoxically involves an accompanying necessary limitation of self. In the manner explained by the forty-fifth lyric, his faith in himself is finally unsure because it is not adequately defined by the world of form outside it. Subjective does not define itself sufficiently strongly against the objective, the world within against the world outside, but in the end it subsumes it, just as assertion outstrips argument and belief overwhelms doubt. In terms of the poetry, this is one reason why Tennyson's reactions should sometimes appear little related to the situations he confronts, why there should be disjunction between tenor and vehicle or 'Between the conception / And the creation'. Lyrics like 'The lesser griefs that may be said' (xx) and 'My love has talk'd with rocks and trees' (xcvii) are prominent examples.

The dialectic process of self-realization is finally circumscribed, it may be said, because *anagnorisis* is not achieved – 'We have but faith: we cannot know.' The hero-speaker shrinks from assessing his experience as a whole, and attempts to bolster his hesitancy by his criticism of form. His lack of total awareness is related also to his passivity, to his helplessness in the grip of a conflict that not he but only time can heal. The poem is one of lyrically celebrated situations rather than of action, its method lies in the juxtaposition of discrete idylls, and this because its hero-speaker lacks the means and the will to control or change the direction of the delineated experience: 'Between the emotion / And the response' falls the Shadow. For the same reason, the passion for the past, the sense of *lacrymae rerum*, was never wholly exorcized and gathered up in present personality: it continued to haunt the 'Laureate' world. One of Eliot's frequently misunderstood comments, that the poem's 'faith is a poor thing, but its doubt is a very intense experience', may be related to another in a very different context, that the spirit killeth, but the letter giveth life: the relation reminds us of the mutual interdependence of Tennyson's belief and art, faith and form.

These suggestions have nothing to do with any failure in 'achieved intelligence', since the issue does not depend upon whether any man can plummet the nature of his own experience, but only whether he thinks he can. 'Intelligence', also, is too narrow a word. The only way to describe the ground of these suggestions is, in the end, to attribute them to a quite distinct and individual sensibility. If it shares some of its qualities with several other poets, it is, as well, itself. For example, whereas Eliot exploits a dissociation of sensibility, a disjunction between appearance and reality, achievement and desire, between what is said and what is intended, in an irony whereby techniques and themes are related at a second remove by the reader; and whereas in the *Quartets* his achievement still depends on his remaining the invisible poet, Tennyson, by contrast, gives his poem form by assuming the dramatic role of hero. Disjunction, though it leads him occasionally into sentimentality or melodrama, in his ideas and his art, is striven against by the man before the poet. The attempt is possibly more difficult to sustain, perhaps it necessarily involves what can only be a special kind of success. At all events, what it certainly means is that in the end one's judgment of the form of the poem is superseded by judgments of its faith – which is the proper moment for a literary discussion of *In Memoriam* to depart.

SOURCE: *University of Toronto Quarterly*, XXXV (1965).

NOTES

1. Valerie Pitt, *Tennyson Laureate* (London, 1962; Toronto, 1963) ch. IV.

2. Miss Pitt, p. 91, suggests on MS. evidence that even 1833 is not an impossibly early date.

3. See for instance, 'Cuthbert Bede' (Edward Bradley)'s 'In Immemoriam', and Thomas Hood the Younger's 'In Memoriam Technicam', conveniently reprinted by J. Postma, *Tennyson as Seen by His Parodists* (Amsterdam, 1926) pp. 143–5. (It should be noted that Postma's identification of 'Cuthbert Bede' with Alfred Bradley is incorrect.)

It may be of interest that only a couple in a large class of fourth-year honour students recognized the Bradley poem as parody when it was read to them and their comments were invited: the large majority missed the nudge, suggested it was a cancelled lyric, and praised its beauty.

4. See supra, pp. 188 ff.

5. R. A. Foakes, *The Romantic Assertion: A Study of the Language of Nineteenth Century Poetry* (1958) pp. 122–3.

6. David Perkins, *Wordsworth and the Poetry of Sincerity* (Cambridge, Mass., 1964). Though Mr Perkins' phrasing has been retained in a number of places, it was not practicable to litter the text with quotation marks and references.

7. It may at this stage again be remarked that the point of comparing the form of Tennyson's and Langland's poems is not to try to establish anything like 'influence' or 'borrowing', but more fully to understand what has been too frequently misunderstood. To approach, for instance, this final lyric in terms of Tennyson's obligations, it is more to the point to think of the place of Will in German or in Carlyle's thinking.

8. Recollection of Keats' *Fall of Hyperion: A Dream*, or Augustine and Dante, are less misleading than *The Friend*.

9. To recall the *Upanishads* here confirms, but does not I think provide the sense. (They are of course one of the many illuminating points of contact between *In Memoriam* and *Four Quartets*.)

10. Clyde de L. Ryals, *Theme and Symbol in Tennyson's Poems to 1850* (Philadelphia, 1964) ch. VI especially.

11. W. D. Paden, *Tennyson in Egypt* (Lawrence, Kansas, 1942) pp. 25, 122, traces Tennyson's source for the reference in the early ode 'On Sublimity' to Clarke's *Hundred Wonders*; but the way in which Tennyson interpreted his source owes a good deal to the early Wordsworth and Coleridge.

12. Besides all the obvious connotations of 'Arden', echoes of *The*

Lotus Eaters, and so on, one suspects Tennyson of interpreting Woolner's story with the biblical Enoch, that is, the seventh from Adam, in mind. The relation of the literature surrounding Enoch and the then recently discovered Book of Enoch to *In Memoriam* is relevant. It not only clarifies the problematical last stanza of xcvi, but throws light on several recurrent themes and images.

13. Joseph Jacobs, *Tennyson and 'In Memoriam': An appreciation and a study* (1892) p. 92; H. C. Beeching, *'In Memoriam'* . . . *with an Analysis and Notes* (1900) p. x.

14. *Tennyson Laureate*, pp. 95–6.

15. W. W. Robson, 'The Dilemma of Tennyson', in *Critical Essays on the Poetry of Tennyson*, ed. John Killham (1960).

16. *Tennyson Laureate*, ch. II.

17. *Letters of Edward FitzGerald*, ed. W. A. Wright (London and New York, 1894) I 263.

18. *The Friend* (1818) I, essay VI.

SELECT BIBLIOGRAPHY

1. Various attempts have been made to establish some chronology for individual lyrics of *In Memoriam* in the relevant sections of Valerie Pitt, *Tennyson Laureate* (Barrie & Rockliff, 1962); Eleonor Bustin Mattes, '*In Memoriam*'. *The Way of a Soul*. *A study of some influences that shaped Tennyson's poem* (Exposition Press, 1951); and *The Poems of Tennyson*, ed. Christopher Ricks (Longmans Annotated English Poets, 1969). This last is a most valuable edition of Tennyson's poetry and provides texts of unpublished lyrics from *In Memoriam* as well as notes on the MSS. and on the relevant evolutionary materials. Since the publication of Ricks's edition, a MS. of *In Memoriam*, dated November 1842, has been made available by the Tennyson Trustees and Trinity College, Cambridge, where it is held. Previously no one had been able to copy or publish any part of the MS., though Ricks discusses it briefly in his edition. A further, short account of this and other Tennyson MSS. at Trinity, including a transcription of an unused section of *In Memoriam*, is given by Christopher Ricks in *The Times Literary Supplement* of 21 August 1969.

2. Further discussions of Tennyson's poem in relation to nineteenth-century science are contained in Douglas Bush, *Science and English Poetry. A Historical Sketch 1590–1950* (O.U.P., 1950 and Galaxy Books, 1968); Lionel Stevenson, *Darwin Among the Poets* (Russell & Russell, 1963); Basil Willey, *More Nineteenth-Century Studies* (Chatto & Windus, 1956); a more discursive and wide-ranging account is that by Theodosius Dobzhansky, 'Evolutionism and Man's Hope', *The Sewanee Review*, LXVIII (1960).

3. Some more general items on Tennyson's life and work are the biography by his grandson, Charles Tennyson (Macmillan, 1949 and Papermac, 1968); the *Memoir* in two volumes by the

poet's son (Macmillan, 1897); and Jerome H. Buckley, *Tennyson. The growth of a poet* (Harvard U.P., 1960 and Riverside paperback, 1966), which remains the best full-length study of Tennyson's poetry and from which Buckley's contribution to this Casebook is taken.

4. Nine further items which could not be used in this volume are:

i) R. A. Foakes, *The Romantic Assertion. A study of the language of nineteenth-century poetry* (Methuen, 1958) pp. 111–39: a most interesting examination of the decline of Romanticism's value-words into empty rhetoric in Victorian poetry.

ii) K. W. Grandsen, *Tennyson, In Memoriam* (Arnold's Studies in English Literature, 22, 1964): a good short introduction to the poem and its problems for criticism.

iii) S. A. Grant, 'The Mystical Implications of *In Memoriam*', *Studies in English Literature*, II (1962): an important discussion of Tennyson's mysticism, with useful references to William James and Evelyn Underhill.

iv) Clyde de L. Ryals, 'The "Heavenly Friend": the "New Mythus" of *In Memoriam*', *The Personalist*, XLIII (1962): Tennyson is related to earlier nineteenth-century idealists, notably Carlyle, and Hallam's metamorphosis into a Christ-figure traced against that background.

v) ——, *Theme and Symbol in Tennyson's Poems to 1850* (University of Pennsylvania P., 1964): the last chapter treats Tennyson's use of themes and symbols in *In Memoriam* which have already been deployed in his previous poetry.

vi) Joseph Sendry, '*In Memoriam* and *Lycidas*', *PMLA* LXXXII (1967): identifies and analyses links between the poems and suggests ways in which Tennyson may be seen to have tried to link his personal song of despair to the long elegiac tradition.

vii) Martin J. Svaglic, 'A Framework for *In Memoriam*', in *Journal of English and Germanic Philology* LXI (1962): discusses the structure of the poem according to the divisions the poet himself established for the elegies (see Introduction, supra, p. 33), as opposed to the structure offered in Bradley's *Commentary* (1901 and Archon Books, 1966), which should also be consulted.

viii) James Benziger, *Images of Eternity* (Southern Illinois U.P., 1962), has a chapter on Tennyson which explores the poet's belief and makes some interesting comparisons with the Romantics.

5. A brief history of Tennyson criticism is given as the introduction to *Critical Essays on the Poetry of Tennyson*, ed. John Killham (Routledge & Kegan Paul, 1960) and a fully analytical list of the criticism by the present editor is available in *Students' Guide to Poetry* (Clarendon Press, 1970).

NOTES ON CONTRIBUTORS

JONATHAN BISHOP teaches at Cornell University.

JEROME H. BUCKLEY is Professor of English at Harvard University, and has written *The Victorian Temper* and *The Triumph of Time. A study of Victorian concepts of time, history, progress and decadence.*

ARTHUR J. CARR teaches at Williams College, Massachusetts.

WALKER GIBSON teaches at the University of Massachusetts.

MANLEY HOPKINS (1817/18–1897), poet, critic, author of books on Hawaii and marine insurance, and father of G. M. Hopkins.

GRAHAM HOUGH is Professor of English in the University of Cambridge and author, among other books and articles, of *The Romantic Poets* and *The Last Romantics.*

HUMPHRY HOUSE (1908–55) taught at Oxford before his death, and was the editor of Hopkins's notebooks and papers and author of *Dickens's World.*

JOHN DIXON HUNT lectures at the University of York and is the author of *The Pre-Raphaelite Imagination: 1848–1900* and a Critical Commentary on *The Tempest.* He has edited a Casebook on *The Rape of the Lock.*

E. D. H. JOHNSON is Professor of English at Princeton

University and is the author of various articles on Victorian poetry and of *The Alien Vision of Victorian Poetry*.

G. H. LEWES (1817–78), a versatile and prolific writer, editor of *The Leader* and later the *Fortnightly Review*; perhaps best known for his relationship with George Eliot.

FRANKLIN LUSHINGTON (1811–90) was the brother of the bridegroom whose marriage to Tennyson's sister is celebrated in the Epilogue of *In Memoriam*.

J. WESTLAND MARSTON (1819–90), dramatic poet, critic and contributor to *DNB*.

J. C. C. MAYS is Professor of English, Victoria College, University of Toronto.

CARLISLE MOORE is Professor of English at the University of Oregon.

F. W. ROBERTSON (1816–53), a clergyman of prominence whose sermons were widely read in Victorian England; his two lectures were delivered to the Mechanics Institute at Brighton in February 1852 and it is from them that his piece is extracted.

JOHN D. ROSENBERG, Professor of English at Columbia University, is the author of a brilliant study of Ruskin, *The Darkening Glass*.

HENRY SIDGWICK (1835–1900) was Professor of Moral Philosophy at Cambridge.

INDEX